MW00976651

the (un)offensive
gospel of Jesus

the (un)offensive gospel of Jesus

Jeremy Bouma

novus·lumen
books

Grand Rapids, Michigan

To my parents, Bruce and Linda,
who have shown me and the world a loving Jesus
and told His hopeful Story well.

The (Un)Offensive Gospel of Jesus

Copyright © 2008 by Jeremy Bouma

All rights reserved.

Published by **novus•lumen books**
P.O. Box 1180
Grand Rapids, MI 49501
www.novuslumenbooks.com

No part of this publication may be reproduced, stored in a retrieval
system, or transmitted, in any form or by any means, electronic,
mechanical, photocopying, recording or otherwise, without prior
permission of the author.

You may contact the author through email or his websites at:
Internet: www.unoffensivegospel.com or www.novuslumen.net
Email: jeremy@novuslumen.net

Edited by: John W. Frye
Cover Jesus art © Luc Freyman from www.freymanc.com. Used by permission.

ISBN: 978-0-615-22414-5

Scripture is taken from the HOLY BIBLE, NEW INTERNATIONAL VERSION®.
NIV®. Copyright © 1973, 1978, 1984 by International Bible Society. Used by permission
of Zondervan. All rights reserved.

Printed in the United States of America
10 9 8 7 6 5 4 3 2 1

About **novus•lumen books**

novus•lumen books is an independent publisher that explores the tension of spirituality and culture, politics and theology, existing and emerging forms of Church, the Kingdom of God and America, modern and postmodern thought, and the gritty drama that is our collective pilgrim story. **novus•lumen books** pledges to offer fresh, relevant, intuitive, and insightful written pieces for Christians and non-Christians alike.

www.novuslumenbooks.com • contact@novuslumenbooks.com

Content

Foreword

I've heard it time and time again: "Before you can preach the *good* news you have to preach the *bad* news." Well, yes, I say to myself: the gospel is good news to rescue humans from their sin, their despair, their problems, our problems, our despair, and our systemic injustices. The *good* news is that God does this for us in Jesus Christ and in the power of God's Spirit. So, yes, there are problems out of which we need rescue.

My problem with the "bad news first" gospel preaching is that it isn't the gospel we find Jesus preaching. Jesus, in other words, was no *grace grinder*, someone who first had to make folks feel miserable before He'd offer them the balm of His good news. There are many grace grinders among us today. For them, grace is the experience of recognizing our wretchedness so powerfully that we clamor for God's grace. Grace grinders, in other words, create a gospel, a theology and a kind of worship service where we must first dig deep into our sin, the deeper the better, so that we can sense how bad we are...and only then, having plumbed the depths of *the (un)offensive gospel of Jesus*

our sinfulness, can we hear the good news of grace. Grace grinders grind us under with the message of grace.

Can you imagine a young man offering a young woman a diamond ring and then saying something like this? "You don't really deserve this. In fact, you're mighty lucky I've chosen you. Be thankful, take my hand, and live with me in love." Love does not work like this. Neither does grace.

Jeremy Bouma is a deep thinker; he's courageous enough to challenge some popular evangelicals and emergents today. Yet, this is not a screed: Jeremy loves the Church and has a passion for the ostracized, like the homosexual community, and he tells us in this book that grace grinding is not the way of Jesus and it is not the gospel Jesus preached. Jesus was not offensive; He was incredibly and beautifully attractive. He fashioned a vision of the Kingdom that brought to expression the deepest yearnings of every human being alive on planet earth, He offered Himself to be loved and to love as the love that sets the heart free, and He pointed to a way, the way of the cross, where He took upon Himself our problems and offered us a way out and a way forward.

This really is good news. And it is good news for more than just *me*. It is good news for *us*—together. God made us to love God and to love others, and Jesus was the Very Presence of God's love and He embodied what it meant to love others. That is the *good* news and it overwhelms the bad news. Jeremy Bouma, in this salty book, may take your breath away at times but he's on a reflective, serious, and stubborn journey to find a way toward the gospel that is *good* news. Many of us are on that journey with him. There is a way to "gospel" without being a jerk; Jeremy shows us a way.

Dr. Scot McKnight
Karl A. Olson Professor of Religious Studies, North Park University
Author, The Jesus Creed *and* The Blue Parakeet

12

Preface

On one of my bedroom walls hangs two precious items: a Christmas ornament cross I co-opted to serve as a spiritual focal point for prayer and meditation and a certified authentic Eastern Orthodox Ikon I snuck-off with during a mission trip to Romania. Well, I didn't exactly steal the thing. I really did pay the Hungarian Ikonography for the finely painted 3x5 inch block of wood. I did hide it, though, from the rest of my mission trip mates because of the uncomfortable questions it would attract. As a thoroughly Western Christian, and (mostly) evangelical one at that, Ikons are a no-no. So I hid it.

I hid "Christ the Giver of Life."

Think about that: Jesus Christ is the giver of everything that is real about Life. And I hid him! What an appropriate metaphor for this book: hiding a physical representation of the beautiful reality of the good, hopeful news about Life available in the Giver Jesus. Over the years I've come to believe that the Church Herself, in many ways, hides "Christ the Giver of Life" from the rest of the world. The Church has taken the life-giving power that is inherent in the hopeful message of Jesus and turned it into something perceived as offensive and actually down right repulsive at times.

Notice I said *Christians* have turned the hopeful message of Jesus into something offensive. The message of Jesus itself isn't offensive, we and the message we carry often are. Neither is Jesus inherently offensive. Rather, His followers are the ones who offend, contributing to a culture that likes Jesus, but not the Church.

Over the years it seems like Christians have forgotten who Jesus is. On the one hand He's a White middle-class Republican who's really only concerned with blessing you with a Jesus-stamped American Dream. On another hand, He isn't really all that concerned with your life (or the entire world for that matter) now, because the real duty of Jesus is to get you and a few others beamed off of earth and into heaven. On yet another hand, Jesus is nothing more than a revolutionary, moral example of love who did nothing for us on the cross, and was not physically resurrected for that matter.

So the Jesus we show is either a middle-class American or a 70's hippie; the story we tell is either escapism or do-gooder moralism. Where is the Jesus of the Bible? The one who said it's necessary to love your neighbor as yourself *and* love God; the one who said we must be spiritually reborn *and* face judgment for what we do in this life. And what about God's Story of Rescue? The one that says heaven is a place on *earth*; the one that says personal sin and death and evil were real objective things that needed to be dealt with, and were defeated through the cross *and* resurrection?

Here's the thing: we the Church are responsible for the Jesus we show and the Jesus people see; we the Church are responsible for the Story we tell and the Story people hear.

Who, then, is the Jesus we're showing? Who is the Jesus the world sees? What is the Story we're telling? What is the Story they hear? What is the portrait of Jesus we are painting and what version of His Story are we penning?

Granted, the Church cannot entirely control how people will react to Jesus and His good news. Even Jesus couldn't do that. I do understand that people will still react, even in offense, to the way Christians show Jesus and tell His Story no matter how well-meaning and good they show and tell. Despite these realities, however, I do think there is space to offer a better showing and telling.

This book is my attempt to show Jesus as He really was, to tell the complete, hopeful Story of Rescue the whole Holy Scriptures sketches. This is the reason for the provocative title: to drive a conversation within the Church about our showing and telling and offer an alternative to both. In Part One, I aim to show Jesus as the One who fully expressed God while also fully participating in all of life by declaring solidarity with humanity and showing them a better, more real way of being human. I also hope to show a Jesus who really, really loves people and really, really loves you, rather than a Jesus who is ticked at the world. Jesus loved the world so much that He willingly went to a wretched cross to rescue the world by paying the penalty for our evil, rebellion, and death. That is good news, indeed! This good, divine-human Jesus is the center of an amazing Story of Rescue that undergirds our collective histories, one that needs a better telling. Part Two hopes to tell a better Story than the one typically told, a Story that is hopeful, life-giving, and thoroughly (un)offensive. This Story carries with it a message that people, when they come across it, are enlivened and beckoned, rather than turned-off or defeated.

Throughout the book you'll meet a cast of characters who add flesh to the skeleton of my theological framework: you'll meet Taylor who is a bisexual atheist and Mykha'el, a gay Christian; Ben, Cameron and Rachel, three recent high school graduates will share their journey through Reformed Christianity; and Andy, a college senior, as well. Their contributions affected me so much that I needed to share their personal stories and spiritual journeys. I trust they will affect you even beyond what my own stories, musings, and attempts at theology could accomplish on their own. These perspectives from my friends, coupled with my own thoughts, will hopefully help solidify a hardy, robust argument and vision for an (un)offensive gospel of Jesus.

I admit, though, that my thoughts aren't all that new. Abraham Kuyper gave us a fourfold understanding of the gospel: creation, fall, redemption, consummation. I've just repackaged them as creation, rebellion, rescue, and re-creation. Plenty has been written in the last few years on following Jesus and living His Way well. I try to package and present some of that in relationship to the Church's efforts at showing and being Jesus to the world around us. But while I admit my thoughts have been written elsewhere by better men and women, how I offer those ideas and the conversation I am trying to spark in these pages is a needed discussion. The only reason I have to writing this book is not because of what I have done or accomplished, but what God did through Jesus Christ; this Story is God's. Openhanded I humbly come, then, to offer my thoughts and musings on the fascinating person of Jesus and His hopeful, (un)offensive gospel, good news that is from the one and only God, who was and is and is to come.

Lest you think that my use of (un)offensive (both as a literal and rhetorical device) means undemanding, think again. While I do not believe the heart of Jesus and substance of His Story is offensive, I do not mean His demands will not irritate our modern sensibilities. A line from *The Lion the Witch and the Wardrobe* comes to mind: "Safe? 'Course he isn't safe. But he is good." Like Aslan, Jesus is very, very good, but He is also unsafe; He is thoroughly unpredictable, unwieldy, and entirely demanding of every ounce of our being. Those who come to the resurrected unsafe Jesus to find rest, rescue, and re-creation do not walk away from that encounter unchanged nor are they able to slink away into their previous way of living.

The gospel of Jesus, then, is both (un)offensive and offensive. Jesus' good news of rescue and re-creation is not inherently offensive, yet people can still react in offense at its demands.

As one apostle author put it, though: "I am not ashamed of the good, hopeful message of Jesus, because that message is the very power of God to rescue and re-create all of humanity, for everyone who believes in Jesus and His Story." A good, hopeful message cannot be by nature offensive. Likewise, a good, loving person cannot offer both an offensive message and good news. While the hearers of that (un)offensive message may react in offense out of pride and self-sufficiency, neither the Story nor its main Character is inherently offensive. This is exactly what my title seeks to convey: neither the loving, gentle, caring Jesus of the Holy Scriptures nor the gospel message He bears is inherently offensive as some Christians seem to insist. Rather, both are hopeful, life-giving, joyous, comforting, rescuing, and restoring to the core. I hope this book casts a vision of a showing and telling of good Jesus and His hopeful Story that is as wonderful, engaging, (un)offensive and healing as the Man and Story themselves, while urging the Church to take partial responsibility for the cultures reaction to their current show and tell efforts.

The more I follow the radical Jesus of the Holy Scriptures, the deeper I dive into His Way, and the more I listen to the spiritual journeys of others, the more I realize both Jesus and His gospel are good, sweet news for all the world. Embedded within the person and reality of Jesus Christ, within the words and way of this God-with-us-God is the very stuff of life, the fountainhead from which all humans can suckle unending streams of the marrow of life.

My only question is this: what's offensive about that?

Jeremy A. Bouma
Grand Rapids, Michigan (October 2008)

Chapter 1
Introduction

"The gospel is offensive!" How many times have you heard that during your life? Growing up I heard it a lot. I would hear it both from the pulpit and from everyday Christians, usually from people who were trying to excuse themselves from personal rejection by the "pagans" they ran into (or rather, ran over) through their life. Just Google "the gospel is offensive" and you'll come up with about 3,510,000 hits, and growing. Apparently, many Christians really want the world to believe the gospel and Jesus are offensive.

Just listen to the attitude and conviction behind this one internet commentator:

> Political correctness has softened us to the point of being salt without effect. Christians are not called to be unoffensive and ineffective. The Gospel is a confrontational message. The minds of our modern society are indoctrinated with worldly, satanic

thought processes that do not let go easily. Sometimes dynamite is required. I am not talking about offending people without love, but come on...let's get back to the truth that Jesus offended just about everyone. The Gospel offends the world. It tells them that unless they turn to Jesus...they are doomed. How can that not be offensive! It's time for a 'Wake Up Call' being sounded until the masses see the one and only Truth! All roads do not lead to God, only through Jesus!! [1]

This one comment is pretty reflective of other Christians who have similarly voiced the whole "the gospel is offensive" rhetoric. In fact, in a recent book outlining the perceptions by young "outsiders" (those not following Jesus or connected to a church community) of the American Church, the authors claimed that, while the ones "offended" by Jesus were the religiously arrogant people (not outsiders), "the cross is offensive to people." [2] Really? Who are these people? Why is the cross offensive? What the heck does that even mean, the "cross is offensive?"

While I too used to believe that the person and message of Christ was inherently offensive, a few years ago I began to wonder if framing the gospel in these terms was really accurate and fit with the Story the Holy Scriptures are telling. Maybe it was because for a whole year I planted myself in nothing more than the four Gospel books for my personal time in the Holy Scriptures. Maybe it was because, after spending so much time with Jesus and the characters of the Gospels, I couldn't help but notice that people flocked to Jesus. Many people! Rather than being repulsed or *offended* by the person of Jesus, I saw people and their stories profoundly affected by this Man. And that didn't jibe well with this whole "the gospel is offensive" business.

For the longest time I just internally mulled over this disconnect between the "offensive gospel" many Christian leaders and teachers push and the very different good message that attracted so many people to Jesus and transformed so many lives. Then one evening I let the proverbial cat out the of the bag, something I wish I really wouldn't have done at the time!

Let me paint the scene for you:

I was at a ministry retreat for congressional staffers on Capitol Hill in Washington, D.C. where I was supposed to train them to share the gospel using an evangelism method called *Evangelism Explosion*. Afterwards we gathered for dinner at a seafood restaurant that served the best crab-cakes outside of Maryland. I was at a table with some staffers, friends, and a coworker and we were having a lively discussion about the evening, our lives, and the American Church. During our conversation, we began talking about the Kingdom of Heaven and what that meant, which lead to a discussion about radically following Jesus and His gospel message.

The conversation was going fantastic until I chimed in with: "And you know what really bothers me? When people say that the gospel is offensive. I hear people saying, 'oh they are not rejecting you the evangelist but the gospel and Jesus, because they are offensive.' That's ridiculous!"

Then nothing but crickets and blank stares.

It was one of those awkward moments when time just stands still, the whole place falls silent, and every eyeball is fixated on you and your brilliant idea!

So I continued, a bit hotter and sweatier: "What I mean is Jesus and His good news is not offensive. When you look at the Scriptures you see people flocking to Him and wanting to be around Him and touching Him. Jesus and His message don't seem all that offensive to me."

At this suggestion people shifted in their seats and mumbled a "yeah" and quickly changed the subject. AWK-ward!

As I've thought about that experience more and wrestled with the good person and hopeful message of Jesus I am convinced more than ever that, understood properly, Jesus and His hopeful message are not in and of themselves offensive, particularly for the people who need Him and that message. For the people who need restoration Jesus' message is hopeful and wholly (un)offensive. While He does seem to pluck the nerves of the powerful, well-to-do, and highly groomed and pampered, those who are at the end of themselves, who are poor in spirit, have found life, healing, rescue, and re-creation in Jesus. The Gospels themselves illustrate this point beautifully.

Take the rich young ruler, for example. In Luke 18, we find a Jewish ruler who asks Jesus, "What must I do to inherit eternal life?"[3] After Jesus explains that he should live out the commandments, the man exclaims he has been doing so since he was a boy. Jesus then asks the Jewish ruler to sell all he has, give it to the poor, and follow Him. Why? Because the man thought he was doing all that was necessary to be on the inside of God's borders; the rich young ruler smugly thought he had it made and was safe because he was a good Jew who was living out the letter of the Law. So when Jesus deflated the mans religious ego and disrobed him for the un-lover that he was, the man turned and ran. The arrogant religious man who supposedly didn't need Jesus' Way of Life because he was a religious insider was the one offended by His hard teachings.

Likewise, another group of apparent disciples and followers of Jesus abandoned Him because of a different set of hard teachings in the Book of John chapter 6. In verses 25-59, Jesus gives a lengthy discussion of the need to intimately receive and accept Him in order to have eternal life. He said, "I am the bread of life. He who comes to me will never go hungry, and he who believes in me will never be thirsty."[4] Further in the discussion Jesus repeats this claim and adds that, while the ancestors of Israel ate the manna (bread of life) in the desert Yahweh provided them, they died; this bread from God in heaven was not enough. He emphasized this point by saying, "Whoever eats my flesh and drinks my blood has eternal life, and I will raise him up at the last day. For my flesh is real food and my blood is real drink. Whoever eats my flesh and drinks my blood remains in me and I in him."[5] The master provocateur pushed these clean, law-abiding Jews to their religious limits. On hearing these teachings, many of Jesus' own disciples abandoned Him, turning back because they couldn't accept these mysterious teachings.

In essence, Jesus was saying that the true food and drink that will alleviate our deepest life-hungers and thirsts are found in Himself. Jesus is what all people have been waiting for their whole life! He calls people into intimate fellowship by receiving Him in the core of their being like they would the finest French delicacies and Italian wines imaginable. Whether these Jewish followers were disgusted by the intense flesh and blood imagery or whether they couldn't really accept the intense demands of relationship with Jesus that He required isn't entirely known. What we do witness, yet again, are religious insiders balking at the claims offered by Jesus Christ. Yet again, the sensibilities of those who claimed a special spiritual status were utterly irritated and disgusted by the good, hopeful message of Jesus.

Contrast these two instances of rejection and irritation with the full-bodied embrace by those who were the weary, broken, and marginalized religious outsiders: a Samaritan woman, after her heart was exposed to the refreshing love of God, embraced Jesus as the Messiah and led her entire religiously and socially ostracized village to belief in Him, as well; [6] a greedy, wretched tax collector who was universally despised by both Jews and Romans found a new life-identity in the Giver of Life Jesus Christ; [7] a woman besieged by a life lived in sin found honor, dignity, and salvation in Jesus, when others in her town shrieked at the thought of being touched by this "sinner;" [8] and lepers, blind men, paralytics, and the demon possessed all found acceptance, love, and restoration in the loving, gentle, caring Jesus.

Those who thought they were on the inside of God's tidy little religious club, who thought they perfectly performed the duties of religion and thus were granted asylum by Yahweh, were irritated, angry, and incredibly annoyed at the claims of this upstart, peasant prophet. Those who were weary, broken, marginalized outsiders clung to Jesus and His wonderful, restful words of life. Interestingly enough, the religious insiders were disgusted by Jesus because of His teachings; what He said offended them. The socially marginalized, on the other hand, were drawn to Jesus because of His signs; they were beckoned to Jesus by what He did, while later embracing His teachings, too.

Wherever Jesus went, He preached the good news of the Kingdom of Heaven and healed every sickness and disease. Matthew 9 says, "When Jesus saw the crowds, he had compassion on them, because they were harassed and helpless, like sheep without a shepherd." [9] That compassion drove Jesus to show and tell of the wondrous reality of God's in-breaking Kingdom Reign, a Reign that centered on a message of acceptance, rescue, and re-creation, while being accompanied by acts and signs of love, healing, and restoration.

Not only is the sweet, amazing gospel of Jesus not inherently offensive to all people who need the holistic rescue and re-creation He offers, His gospel isn't offensive for another reason: the word (offensive) used to paint an entire theology of the gospel has been misinterpreted and ripped from its context.

Reading Offense Into the Text

What do I mean by the gospel being offensive, or better (un)offensive?

At this point let me better define what I am and am not saying: I am saying Jesus and His gospel message are not inherently offensive, not defined by offense nor intended to offend; I am not saying that people will not react in offense because of the demands and requirements of Him and His message.

Yes, there is a difference!

When a parent instructs his or her child out of love, care, and affection, that child isn't usually all that enthusiastic for mom or dad and their 'hopeful' message at the time. Children want to run into the streets, eat cookies before dinner, and do a whole host of things that are forbidden for good reasons by their parents. Neither parents nor their message are offensive. Both are good and loving and for the benefit of their children. The hearers of those instructions do react in offense, though, out of pride, confusion, and self-sufficiency. The same is true for Jesus, His gospel message, and us humans.

While people do react to the demands of Jesus and His message, neither are inherently offensive. For all of us humans who are broken and spiritually disconnected, Jesus and His good news of the Kingdom of Heaven is what we all deeply need, what humans deeply desire. Restoration and re-creation are what all humans long for from birth to death. A better way of living and being human, a way that makes sense to our created order, are what people need and want and crave. Jesus and His message point to that better Way of Life and satisfy our deepest inner longings.

Jesus is what a person has been waiting for their whole life, even if they may not realize it yet.

This is why Jesus and His message are so (un)offensive.

When the good news of the Kingdom of Heaven is properly communicated and embodied as Jesus has commanded His people (see Matthew 28:19-20), it will not be offensive to people, but will instead be what they've been waiting for their whole lives. A good, wholesome, and healing message cannot be inherently offensive. Impossible. An offensive gospel is absolutely oxymoronic, a contradiction of terms! How can good news be offensive? How can the cross, which embodies the amazing news of rescue from the consequences of rebellion, be offensive?

Uncomfortable? Maybe. Countercultural? Definitely. Demanding? I'd say so! Offensive? Absolutely not possible.

There are Christians, however, who insist Jesus, His gospel, and the cross are inherently offensive. Several Christians have confused the good, hopeful, life-giving message of the cross with something that is repulsive and obnoxious, all the while insisting God framed His Story in this way. The passage from the Holy Scriptures that is used to paint Jesus and His good news as offensive is found in 1 Corinthians 1:18-25. Here is what is written:

> For the message of the cross is foolishness to those who are perishing, but to us who are being saved it is the power of God. For it is written:
>> "I will destroy the wisdom of the wise; the intelligence of the intelligent I will frustrate."
>
> Where is the wise man? Where is the scholar? Where is the philosopher of this age? Has not God made foolish the wisdom of the world? For since in the wisdom of God the world through its wisdom did not know him, God was pleased through the foolishness of what was preached to save those who believe. Jews demand miraculous signs and Greeks look for wisdom, but we preach Christ crucified: a stumbling block (skandalon) to Jews and foolishness to Gentiles, but to those whom God has called, both Jews and Greeks,

Christ the power of God and the wisdom of God. For the foolishness of God is wiser than man's wisdom, and the weakness of God is stronger than man's strength.

Christians typically translate *stumbling block* into 'offensive.' While the range of meaning of this Greek word can include this translation, a better understanding is scandal. *Skandalon* is something scandalous, something that is repugnant to one's categories of reality, not an offense at an emotional or personal level. In fact, it is from this Greek word that we get our English word "scandal." In the 1 Corinthian context, the cross wasn't offensive to the Jews or Greeks because of what it demanded from them, but because it was an affront to their long-held ideas of what the Messiah or a god should be. [10]

This passage has nothing to do with the personal offensiveness or (un)offensiveness of the cross. In his letter to the Church at Corinth, Paul proclaims a "wisdom" (which is a rhetorical device) from God's revelation and God Himself that counters human categories about the character of wisdom for salvation. This wisdom has to do with the salvation made possible through Christ's apparent weakness in being crucified. The Jews were scandalized by the notion of a nailed-up Messiah; the Greeks and Gentiles screamed "foolish!" at the thought of a Powerful One succumbing to the ultimate penalty of god Roma. Both camps in Corinth were trying to accommodate the "Scandal of the Cross" to human wisdom and expectations, which simply does not work. For Paul, any wisdom or philosophy that emptied the cross and gospel of its content and power, and did not connect with the countercultural, alternative way of Jesus, was a big problem. [11]

Considering the story of the children of Israel, however, we should at least sympathize with the "Scandal of the Cross." They were waiting in eager expectation for the promised Messiah who would fight their last fight, restore temple worship, and come riding in on a white horse as their king. They were expecting him to defeat their Imperial Roman oppressors once and for all, not be slaughtered at the hands of Empire. The idea that the Messiah should be crucified and butchered on the very symbol of an Empire He was supposed to defeat was not subversive; it was grossly obscene. A crucified Messiah was an oxymoron, a complete contradiction of terms. In the words of my friend and mentor John Frye: A crucified Messiah "does not compute!"

Likewise, the idea of a crucified god defied Greco-Roman categories of a Deity. How can one be divinely powerful if one succumbs to the ultimate penalty of Rome? If you think of Rome in god-like terms, it becomes even more absurd. Roma was the God of Rome. In battles people would pray and give burnt offerings to Roma beforehand to ensure victory. Thus, when Roma and Britainia went to battle and Roma won, it was thought that Roma was a more powerful god than the god of the Isles of Britain. To suggest, then, that another god actually triumphed while dying at the hands of Roma was foolishness!

From human understanding and wisdom you can have a Messiah or you can have a crucifixion, but you cannot have both, at least not from any human perspective. A Messiah equalled power, splendor, and triumph. A crucifixion equalled weakness, humiliation, and defeat. No human in his or her right mind could conceive of such a rescue event: a crucified Messiah. [12]

In contrast to the Jews and Greek Gentiles, Paul declares a paradoxical notion of a crucified god: this apparent foolish and weak and powerless God dies at the hands of Roma—a scandal to the Jews and foolishness for "pagans." This crucified Messiah is the Wisdom and Power of God for salvation, so that a rescue not of human effort or wisdom is possible. [13] The gospel is not some new human wisdom and philosophy. How could it be? The (un)offensive gospel completely obliterates all human categories of wisdom for both God and human rescue.

What's interesting is that modern day people are befuddled by this crucified God, too. Through his character Pi Patel, Yann Martel in his book, *Life of Pi*, says the Jesus Story is downright peculiar. Martel writes:

> That a god should put up with adversity, I could understand. The gods of Hinduism face their fair share of thieves, bullies, kidnappers and usurpers...Adversity, yes. Reversal of fortunes, yes. Treachery, yes. But *humiliation? Death?* I couldn't imagine Lord Krishna consenting to

be stripped naked, whipped, mocked, dragged through the streets and, to top it off, crucified—and at the hands of mere humans, to boot. I'd never heard of a Hindu god dying. It was wrong of this Christian God to let His avatar die. That is tantamount to letting a part of Himself die. For if the Son is to die, it cannot be fake. If God on the Cross is God shamming a human tragedy, it turns the Passion of Christ into the Farce of Christ. The death of the Son must be real. But once a dead God, always a dead God, even resurrected. The Son must have the taste of death forever in His mouth. The Trinity must be tainted by it; there must be a certain stench at the right hand of God the Father. The horror must be real. [14]

In the end, Pi wonders how on earth God would wish this upon Himself. "Why make dirty what is beautiful, spoil what is perfect?" [15] Why? "Love. That was Father Martin's answer." [16] That is God's, too.

Do you see the beauty in this? My wonderful friend, Mykha'el, said the most amazing thing about the anti-wisdom that is found in the cross: "What God did through the cross and Christ was creepy!"

I love that. The cross *is* creepy!

When he said that I laughed so hard and marveled at both the simplicity and complexity of that statement. So much is conveyed in Mykha'el's observation that God through Jesus is "creepily in love with humanity. What God did was creepy, because it demonstrated intense, obsessive love for humanity." What Mykha'el means here is that, just like a lover might obsess over his or her object of affection—an obsession that might look creepy to the outsider—so too was God's love for humans. God was obsessive to the point of coming to earth as a human and being slaughtered on a cross for our rescue and re-creation.

"We're part of the greatest scandal ever!" Mykha'el said.

He is exactly right!

Who would have ever conceived of God coming to earth as a human, denying the powers of His divinity to live in humiliation as a full human, and eventually suffering at the hands of the very ones He came to rescue? Even more:

Who could have anticipated that the crucified Messiah/god would actually defeat evil, sin, and death by triumphing over them all through resurrection? That's exactly what Paul is saying here in 1 Corinthians: a crucified Christ is a contradiction in terms the same way that wet fire is impossible! Yet, through the creepy, obsessive, and furious love of God, all humans can find rescue and re-creation in His death and resurrection,

What incredible news! What a hopeful message! What a thoroughly (un)offensive gospel!

Defining "Gospel"

Please understand that I am only pouring out and studying a thimble size of the massive ocean that is the hopeful message of Jesus. The conversation within these pages is really a conversation about the gospel. It probes the question, "Just what is this hopeful message of Jesus?" Because the good news that Jesus taught, embodied, and for which He sacrificed His life is so deep, thick, meaty, luscious, weighty, beautiful, lovely, and magical I approach this (un)offensive gospel humbly and (hopefully) with great care.

The Greek word for 'gospel' is *euangelion*. This simply means "good news." In Mark 1:15 that's what Jesus calls the invasive presence of the Kingdom of Heaven, *euangelion*. Some people have reduced the entirety of this good news to Jesus dying on a cross to pay the penalty for human sin and purchase a place for humans in heaven after death. While this description sounds like an oversimplification of *this* version of Jesus' message, this manner in which the gospel is communicated and understood is the foundation of much of the conservative Christian world.

Another version of the good news is about communal liberation from oppressive powers to bring freedom and justice to the earth. This is the foundation of liberation theology and the more social gospel flavors. In this version there is little focus on the individual sinful acts by all humans, but rather it focuses on broad social structures that perpetuate the sin of oppression, injustice, and social inequality. Jesus is said to have come to destroy and subvert these Powers to raise-up the least of those in society. For them, the cross is a subversive symbol of the systemic evil of Empire Rome and a moral example of love.

These are two ends of a broad spectrum of the meaning of the gospel with varying degrees in the middle.

Last year on my blog, novuslumen.net, I asked the open-ended question: "How does Jesus define the gospel?" I left it open for people to sound off and articulate *Jesus'* articulation of the gospel. Not John Piper's or Paul's, but Jesus'. In our emerging, postmodern culture we need to recapture how Jesus defined His own gospel. The reason I posted this question was really for a series of posts which led to this book. I wanted to get some ideas about how people defined the gospel in relationship to Jesus.

Here were some great responses to that probing question:

"For God so loved the world that He gave His only Son …" –Alden

"Jesus wants us to unconditionally love each other, help each other, and be good to each other. This means feeding the poor, clothing people, helping to heal people, caring for people, and trying to help those that are (in the eyes of society, irreparably) screwed up, etc. Another part of the gospel is loving God. For me, this means trying to see the good in the world that God is/could be responsible for, and also doing all of the things listed above for other people." –Maria

"'The Kingdom of God/heaven is at hand.' In this way, Jesus offers us all a new way of being human, the way that we were created to be. The good news is that it is here, now." –George

All of these responses revolve around the essence of the good, hopeful news that Jesus shared throughout His ministry: the Kingdom of God.

Here is, I believe, Jesus' articulation of the gospel: "'The time has come,' he said. 'The Kingdom of God is near. Repent and believe the good news!'" (Mark 1:15.) When I say *gospel* (meaning good news), I mean the Kingdom of Heaven and Reign of God. As I have wrestled over the past three years with the good news of Jesus, much of my understanding of what it is has centered on the central teachings of Jesus on the Kingdom of Heaven. I truly believe the fulcrum upon which the broad idea of the gospel/good news of Jesus rests is the Kingdom of Heaven. In short, it is God's movement through the life, death, and resurrection of Jesus to restore both the God-Man relationship and all of creation to the way they were intended to be at the beginning.

The gospel is not simply that humans sin or are sinners and need a savior. The gospel is not simply social liberation. The gospel is not simply that Jesus died on the cross for the sins of humans. The gospel is not simply the destruction of injustice. The gospel is not simply about being saved from hell and salvation into heaven. All of these things reflect aspects of His gospel, but none of them (by themselves) are the fullness of the good news of Jesus. Rather, the fullness of the good news that Jesus taught throughout His ministry and life is the Kingdom of Heaven, an idea that is not inherently offensive, and when communicated properly is (un)offensive.

Indeed, the good news that all of creation has been groaning for since the dawn of creation is this declaration by Jesus: "The Kingdom of Heaven has now invaded the world! My movement to rescue and re-create the world anew is beginning. This is good news, and comes by denying and giving up the Way of Self and rhythm of this world and following Me."

How is this offensive? If the whole world is groaning for re-creation as Paul says in Romans 8, and if all people thirst after Life and deeply desire re-creation, why would we Christians automatically assume the hopeful message of Jesus would be offensive to people? Why would we *insist* this good Jesus and hopeful message are offensive?

Throughout the Gospels, wherever Jesus went this invading Reign of which Jesus spoke trailed like a rainbow from a pot of gold. Throughout Galilee He restored the social dignity of people, He healed diseases, brought sight to the blind, and made the lame walk. All of these acts resulted from the good news of Jesus.

These "events" of rescue and re-creation were not the gospel, but the result of the spread of the good news of the Kingdom of Heaven through Jesus.

When John the Baptizer asked if Jesus was the Messiah, here was his response: "Go back and report to John what you hear and see: The blind receive sight, the lame walk, those who have leprosy are cured, the deaf hear, the dead are raised, and the good news is preached to the poor." [17] These were the very words Jesus said were prophesied in Isaiah concerning the in-breaking of God's Reign and Kingdom. Jesus told John's followers to report this so that he would know that the gospel had finally come.

But to say that Jesus and His beautiful, hopeful, life-giving news of the Kingdom of Heaven are not inherently offensive doesn't mean people will not react in offense. In summarizing the idea of the (un)offensive gospel, my friend Andy said, "The (un)offensive gospel of Jesus is the amazing news given to us by the historical event of the cross and resurrection that God is actively working to rescue us and our world and reconcile all things to himself. People shouldn't fear because of God's active work to rescue and restore the world, but they might be made uncomfortable because it makes them aware of their situation: sin and the consequences of rebellion. Those are uncomfortable, not the gospel."

The (un)Offensive/Offensive Gospel

Andy is onto something in that previous quotation: the good news that Jesus came to embody, demonstrate, and proclaim is God's active work to rescue and re-create us and our world. But while Jesus' own life, teachings, and Way provide the life and hope for which all people are searching, His demands and confrontation of the rebellion in us all often meet with resistance. Sometimes people don't want to listen to what He and His hopeful Story offer, and they respond in offense.

In this book, I am arguing that Jesus and His gospel Story are not inherently offensive, but instead hopeful, beckoning, and life-giving—both are what a person has been waiting for their whole life. If this is the case, if the gospel is *not* offensive, why do people still resist Jesus' good news? The disciples would have wondered the same thing, actually. After Jesus begins His ministry, sends His disciples to do what He was doing throughout Galilee, and begins to receive great opposition from the very people to whom He was sent, many of His followers would've been wondering why He and His message were not being welcomed or acted on by everyone who heard. If the Kingdom of Heaven really was the good news for which all of Israel and the world had been waiting, where was the triumphant response? If the message is good and the bearer of that message is God's Messiah, why did people refuse to listen and respond?

To answer these question, Jesus illustrates the receptivity of people by telling a story about four soils in Matthew 13. In it, He tells of a farmer who went out into his property to sow seeds in anticipation of a bountiful harvest. As he was scattering the seeds, some fell along the path and were eaten by birds. Other seeds fell on rocky places without much soil. Some seed fell among soil with thorns, which grew up and choked the seedlings. Still other seeds were sown in good soil which produced a crop yielding thirty, sixty, and a hundred times what were sown.

Jesus ended the parable by urging the listeners: "Let the person who has ears to hear—listen!"

Understandably, the disciples wondered aloud why Jesus spoke to the crowds like this, rather than plainly. Jesus explained the parable in this way: when some people hear the good news of the Kingdom of Heaven and they do not understand it, the Evil One snatches what was sown; some people receive the teachings with joy, but fall away because they have no "roots" like seeds on a rocky path; still others receive the good news, yet the worries and cares of life choke it and make it unfruitful, like thorns; and finally, the one who receives the seed of the Kingdom, hears it, and understands it produces a bountiful crop. As cryptic as Jesus might sound, this is *the* parable for understanding the good news of the Kingdom of Heaven, the gospel. [18]

Here, Jesus explains why people are not responding to Him and His hopeful message like the disciples thought they would: not everyone will hear by receiving the Kingdom and respond by actively living it out. The gospel (good news of the Kingdom of Heaven) is a verbal challenge to us to reorient our lives around Jesus and His Way. People must "hear" and respond with a lifestyle that bears fruit in obedience to the message of God as revealed in Jesus Christ. For reasons explained in Jesus' parable, people will not always receive the hope of the gospel. This realization, however, does not give the Church license to be jerks. Just as the sower took care to distribute the potential little plant life in his surrounding world, so too is the Church to take great care in distributing the good news of life in the Kingdom through Jesus Christ.

In the Parable of the Soils, Jesus' emphasis was on the "soil," those who hear His teachings and hopeful message. While something could be said about the sower and the person who scattered the seed, Jesus spoke directly to the people who encounter Him and His gospel. The apostle Paul, on the other hand, sketches a wonderful portrait of how that sower should look. In a letter to the Thessalonians, Paul described the way in which he, Silas, and Timothy related to the believers and unbelievers in this community:

> As apostles of Christ we could have been a burden to you, but we were gentle among you, like a mother caring for her little children. We loved you so much that we were delighted to share with you not only the gospel of God but our lives as well, because you had become so dear to us. Surely you remember, brothers, our toil and hardship; we worked night and day in order not to be a burden to anyone while we preached the gospel of God to you. You are witnesses, and so is God, of how holy, righteous and blameless we were among you who believed. For you know that we dealt with each of you as a father deals with his own children, encouraging, comforting and urging you to live lives worthy of God, who calls you into his kingdom and glory. [19]

As apostles, they could have used their "apostleship card" to demand conformity to their teachings and instructions. Because of their positions in the Church, Paul, Silas, and Timothy could have used their power to force change and conformity. But they didn't. Instead, they lived among the Thessalonian community as "mothers" and "fathers." They scattered the life-giving, hopeful seed of the (un)offensive gospel of the Kingdom of Heaven like mothers nursing their young. This imagery replaces any claims to power and authority with service and love. Rather than simply preaching at the Thessalonians and demanding repentance and change, these early Christians labored among them night and day as fathers caring for and encouraging their children. Through these power-denying, nurturing efforts, many people throughout Asia minor and beyond met the loving, gentle, caring Jesus and His hopeful gospel Story.

What a great example for showing and telling. While people are responsible to listen to and respond to Jesus and His Story, we are called to show and tell both as nursing mothers and encouraging fathers. Though Jesus explains why some people in His own time did not respond as hoped to the announcement of the good news of the Kingdom of Heaven, plenty of people did and found the Life for which they had been waiting all along.

If everywhere Jesus went the people who needed it found holistic (social, economic, physical, and spiritual) healing and restoration, and people followed Him as a result of this restoration, who then were the offended ones? Were they not those in religious and political power who sought to destroy Jesus' Kingdom movement? It seems like those who were especially offended by Jesus were the religious leaders of the day who were threatened by Jesus' teachings and re-creative power. Those in power sought to maintain power by killing the man who threatened that power, Jesus of Nazareth.

So what of this notion that people are offended by the gospel and Jesus? If the power inherent in this good news is the rescue, re-creation, and life all people are seeking, why would we think people would be offended? Could there be *another* reason so many are turned off to Jesus and that good news?

Let's face it: in this emerging, postmodern culture we Christians are at times offensive; those whom Jesus sent to bear witnesses to Him and His message offend. Jesus isn't offensive, the version of Him perceived by the world is. The gospel isn't offensive, the versions of that hopeful message we tell the world often are. How is this the case, you ask? Let's wrestle with this throughout the next several chapters. If you're a follower of Jesus, I don't know about you but I want to show and tell the world about a Savior and Kingdom that is real and deep and magical, rather than fake and thin and drowsy, let alone...offensive. Before we get there, however, we the Church need to understand how we are currently showing and telling, and how the world perceives both.

Chapter 2
the Jesus we show, the Story we tell

"The Church is f–ed up!" What a great way to start a conversation about my future profession as a pastor!

Usually when someone asks me about what I am studying, I dodge the question with a vague "I'm studying theology" response. That's usually enough to change the subject. Not for Beth. While working with her at Starbucks, she asked me outright if I was studying to be a pastor. Apparently, the rumor mill being what it is, churned out a juicy morsel that I was in seminary studying to be a pastor.

I answered, "Sort of." For me words matter and knowing the context of West Michigan, the Mecca of all things Christian, I am usually deliberate with the words I use to describe who I am in Christ and what I am pursuing in my studies. Maybe I learned it while working in politics and ministry on Capitol Hill in Washington, D.C. where people immediately peg you as either "this" or "that" with two, ten-word sentences. I wanted to nuance my future pastoral pursuits and describe what exactly shepherding a church meant for me.

That's when she offered up her analysis of the Church. Did you feel the jolt of profanity at the beginning? I think this anecdote is important, because it sketches a picture of what the Church is doing in the eyes of the rest of the world around Her. For an entire generation of young adults, Christianity has become something to despise and view with skepticism at arms length. When young outsiders (age 16-29) think about the Bride of Christ, recent studies show they perceive her as anti-homosexual, judgmental, and hypocritical. [20]   While perceptions never define reality, they sure do help us understand it. Rather than being understood solely by good Jesus and His hopeful Story, the Church is dismissed and completely irrelevant to our world.

In their words, the Church is f–ed up!

Why? What has happened to cause this seismic shift? A hundred years ago the Christian community was at the center of society and culture, making large contributions to the arts, science, and civic good. Even until the last decade 85% of adults were favorable toward Christians, with young adults closely mirroring that perception.[21] Now people are extremely concerned with the Church's involvement in the affairs of society and believe She has little to offer. In fact, now only 16% of young outsiders have a favorable impression of Christianity, nearly two out of every five (38%) have a bad impression and one out of every six (17%) indicate he or she maintains a very bad impression of Christianity. [22]

Unfortunately, the Church has lost Her voice and prophetic authority. Instead of being entirely understood and known for love, rescue, and re-creation, Christians, as noted in the above statistics, have a nationwide reputation for being anti-homosexual, judgmental, and hypocritical. Consequently, the Jesus people perceive in His followers is exclusive, inhospitable, condemning, rude, and angry.

Instead of marching down the streets of our broken urban communities and depressed suburban shopping malls waving the banner "God Loves You!" America perceives the Church as prancing around in t-shirts emblazoned with, "God Hates Fags!" Instead of being known for love, gentleness, and care, the Church is often viewed as hateful, harsh, and judgmental.

That's too bad.

Antigay and Judgmental

The Fall I returned to Grand Rapids from Washington, D.C., the Grand Rapids community college featured a play production called *Seven Passages: The Stories of Gay Christians*. The play was a 100 minute dramatic piece incorporating twenty-eight stories from gay Christians in the West Michigan area. It told of their first realizations

Most Common Perceptions of Christianity:

•91% – Anti-homosexual.

•87% – Judgmental.

•85% – Hypocritical.

of same-sex attraction, how they wrestled with those attractions and implications in light of their Christianity, and subsequent fallout (both good and bad) from coming out to their communities. It also discussed the response from their Churches, their prevention to participate in the life of the faith community post-outcoming, and the hopes and dreams for their lives (existential and spiritual) and the life of the Church concerning this "issue."

The last place on God's green earth I thought I would find a constructive dialogue piece on homosexuality and the Church was Grand Rapids, Michigan. Washington, D.C. certainly, but absolutely not *the* bastion of all things conservative and Christian!

That's exactly what I found, however, in this production.

The play was not so much theological as it was existential. While it did address some of the theological and biblical issues surrounding homosexuality (hence the use of the seven often quoted Scriptural passages as a springboard for the dramatic dialogue), the whole of the production centered on the dual experience of Christians living as followers of Jesus and gay people, and the tragedy and comedy that befell their lives.

Obviously, the issue of homosexuality and the Church is a hot potato. What often happens, though, is that the discussion is completely divorced from real people and their stories. Maybe that's why the Church is known for being anti-homosexual and judgmental. Maybe the American Church is perceived in this way because our trumpeted ideas about what is real about sexuality are completely divorced from the stories of individual people. Because our response to the *issue* of homosexuality is often divorced from *people* within the gay community, the very community that is supposed to be the entry point for all humans (LGBT included) to experience Jesus' Kingdom of Heaven and *shalom* often respond with un-love.

In response and reaction to these featured stories, the community that should have provided space for them to wrestle and journey toward wholeness in Jesus can be categorized by one word: hell. Their communities responded with hell, as in "you're going to burn in hell for this." Literally, their family and church (especially their church) said that God would send them to hell for having this aspect of them that was attracted to "their own kind." Of course the Bible (and variations of the seven passages in particular) was used to set them straight (pun intended!), but usually only had the effect of driving these men and women far from God, far from the only source of Life that would have provided the *shalom* for which they (all of us) longed.

One woman said that the reaction from her Christian parents reduced her to "a thing." She was "a thing living in the basement." After she came out to her parents, they were so repulsed that they didn't speak to her for days and weeks. Their relationship disintegrated and her humanity was leveled to below a kitchen roach.

The Church's response was no less unfortunate.

Even though they weren't necessarily sexually practicing, most were barred from participating in the life of their church. No one was available or willing to talk with them within their communities and the pastors were horrified and disinterested, not even desiring to help them sort through their confusing feelings. A pastor I know who was featured in this play lost his ministry of 18 years after it came out that he believed himself to be gay, even though he was not practicing. These churches perfectly lived up to our cultures perceptions.

I think the thing that struck me the most was how shutout they were from Jesus' table fellowship. In the ancient Jewish culture, dining with someone was a sign of intense acceptance, hospitality, love, and commitment. If you said, "I want to have a meal with you," what the other person heard was, "I want to do life with you!" Throughout all four Gospels, we see a Jesus who pursued meals with people from all backgrounds: Jesus dined with greedy tax collectors, wretched prostitutes, and plenty of other unclean "sinners," as they were labeled by the tidy religious elite of Jesus' days. In other words, Jesus *did life* with everyone whom society *and* the religious community intentionally marginalized and bordered-out as "sinner."

In the stories of these gay Christians, the communities who should have mirrored Jesus' table fellowship practices were completely unwilling to engage in dialogue to hear their story, even if they disagreed with them and their life choices. There was no interest to engage them as people created in the "image of God" nor was there any desire to listen to how their journey brought them to their place. No dialogue. No care. No dignity.

No love, only walls.

To be sure, there were some parents that reassured their children of their love and even came to the point of embracing the reality of this aspect of their son or daughter. I do not recall a single story, however, where a community of Jesus embraced them and their story, wherever they were and whatever the story was.

How sad.

I don't mean to belabor the point that we the Church are perceived as anti-homosexual and judgmental. In twenty-first century America where the Culture Wars continue to stoke the flames of anti-homosexual sentiments and judgmentalism, Christians need to come to grips with the fact that the Church often shows a Jesus who marginalizes and condemns, rather than accepts and loves. I can imagine that in a decade someone will find this book for a buck at a used books store and chuckle in amazement at my emphasis on the gay and church communities. This issue, however, is probably the single most pressing issue that is currently influencing our cultures perceptions of Jesus, His people, and His Story. I don't believe the content of our reaction is necessarily to blame, but rather the way in which we've handled that content; the *what* is not the problem, the *how* is the reason Jesus and His community is viewed as angry, judgmental, controlling, and disinterested in, even hostile to, the lives of real people.

Here is one more story to make my point of the judgmental, condemning Jesus we are showing; the judgmental, condemning Jesus the world is seeing.

This summer I went to my ten year high school reunion. Yikes! It really was a wonderful time even though I literally hadn't seen most of them in a decade. In between drinks and hors d'oeuvres were conversations about life, family, jobs, and...church. Because I am a graduate student studying theology and I help pastor a small church in the Grand Rapids, MI area, the topic of religion and church naturally came up. It was fun to hear some of the stories from people I never would have thought growing up would be small group leaders or even involved in the Christian scene in Grand Rapids. I was pleased to hear about several who attended a few of the churches for which this area is known.

Others, though, have dropped out. Completely.

After living in one of the most Christian saturated parts of the country, several people whom I knew well growing up are now completely disconnected and disinterested in Jesus and His community. While they were embedded within the fabric of West Michigan Christianity as kids and teens, as adults the Church and Jesus are the least of their concerns and completely off their radar.

Why? What were their reasons for dropping out? Too judgmental, closed-minded, and hypocritical. This follows national patterns where fully one in four young adults have completely disconnected from American religion in general, including Christianity. [23] In fact, they are the least likely to identify with being Christian (68%) in comparison with those 40 and older who overwhelming (80% or higher) identify with Jesus and His Story. [24]

One of the guys at the reunion told me about how his gay uncle recently died of Lou Gehrig's Disease and was completely ostracized from his Christian family and church community because of his orientation. For fifteen years, the uncle struggled in a game of tug-of-war between his sexual attractions and Christian family who were all trying to "save" him. Leading up to his death, the guys father, a Protestant pastor, would preach to the uncle trying to convert him from his "condition" and save him for Heaven, even though the uncle considered himself a Christian.

For this high school acquaintance, the Jesus displayed through countless churches and Christian family members was enough to send him packing from Jesus and His community of "followers." Even now it's really hard for him to think about following Jesus and getting involved in a community after he witnessed what his family and countless other Jesus followers did to his dying gay uncle.

To some Christians, this might seem an appropriate response. For some, taking an active stance against sin within the Church through exclusion and discipline is entirely consistent with the role of a local church. The apostle Paul himself actively wrote against those within the Church who were actively and deliberately continuing in rebellion, urging his brothers and sisters in Christ to root out willful sin. While I understand, and even embrace, such serious handling of continued, willful sin, this response must be tempered with the relational example Jesus Christ Himself set in His interaction with and embracement of those labeled "sinner" by the community.

Consider His example found in Luke 7:36-50. In this passage, a woman who "lived a sinful life in the town learned that Jesus was eating at the Pharisee's house." [25] This characterization marked her as a prostitute by vocation, a whore by social standing, and ceremonially unclean. [26] For reasons not mentioned in the text, she buys an expensive jar of perfume, wets His feet with her tears, wipes His feet with her hair, and pours the expensive perfume all over them. Given her social standing and vocation, these actions would have been regarded as highly erotic: as a woman she was already viewed as a temptress and sex object; letting her hair down would have been like removing her top; and she would have appeared to be fondling Jesus' feet like a prostitute eliciting sexual favors. [27] Yet despite who she was before and what she did during the visit and meal, Jesus did not flinch.

How did the religious elite respond? "I can't believe Jesus is letting this 'sinner' touch him! If He really is a prophet, surely He would know the scandalous, sinful life she leads. If He did, there is no way He would allow such close, intimate fellowship with her. He should have kicked her out of the house!"

the (un)offensive gospel of Jesus

Typical. This response is all too reflective of many within the Church who react to the full range of sinners who desire intimate fellowship with Jesus and His community. Jesus responded quite differently, however. After challenging Simon, His host, with a parable on love and forgiveness, He reminded him that this 'sinner,' as Simon put it, did everything that he, the religious elite, failed to do. Therefore, because this woman loved Jesus much, her sins would be forgiven. Despite who this woman was and what she did, Jesus embraced her in fellowship, forgave her sins, and sent her away in peace.

Between the guy at my high school reunion and several others I've recently met, I get the feeling that they have better things to do than get involved with what they perceive as an anti-homosexual, judgmental Jesus, much less a community reflecting these understandings of this version of God' Son. What's interesting (and sad) is that there is growing evidence that people are rejecting Jesus precisely because some of His followers show a terribly poor Jesus who draws thick borders around Himself and His Kingdom.

In a study on the spiritual patterns and perceptions of Christianity by young outsiders and young adults, David Kinnaman and Gabe Lyons reveal in their book, *unChristian*, that one out of five of all adults have had very negative experiences in the Church and with Christians that have negatively influenced their view and image of Jesus; 50 million adults view Jesus negatively because of negative experiences with His followers. [28] Among those between the ages of 16 and 29, three out of ten had negative experiences with Christians leading to a negative image of Jesus; in fact, they are two and a half times more likely to say those negative experiences have degraded their impression of Jesus. [29]

Is this really what we the Church want to be known for? Do we really want to be known for our antigay sentiments? Do we really want to be known as a condemning, judgmental community who can barely keep its *own* pants on, let alone keep track of who are taking their pants off when and with whom? Do we really want to be responsible for an entire generation disconnecting from Jesus and His Story because of their perceptions of our un-love?

•20% of adults have had a negative experience with the Church and Christianity that has influenced a negative view of Jesus Christ.

•30% of young adults have had negative experiences with Christianity that have influenced their perception of Jesus Christ.

•Young adults are 2.5 times more likely to have a negative image of Jesus Christ because of experiences with the Church.

Thanks to some within the Church, not only does rebellion stand in the way between a person and God, we Christians do, too.

Blow Horn Guy (Or Gal)

If you are a Christian, you've probably seen or heard the classic *Bridge Illustration* evangelistic tool to help tell God's Story of Rescue. In this illustration there is a great chasm with two sides: humans are on one side and God is on the other. The illustration explains that sin separates humans from God, but that great gulf is "bridged" by Jesus, who provides a bridge between the two. While that may be true, our postmodern, post-Christian context has another problem besides sin. Now a second gulf has opened between non-Christians and God's Story itself, a gulf that inhibits them from even considering a Story that explains their rebellion and God's rescue.

In his book, *They Like Jesus But Not The Church*, author and pastor Dan Kimball writes about the new challenges facing the Church in our postmodern, post-Christian culture. He explains that in the Judeo-Christian world of the midtwentieth century, the *Bridge Illustration* worked well because most people understood the idea of one God, generally understood what sin was, and respected church leaders and Christians enough to listen readily to their explanations of Jesus. [30] While this may have been true a generation ago, this has all changed in our post-Christian culture. Before people are willing to hear the Story that explains the first "chasm" between humans and God (sin and rebellion), they come across another chasm: Christians.

The attitudes and rhetoric of many Christians have created another chasm between non-Christians and God's Story of Rescue. Even before people are willing to listen to Jesus and His hopeful message, they need to get through the barriers we erect that prevent them from listening in the first place. The negative perceptions presented earlier in this chapter create this new chasm and prevent them from listening to God's Story of Rescue that tells them of the second chasm of rebellion and need for God's rescue. And as Dan Kimball says, "Because we have become citizens of the bubble, having lost our understanding that we are missionaries in our culture and staying comfortable within our church walls and networks, the new chasm only continues to grow." [31]

Look at the illustration below to get an idea of the problem:

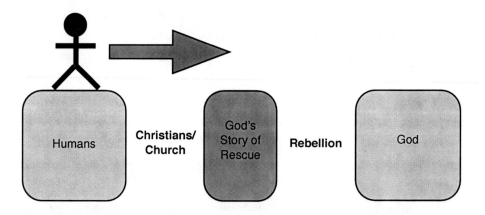

The way in which the Body of Christ has interacted with and responded to the world has contributed to their disinterest and disconnection from Jesus and His Story. The way in which many Christians have shown Jesus has negatively affected Americas perception of Him and His hopeful message. In fact, people never even get to interact with both, because of the distance we've created between them and God's Story of Rescue through our actions and attitude.

Who's chief among the offenders? Blow horn guy.

You know who I'm talking about. I'm referring to those people who insist on standing on milk crates in the middle of rush hour downtown, blow horn in tote, to let the world know that every one of them are skipping straight into hell unless they repent and turn to Jesus. I realize most Christians aren't as dramatic. Most Joe-Sixpacks and Ms. Hockey Moms aren't berating their coworkers, friends, or fellow commuters about their sin and labeling them "evil doers, hypocrites, and sodomites." Others, however, are doing a tremendous job of destroying the credibility of Jesus, His community of followers, and Story of Rescue through their reckless, non-Jesus acts of un-love.

A recent article in a local state university student newspaper illustrates this point. On September 20, 2008, the student newspaper reported that a Lansing, Michigan man, his family, and group of local supporters spent the weeks condemning gays and other groups under the campus' central square. His message claimed each student was going to hell for homosexuality, listening to rock and roll, wearing "slutty" clothes, smoking cigarettes, and other "sins." [32] Here is some of what the newspaper reported:

"You all are headed to hell," he shouted at a group of students who gathered around him. "You are all hypocrites. You all are heathens. I am not a sinner, I am perfect. But you're not; you're all headed to hell."

"The message in a nutshell is obey Jesus, or burn in hell," Venyah told the Lanthorn Tuesday. "The way people respond to the message is, in general, very resistant. The majority of people don't like to hear our message. But the Bible shows us that when prophets preach, most will show resistance."

Opposition has come in a variety of ways.

Signs, like "Hate does not represent me, my faith or my community," have dotted the crowd. Some broke out into hymns or formed prayer groups, while other students engaged the speakers in verbal confrontations and arguments.

Film and video student Dan Rickabus led a group of musicians Wednesday that began playing music under the Transformation Link, forcing the speakers to the grass near the VanSteeland Arboretum.

"Everyone was so angry (Tuesday), so we're just trying to bring some love to the scene instead of crazy amounts of hate," Rickabus said. "And what has love? Music. That's a lot better than just being pissed, (which is) what they want."

Soulwinners plans to continue speaking through Friday, but some are claiming the university should step in before then. Sophomore Becky Takacs said the group should be removed from the campus for committing bias crimes.

"These are hate crimes disguised as free speech," she said. "They are persecuting everyone. He called me a 'lustful individual' because I'm engaged. I saw another girl break down in tears because he pointed at her and said 'You're nothing but a pervert.' We should have the right to go to class without feeling intimidated and threatened." [33]

On the website version of this article, the newspaper posted a YouTube video of highlights and student interviews throughout the week. The comments of one student caught my attention: "I believe they have a right to be here. Any protest has the right to be anywhere. I just feel this is outlandish!" The student reporter followed up his remarks by asking, "Do you think they are taking their right to free speech and right to be on campus and protesting too far, by causing this disruption?" The student replied, "All protests are met with opposition. You can't really have a peaceful protest without people coming in and saying, 'You can't tell us this. We don't believe in this,' or people coming and saying, 'We believe exactly what you are saying.' But to tell you the truth I haven't met a single person here who is saying, 'I believe what this person is saying.' We all feel opposed to this. So yes people have the right to protest here. But is it working? No." [34]

I found it incredibly interesting that the word this student used to describe the activity of this group of people was *protest*. In the eyes of this student, the Christians who were shouting at the crowd and proclaiming "the truth of God's Word" were not offering anything remotely close to the good news of the Kingdom of Heaven of which Jesus and the apostles spoke. To him and others their actions were nothing more than a protest, a protest against gays, rock and roll, "slutty" clothes, smoking, and other "sins." Life was not offered in the words of these supposed followers of Jesus. These "Christians" were not defined or known by the loving, gentle, caring Jesus of the Holy Scriptures nor by His hopeful, (un)offensive gospel. Instead, they were viewed as hateful, persecuting protestors who offered the students nothing more than a bitter elixir of judgement and condemnation.

Maybe this is why only 16 percent of young outsiders say the phrase "consistently shows love for other people describes Christians a lot." [35] This is incredibly ironic, because I thought we Christians were to be known *entirely* by our love, the same love that Jesus Christ showered on those with whom He came into contact, the same love that drove Him to the cross on behalf of all humans.

I thought we were to be known by our hospitality, the same hospitality that demolished the barrier between Jew and Gentile and expanded Jesus' table fellowship to include all people from every corner of the world.

I thought we were to be known by a basin and towel—these simple objects of service—rather than by swords and shields, by objects of attack and defense.

I thought we were supposed to follow Jesus into His countercultural, alternative way of living and being, rather than responding like every other divisive pattern of life found in the world.

My young adult friends, Cameron and Ben, intuitively know that this is what Jesus' community of followers is to be about. Cameron said, "The (un)offensive gospel of Jesus is something that's inviting for everyone. Therefore, the Church is to be a place where everyone feels accepted and secure, regardless of looks and color and actions." Ben chimed in with, "We are to be about unconditional love." These guys are spot on!

In response to the acts of un-love by the group of people at the state university, one of the Christian students interviewed by the newspaper nailed it: "I am compelled to wonder how many people they have ever converted with their threatening message, verbally abusive tactics, and down right disrespect for people," said senior Derek Plumb. "How can they misinterpret the Bible so badly where they are claiming to represent a man so loving and peaceful and forgiving, but in ways that are disgraceful, rude, and hurtful?" These offensive "Christians" showed an offensive Jesus and told an offensive Story, neither of which were the real deal.

After I found out about this incident I shared the article with my friend, mentor, and colleague in ministry, John Frye. We both sat fuming at the arrogance, pure un-love, and destruction this group caused. We wanted to run to this university and cry, "This man and his group does not represent us! They don't represent Jesus and His hopeful, (un)offensive gospel message!" We wanted to instead take up the example of one author and erect a confessional on this campus to confess all the sins of the Church to them and our American culture. [36]

Later, John said we Christians often offer Jesus like a father introducing his daughter to a potential suitor who says, "This is my daughter and you *will* love her! In fact, you need to change everything about who you are right now before you can marry her, but you *will* marry her!" Guys, would any of us jump at such an "invitation?" I sure wouldn't! In any relationship, love and affection for another comes through a journey of discovery, through belonging to that person and becoming better aquatinted with them and their "story." Only through countless dates, late night phone conversations, heated arguments, and even discussions with the friends of potential mates do any of us fall in love. None of us make immediate changes for our "earthly" relationships nor do we embrace them through strong-arm tactics of excessively assertive fathers. Why would we Christians think people would embrace relationship with Jesus without the same journey?

Just as we grow into relationships, romantically or not, I think the same is true for anyone who encounters Jesus and His Story. So often Jesus is shoved on people with little sensitivity to the courting, journey process of those who would follow after Him. The Church has no right to simply insist that people embrace Jesus and His Story, while completely changing beforehand. She needs to be more sensitive to the belonging and becoming that occurs before believing.

While I readily admit this university example does not entirely reflect the actions and attitudes within the Church, I think it illustrates well why Christians are not all that well liked and why many people simply do not care to see or hear what Christians have to share. How we often show Jesus and tell His Story—more importantly, how the world sees and hears both—is contributing to a mass exodus toward post-Christendom, not simply the culture's slide into postmodernity or secularism. Though some Christian leaders may try to shift the blame, we cannot simply lay this disconnection on cultural corruption. While people do react to Jesus and His message in offense and selfishly desire to continue in their own way of living, their disinterest in them is not exclusively their fault.

It's the Culture Stupid!

I realize some of you reading this believe the reason our culture thinks Christians are repulsive, judgmental bigots is because it has slouched so far toward Gomorrah that it can neither discern truth nor appreciate it. This was the argument someone made recently when I shared the idea of this book and data, both statistical and anecdotal.

After talking about the huge swing in appreciation of Christians, by young adults particularly (84% in 1996 versus 16% in 2006), he said that, while the church has definitely failed in some ways, we cannot be blamed for drastic cultural shifts. He said that because the culture has decayed so much in the last 10-12 years, of course it will label us antigay and judgmental; since the American culture has darkened and become more polluted, it is no wonder that they find Christianity repulsive.

I took major issue with this analysis. On the one hand, I certainly agree that we the Church should not go masochistic and endlessly punish ourselves for past misdeeds. I agree that people do react negatively to Jesus and His message because we are rebels and insist on living according to our own Rhythm of Life. On the other hand, to simply chalk American culture's skip toward post-Christendom as sinful decay is at best simplistic and at worst completely dishonest. While cultural conditions have contributed toward our post-Christendom slide, is our culture more powerful than the Church? I thought Jesus said the Gates of Hell would not prevail against the Body of Christ as it moves into polluted territory to bring rescue and re-creation through the Reign of God. Is the Zeitgeist of American Culture more powerful than the Spirit of God? Can darkness extinguish the light? John doesn't say so in His Gospel!

In response I offered up anecdotal evidence from West Michigan as evidence for the American Church's failures to show Jesus well. A year ago in May 2007, I returned to a place I fled five years prior. After graduating from a liberal arts university in Ohio, I moved to Washington, D.C. to work for a United States Senator and later a ministry on Capitol Hill. Between my D.C. experience and undergraduate time, I was very disconnected from the Grand Rapids area for a good nine years. After returning, I was amazed to see the incredible amount of change this place had undergone, not least of which was the incremental shift away from the Church and Christianity among an entire generation.

As I mentioned earlier for those not familiar with West Michigan, it is seriously the Christian Mecca of the world. Three of the top Christian publishers (BakerBooks, Zondervan, and Eerdmans) operate here, devotionals like *Our Daily Bread* are produced in this city, there are more churches than gas stations, and two versions of the Bible (NIV and tNIV) are published here. West Michigan is a very culturally Christian community, which is both a blessing and a curse. So of all the places that should be immune to cultural decay and influence, it should be West Michigan. If one pocket of the country should create long-term generational appreciation for and devotion to Jesus and His Story it should be the Grand Rapids area.

After returning home after being away for nine years, I am amazed at what is occurring among an entire generation of West Michigan young adults. In a place as 'Christian' as Grand Rapids, the Church should not be disaffecting and disillusioning an entire generation of young people. If She was truly 'being the Body' and showing Jesus and telling His hopeful, (un)offensive gospel well, why are sanctuaries across West Michigan hemorrhaging an entire generation?

I realize that we Christians are human. I understand that the Church is filled with struggling, broken people who are trying their best to live like Christ. I get that we will never act perfectly until we are fully re-created upon Jesus' return. I get all of that and do not at all wish to heap upon the shoulders of Christians the responsibility of acting perfectly. (By the way, this is exactly why only one chapter is devoted to unpacking how we are not acting well.) Yet, if the West Michigan Church were truly living out Her identity as the Body and Bride of Christ, then would She still loose an entire generation? If She were telling Jesus' hopeful story and message with conviction and love, while also showing Jesus well, Grand Rapids would not now see an entire generation somersaulting toward post-Christendom.

West Michigan of all places should not be moving toward a post-Christian condition like some places, such as Seattle or San Diego. A place that is saturated with church communities should not be leaving an entire generation of people, let alone Christians, thirsting for a more authentic encounter with their Creator. How exactly are we telling God's Story of Rescue? If Jesus and His gospel message are the power of God for salvation for all people, what exactly are we doing with this hopeful message? The Church's contemporary problem does not simply stop with poorly showing Jesus, for Her problem is also with the way in which She tells His hopeful Story. And the problem with the way in which we tell it is in the place we start. Rather than starting at the beginning, we start in the middle. This messes the whole thing up completely!

Getting The Story Wrong From The Beginning

Part of my problem with the whole "offensive gospel" thing is its starting place: this distorted version either begins with heaven or sin. One of the most well known tools for sharing the gospel begins with sin: *Romans Road* begins at

Romans 3:23 and emphasizes our screwed-upness. Another well known method, *Evangelism Explosion*, starts with heaven as the entry point into the gospel of Jesus. The first two questions of this method ask if a person knows for sure if she will go to heaven when she dies and what she will say to God in heaven when He asks why He should allow her to enter. The rest of the 'presentation' begins with heaven being a gift that isn't earned or deserved.

On the one hand the world is so screwed-up that we better be sure we're not going to a *more* screwed-up place (hell). On the other hand, we are so screwed-up and in need of help that we do not even realize our screwed-upness and need for redemption apart from God, if we are lucky enough to be among the 'chosen' to realize it in the first place. These understandings and articulations of Jesus' gospel message start at the wrong place. While I do believe in everlasting life and appreciate the concern that individuals understand they rebel against a Holy God, this is where I differ: God's Story of Rescue neither begins with sin nor heaven. Rather, the starting place is *creation* and the fundamental nature of humans as Image-Bearers of God.

At the beginning of the Story God tells, humans were created good. They were creatures crafted after their Creator and were by nature Eikons, Image-Bearers of the Divine. [37] Genesis 1 and 2 paints the picture of how the human story began, what that story is fundamentally, and where God wants to return the human story. If the human story begins with Genesis 1 and 2, then people are not fundamentally sinful nor are we fundamentally sinners. Instead, we are fundamentally Image-Bearers of the Creator; fundamentally we are beings that are called to reflect and in fact *do* bear the reflection and Image of God, an albeit faded one. Furthermore, God created a good world and called us to be co-creators with Him to steward, explore, and enjoy the very good earth now and in the future.

Storytellers who believe the human story starts with Genesis 3 and the "Fall" say humans are so screwed-up that they really need to be told they sin; sinners cannot realize they do things which they should not do, that the way they live is not the way it's supposed to be. Humans are fundamentally sinful and cannot desire anything else but sin and any way other than the rhythm of this world. A

Story that begins with heaven says that the only thing that matters is where people are going to go when they die. It says that all we should be concerned about is some magical world in outer space down the road, instead of figuring out life right now. For these Storytellers, this world is not our home and we're just a passin' through, the world is evil and bad, and the point is get to heaven and escape out of *here* to a home out *there*. Both Storytellers transform Jesus' good news into a message that is either drained of love and compassion or completely unappealing and uprooted from real-life circumstances right now.

Now to be sure, I believe the Scriptures teach that humans sin, that they choose the Way of Self over against the Way of God. All humans are born with the capacity and desire to do sinful things. Any front page of the newspaper will attest to this. But humans are cracked Eikons, meaning they are broken Image-Bearers of God and in need of rescue and re-creation; like Humpte Dumpte, we need to be put back together again! We also exist in a world that is controlled by Deep Magic, an evil power that dulls the senses to fully understanding God and His reality and a magic that entices people to do things they know deep down just aren't in line with the way life is supposed to be lived. Jesus said this when He revealed that human hearts are blinded by the darkness of this world. So while humans do things that are sinful, humans are also profoundly influenced by the Deep Magic of the world.

As equally important to affirm is the reality of a new world that will eventually burst forth upon the return of Jesus Christ. The Book of Revelation reveals that Jesus will come to make all of this stuff new, humans and all. The picture that Revelation paints is of heaven coming down to earth, not earthlings going to heaven; God will eventually dwell with humans in the world He created, which was His original, created intent from the beginning. So in affirming a final re-creative act, we must point back toward creation to how the Creator intended us to be and the *shalom* that will finally and ultimately permeate God's good world.

The real problem, though, is not simply with where we begin in retelling God's Story of Rescue, but in the substance of its actual retelling. While beginning in the wrong place can seriously warp Jesus' hopeful, (un)offensive message, *how* we tell it can have disastrous consequences.

How We Tell The Story

When I was certified as an *Evangelism Explosion* trainer (although after this book they may decertify me!), I remember a very odd and disturbing occurrence. One of the sessions, led by EE founder Dr. D. James Kennedy, was entitled "Handling Objections." It was designed to help equip people with the tools to, well, handle the objections people have to the presentation of the gospel message. It was part *Evidence Demands A Verdict,* part *Law and Order* because it ran through the factual reasons Christianity was valid, while helping "the evangelist" evade the questions of the "prospect" like most of the characters in the "whodunit" TV show. That last part still concerns and disturbs me.

When Dr. Kennedy addressed the section on dealing with prospective questions, I'll never forget what he said, it went something like this: "If someone interrupts your presentation to ask a question, don't let him distract you from the gospel message. Instead say this: 'Well, that's a great question, Johnny or Susie. I can really tell that it's important that I answer that for you and I will at the end, after I share what I was going to tell you. So, if you will just put that question in abeyance and ask me again at the end, I'll be sure to answer that important question for you when I'm finished.'"

He said feeding them that line would do one two things: First, it will force *them* to re-ask the question at the end when *you're* finished, which normally never happens because they usually forget. Second, they will be so confused and distracted by the meaning of the word *abeyance* that they will be happy to move the conversation along, drawing approving laughter from those attending the seminar.

So when we're telling God's Story of Rescue, we're supposed to nip any potential dialogue in the bud and assume our friends have nothing to contribute to the conversation? And we're supposed to play mind games with them so they forget their questions and leave the Jesus Story well enough alone?

Not only is this just rude and entirely presumptive, it outright denies what Paulo Freire calls, "the epistemological relationship of dialogue." In an article he wrote for the *Harvard Educational Review* entitled, "A Dialogue: Culture, Language, and Race," Freire describes how dialogue isn't merely a technique to arrive at information. Instead, dialogue and conversations are an entire epistemological relationship, an entire *way* of knowing and a process of gaining understanding and insight into what is real about life. [38] So rather than discourage conversation and dialogue, both should be the starting point. Rather than evade questions and play Jedi mind tricks with our coworkers and relatives, questions should be our playground, not our cemetery. Followers of Jesus should seek every opportunity to engage and sit in the questions of our friends, rather than killing and burying them.

When we evade questions and remove dialogue, what happens instead is a monologue, and Jesus is sold like a vacuum cleaner or set of kitchen knives, sans nifty accessories. So instead of preaching and selling Jesus to our friends, God's Story of Rescue needs to be told in conversational dialogue with them.

This idea of dialogue and presentation was driven home for me my last year of ministry on Capitol Hill. Through one of our larger events, I was connected to a Democratic staffer named Clay. He was interested in dialoging over spiritual things. We started meeting regularly for lunch for almost eight months straight and had the most amazing conversations about life and the spiritual. This intelligent, learned 22 year old grew up Catholic and was deeply committed until his freshman year of college. At a state school in Florida, he was challenged by a friend to deconstruct his faith and reconsider the dogma of the church in light of modern philosophy and scientific discoveries.

So he did. He deconstructed everything and built for himself an a/theistic religion apart from the Bible, Church, and Jesus. In fact, the last time we chatted he considered himself an agnostic/non-theist who appreciated Jesus, but wanted nothing to do with the institution of the Church.

For eight months we dined in one of the Senate dining rooms and talked theology, philosophy, politics, and theology again. I really never had an agenda with our conversations, meaning I never intentionally steered them to "the way of God" each afternoon, but somehow that's where they ended up. Dialogue does that you know. It's like a droplet of water that winds its way down the back of your hand; when it drops loose from an eyedropper you never can tell where it's going to end up. The same was true for our conversations.

Though he challenged my beliefs and assumptions about Christian spirituality, I also pushed back and constantly pointed him toward Jesus. Rather than making the conversation about whether the Bible was true or not, I was really only concerned with what he did with Jesus and His Story.

One day on our way back from lunch, Clay asked me something I'll never forget: "Why don't you ever get offended by my questions and our conversations?" At first I didn't really understand where he was going with his question. He said that for months we had been dialoguing and he had been saying much of what I and the Church believe is a bunch of crap. He was very confused why I never reacted negatively to his ideas or intellectual attacks.

I was stunned. Not only had I really not thought about it, but I didn't know why I had responded in a non-defensive way. I guess I valued the conversation more than I did Clay's conversion. Don't get me wrong. Every time we met I hoped he would inch closer toward relationship with God through Jesus and ultimately follow Him with his life. But in the journey toward following, I wanted to show Jesus and tell His Story well so that I wasn't a barrier between good Jesus and the hopeful message of Christ.

You see, the problem isn't that young outsiders are unfamiliar with Jesus or His Story and message, the problem is what the Church does to create barriers for them. More than four out of every five young outsiders (82%) have gone to a Christian church at some time in their lives, most attending for at least three months. [39] Two-thirds of non-Christians (65%) said they have had conversations with Christian friends in the last year about issues of faith, and around half (53%) had been specifically approached about becoming a Christian. [40] If this is the case, then why do only 23% of young outsiders age 16-29 believe Christianity offers them hope for the future? [41] What is the Story we are offering the world as we explain why things are the way they are? What is the remedy we are offering? Especially in the midst of evil and tragedy, how are we handling the brokenness of the world when it screams at us through every CNN headline?

•82% have gone to a Christian church at some time in their life.

•65% have had spiritual conversations with Christian friends.

•19% believe Christianity offers them hope for the future.

Again, what is the Story we are telling our broken world?

Telling the Story of Our Broken World

Like many Americans, I was fixated on the events from the summer of 2007 in Minneapolis after an interstate bridge collapsed. What especially intrigued me, however, was the response from the Christian community. Unfortunately, the Church has a soiled track record with responding well to pain, tragedy, and hopeless world events. Let's have a little review: a few days after 9/11 a certain Christian leader blamed this tragedy on gays and feminists; after Hurricane Katrina, some other prominent Christian leaders said God wiped out New Orleans as judgment for their sins, mostly because of Bourbon Street shenanigans and abortionists; and yet others swear the catastrophe in Iraq is an omen (well, I guess Christians don't call them omens, but rather "signs of the times") of the imminent return of Jesus and impending Seven Years of Tribulation, complete with 666, Armageddon, and all. Like doctors next to patients in trauma, we really need to brush up on our bedside manor!

Shortly after the events in Minneapolis another national Christian leader, author, and pastor, John Piper, wrote an equally interesting analysis of the spiritual implications of the Minneapolis bridge collapse for that community. I guess it made sense for him to respond since his church is within sight of the bridge and his ministry offices within a mile. His response was both pastoral and theological, with a bit of a theological tilt minus the pastoral sensitivity.

I respect John Piper and know plenty of people who have been helped by his books and messages. I appreciate his heart for people and commitment to Jesus and to seeing people restored to relationship to God through His life and death. So I do not have many bones to pick with Pastor Piper. His blog post on www.desiringgod.org really confused me, though. His response and analysis was all too typical of Christian leaders during times of tragedy.

Here is some of what he wrote that caught my eye:

> Tonight for our family devotions our appointed reading was Luke 13:1-9. It was not my choice. This is surely no coincidence. O that all of the Twin Cities, in shock at this major calamity, would hear what Jesus has to say about it from Luke 13:1-5. People came to Jesus with heart-wrenching news about the slaughter of worshipers by Pilate. Jesus implies that those who brought him this news thought he would say that those who died, deserved to die, and that those who didn't die did not deserve to die. That is not what he said. He said, everyone deserves to die. And if you and I don't repent, we too will perish. This is a stunning response. It only makes sense from a view of reality that is radically oriented on God. [42]

First, I found it very odd that John Piper would think there was some special message for the Twin Cities through Luke 13:1-9. When I read this I thought, "This is what God wants to say to Minneapolis? If Jesus was walking around the twisted metal jutting from the ends of the bridge, wading into the Mississippi around the chunks of concrete, and moving through the throngs of injured, *this* is what he would say in the midst of this gut wrenching scene?"

I'm sure there are other passages to point toward, but John 11 is very instructive. In this narrative Lazarus, "the one [Jesus] loved" was sick. Jesus didn't tend to him immediately, because He knew this future moment would be a glorifying moment for Him and His Father. But when He later went to Lazarus' house, He was met by Martha who was beside herself and angry that Jesus had not come sooner. And when He left her and entered the village, Jesus was met by Mary.

John writes, "When Jesus saw her weeping, and the Jews who had come along with her also weeping, He was deeply moved in spirit and troubled." [43]

Then He wept.

When Jesus encountered the scene of emotional chaos, saw the emotionally fragile Mary, and felt the lament of Lazarus' friends over his death, Jesus' soul was overcome by the moment and in a very authentically human response Jesus cried. He had no words when He stepped into the confusion and chaos. He simply sat with Mary and Lazarus' friends, joining in their weeping.

I can't help but think Jesus would have responded to Minneapolis in the same way, not with a lecture or scroll full of words about sin and instructions on their eternal destiny, but rather with the raw human response of tears and embrace.

John Piper continued:

> The meaning of the collapse of this bridge is that John Piper is a sinner and should repent or forfeit his life forever. That means I should turn from the silly preoccupations of my life and focus my mind's attention and my heart's affection on God and embrace Jesus Christ as my only hope for the forgiveness of my sins and for the hope of eternal life. That is God's message in the collapse of this bridge. That is his most merciful message: there is still time to turn from sin and unbelief and destruction for those of us who live. If we could see the eternal calamity from which he is offering escape we would hear this as the most precious message in the world. [44]

Really? The meaning of the collapse of this bridge is that we are sinners and need to repent? God's message in the collapse of the bridge over the Mississippi River is that He is merciful, we are sinners, and there is still time to turn toward Jesus to be saved, or burn? Now I do not necessarily disagree with any of this theology, but to say that the meaning and message inherent in this tragedy is to "get saved" is just silly and wretched. I would go so far as to say the story John Piper told Minneapolis during this time of tragedy was equally silly and wretched.

The story of Job has a similarly wretched encounter with people who wanted to label the reason for Jobs life tragedy. Several "friends" tried to blame Job by claiming he was living in sin and was being punished by God. Job responded by unmasking these "friends" for who they were: miserable comforters!

On my own blog in response to Piper I wrote, "Why must we preach to Minneapolis in this time? Why can't we just sit with them in their grief, hold them, cry with them, and listen to their stories? Why must we insist on slapping *The Passion* all over this and insist that unless the Twin Cities repents, God will keep sending more messages through more collapsing infrastructures until they get the hint that God is ticked at their screwed-upness?"

I still feel the same way.

Christians are all to quick to tell stories and talk and blabber on about why certain events occur, rather than just sitting with people in their chaos and weeping over the devastating, confusing evil in the world.

Unfortunately, Piper's silly, wretched storytelling continued:

> You and I know that God did not do anything wrong. God always does what is wise. And you and I know that God could have held up that bridge with one hand." Talitha said, "With his pinky." "Yes," I said, "with his pinky. Which means that God had a purpose for not holding up that bridge, knowing all that would happen, and he is infinitely wise in all that he wills." [His daughter] Talitha said, "Maybe he let it fall because he wanted all the people of Minneapolis to fear him." "Yes, Talitha," I said, "I am sure that is one of the reasons God let the bridge fall." [45]

Sorry John Piper, but that doesn't jibe. You mean to tell me that you would say to the mother who accidentally ran over her 5-year-old son as she moved her minivan to a different location outside her home, killing the boy, that it was willed by the purposeful "pinky" of God in all His infinite wisdom? You would tell the adult crack addict that God wanted him to be ravished by years of abuse? You would tell my friend who was sexually abused as an infant that his Creator deliberately crafted that heinous life event to use for His glory as an adult?

While I support God's general sovereignty and His full participation in the human story, the tragedy of a mother backing over her son or the evil of a sexually abused child are no more directed by God than the collapse of a bridge that results in seven deaths and over seventy injured. God participates in reality as Immanuel, the God-with-us-God, not as a programmer who robotically controls and programs all the events of the world. I am thankful that Jesus is the complete expression of the character of God we find throughout the Holy Scriptures, rather than the angry gods of Greek mythology. I'm disappointed that Piper seems to respond with the latter. I am equally dismayed that he and others have told the Story of God in this way, a telling that continues to drive people away.

I could go on, but I think I'll stop. Rather than simply critiquing John Piper, I hope this section is more about the typical story Christians tell our world regarding tragedy and evil than it is about one man who does love Jesus and is trying his best to be a pastor. Needless to say, the Church needs to seriously rethink not only *how* it tells God's Story of Rescue, but also the Story itself, the "what" She tells the world of God and His reality.

As I wrote earlier, this book is about wondering about the Jesus we are showing and the message we are telling the world. I guess in large ways, I feel the twenty-first century Church is not doing a very good job at either. It isn't necessarily about the Church simply failing at doing something well, but more about our modern expressions of Jesus and His good news being incomplete, inadequate, and just plain missing the mark. No, actually it isn't about the arrows falling short of a target; we're aiming the bow in wrong directions!

Three recent high school graduates—Rachel, Cameron, and Ben—voiced these same frustrations at lunch one afternoon. In our conversation I asked, "If you could say one thing to the Church, what would it be?" Rachel said, "Don't be so judgmental." Cameron asked, "What are you doing? Are we reading the same Book?" Ben questioned the trajectory of the Church in asking, "What happened guys?" In each of these responses is embedded a deep awareness that something is not quite right in the Jesus and Story the Church often offers to the world.

Again, rather than simply critiquing and attacking the Church, I hope to sketch a possible alternative to our show and tell efforts. I hope to add a bit to the larger emerging-missional conversation happening within the Church that is reshaping our understanding of the gospel and how we can see what this gospel is through the life and teachings of Jesus. I contend that the life we see and teachings we hear point to an (un)offensive gospel, good news that is wholesome, healing, and attractive rather than unhelpful, unhealing, and repulsive.

So what are we to make of this (un)offensive gospel of Jesus? Where do we begin? And how about this good Jesus? What is He like?

I'll tell you this much, both Jesus and His Story are much more hopeful than you think.

Part One

Jesus-Show

"Who is the Jesus we show;
who is the Jesus people see?"

Chapter 3
the (un)offensive Jesus

It's been said, when a person takes leave of God, we need to ask what sort of God did they take leave of. [46] One could easily say the same thing for Jesus: when someone rejects Jesus, we should ask which Jesus did he or she reject? Central to the (un)offensive notion of Jesus and His Story and message is the idea that in many ways we've shown a bad Jesus and told a bad Story. We've either portrayed Jesus as a Superhero who is entirely unaffected by the stuff of life or made Him out to be a manly Mother Teresa without any concern for who He is as God. So before we understand how to show Jesus well, and way before we retell His Story, we need to understand how the Holy Scriptures show and tell Jesus.

Before we get to Him, however, we need to talk a bit about God. If Jesus fully expresses God, if the entirety of God's divine self-disclosure has been poured into Jesus Christ of Nazareth and He truly is God, then we need to examine this God. In our emerging post-Christian world, we need to ask hard questions about the idea of God which people are abandoning, and why and how we the Church are offering this conception. Now is the time to reevaluate how we speak about the character of God.

Such a reevaluation of the Church's idea of God already began in the mid-1990's with the landmark book, *The Openness of God*. Through this book, the authors offered an innovative, well reasoned argument that the God known through Christ desires responsive relationship with His creatures. I call this *relational theism*. They also argued it was necessary to reconsider such classical theistic views on God's immutability, impassibility, and foreknowledge. Seven years later, Clark Pinnock wrote to extend and revise their original conversation in his equally pivotal book, *Most Moved Mover*. In his book, Pinnock says we need to re-understand and re-articulate our idea of God as a hyper-relational Lover who intimately participates in our world. I agree.

I realize that this discussion of the Church doctrines of God is deep, complex, and multifaceted. Unfortunately, I can't go into greater detail in these pages regarding this important conversation. You should read *The Openness of God* and Pinnock's follow-up work to gain a greater appreciation for and understanding of this dialogue. I still want to offer an alternative, relational portrait of God in contrast to the problematic classical depiction of the God who has revealed Himself in Jesus Christ.

The Unblinking Cosmic Stare

In telling the Story of the version of God found in much of Western Christianity we begin with Greek philosophy, whose god was considered to be the ultimate source and origin of everything, the origin of creation's order and design. According to Roger Olson, author of *The Story of Christian Theology*, "[The Greek Philosophy] god is simple substance, completely free of body, parts, or passions, immutable (unchangeable) and eternal (timeless). He (or it) is everything that finite creation is not—the epitome of metaphysical and moral perfection untouched by finitude, limitation, dependency, emption, passion, change, or decay." [47] Eventually, this god of philosophy seeped into our understandings of God, beginning with Judaism.

Thanks to Philo, a Jewish scholar who attempted to synthesize Judaism and Greek philosophy, Greek philosophical theology began to sink its claws into the Hebrew understanding of Elohim. Gone were the ancient Hebrew relational categories for defining God. The ancient explanations of Old Testament ideas about God could not survive the militant expansion of Platonic theology. "Philo saw many similarities between the god of Greek philosophy who was one, metaphysically and morally perfect, and the creator and judge of all souls, and Yahweh of the Hebrew tradition, who was Creator, lawgiver, and judge of everyone." [48] Thus, Moses and Plato were Siamese twin. This Jewish precedent became the catalyst for early church apologists who superimposed a Greco-Christian costume over Philo's Greco-Jewish foundation. Unfortunately, as we'll see, the God we present to people is still thoroughly Hellenistic, a shadow of His Hebrew lineage.

The traditional, classical view of God reduced Him to an "unblinking cosmic stare," described by Dallas Willard in his book *The Divine Conspiracy*. In this classical view, held today by certain pockets of modern American Christianity, God does not grieve over the suffering of the world nor experience compassion, He is distant from His creation, and has determined its course like a Master Programmer. The classical view insists that the language the Bible used to describe a personal, relational God merely accommodates to finite human understanding rather than viewing the biblical metaphors as real descriptions of the character of God. If Jesus is the fullest expression of God, though, does this really jibe with the divine self-disclosure (Revelation) we find in Him?

During one of my interviews with a young atheist, Taylor had this to say about the God who was presented to her: "In the beginning when I didn't really think about religion and Christianity, I thought God was some guy in the heavens and sky who controlled all my actions, and that's what I didn't like. I didn't want to think life was all planned out. That's how God was presented, someone who was very controlling." I wonder if the reason Taylor has taken leave of God is because of *this* sort of God who was given to her by those who tried to show the God behind Jesus and tell His Story?

A new, relational view of God, however, describes the God of the Holy Scriptures in these ways: it portrays God as a hyper-relational, hyper-personal Lover who seeks relationships of love with humans, having bestowed upon them genuine freedom to relate to God with the same love; love and freedom are central concerns because God is wooing humans into a loving relationship, which requires freedom; it envisions God making a world where the future is not yet completely settled in order to make room for His creatures to freely exist and choose, rather than treating them like puppets whose every move is planned and predetermined; it recognizes that creating such a world was risky, but for some mysterious reason it was better to have a world in which humans could freely love God than one where He always gets His way. God grants humans significant freedom to partner with or against His will for their lives and enter into a dynamic give-and-take relationship with Him. Finally, while God takes a risk in such a give-and-take relationship, He is endlessly resourceful and capable of bringing the world and His plans to an ultimate goal. [49]

We need to be more affirming of God as a living Person involved in history and less as a remote, distant Being. The Church tends to show a God who is immobile, transcendent, and distant, a God who is not affected by life and is far removed from it even though the Scriptures point to a thoroughly hyper-personal and relational God. Unfortunately, our understanding of God was influenced by the Greek pagan *Unmoved Mover* god of Aristotle. Rather than offering the God we find in the Holy Scriptures, who responds to changing circumstances and is passionately involved in the gritty drama of human history, the god typically offered is carved out of the image of a forgery who is distant, unaffected by humans, and removed from their gritty drama.

The Holy Scriptures, however, reveal a hyper-relational God who is not only interested in humans and their lives, but is furiously, creepily in love with them. By creating humans as free agents, God left open the possibility that we would choose relationship with Himself and obey His ordered Way, or reject both. This creative act by God (crafting beings after His Image who had the freedom to choose or reject relationship with the Creator) was incredibly, incredibly risky.

The God Who Risks

Risk. Undefined future. Hyper-freedom. Have you ever thought of God in these terms, as a risky Creator who left the future wide open by injecting His creatures with the freedom to choose how to act and live?

Probably not. Most of our ideas of God are incredibly concrete, deterministic, and entirely un-risky. I mean, who could trust in a God who allowed for uncertainty and risk in the experience of life? Consequently, our modern understandings of God are closer to Aristotle's *Unmoved Mover*: God is like one of the granite faces of Mt. Rushmore, stayed and unmoved through thousands of storms and millions of visitors. But risk, open future, and creaturely freedom is the wonderful world created by a living, creative, *risky* God. A classical view of God, however, suffers from a monarchic view where He is the "sole performer" of the story and dictates the script like a ruler from above, rather than a Being who is intimately involved in and affected by a story in which other characters exist, too

The narrative of the Garden in the Scriptures, however, paints a realm of unlimited possibility, because God created other characters with the freedom to choose. Because true freedom demands real, actual choice, both in relation to God and creation, how could God not be affected at some level by those real choices? Furthermore, because God freely and deliberately loves humans and is conditioned by human acceptance or refusal of that love, God is affected by the objects of His love and made vulnerable by them.

In the Sodom and Gomorrah narrative in Genesis, for instance, we see a God who changes His mind in light of his relationship with Abram; God allowed Himself to be influenced by a human in intimate relationship. God wasn't influenced because the human was stronger than God, but because God chose to be in relationship with Abram, the essential posture of the nature of God was Love, not control. The same is true with us and our current time and space. While God is generally sovereign and is capable of working with all of our messy life choices and circumstances, He is not a computer programer.

Because God is hyper-relational and purposefully created beings after His Image to exist eternally with Him in relationship, the Holy Scriptures reveal a God who is generally sovereign. While the Psalms and Job portray God as above and outside creation, the Holy Scripture's portrait of divine sovereignty is not of a single, all-determining divine will that calls all the shots. Rather, we see an all wise, resourceful, and creative God who can handle all the possibilities that result from the choices of His creation.

A relational view reveals a God who shares power with His co-creators and limits His own power through human freedom, which contrasts against a Greek idea of a domineering, all-controlling despot typically articulated by a more classical understanding of God. While this relational view has a place for God's ruling sovereignty, it recognizes the universe is filled with dynamic forces and events outside God precisely because He risked by creating humans with real freedom. Thus, history unfolds accordingly because God chooses to share His power with beings outside Himself (both human and non-human beings). In fact, this re-understanding of the character of God is helps us understand the problem of evil, a contribution to theology and Christian discussion that is long overdue.

Like the European philosopher-theologian LeRon Shults, I believe "absolute evil" exists in the world. This genuine evil resulted not by the willing hand of an all-controlling God, but rather out of the risky possibility of genuine human freedom. "If love requires freedom and if freedom entails risk, God could not create such a world and be absolutely certain what the creatures would do with it."[50] "Bad things happen to good people" precisely because God is not hyper-controlling nor does he hold a monopoly on power and the affairs of the world. As Pinnock says, "If God had such a monopoly, one would have to deny the existence of genuine evil because evil is something God wanted to happen." Think about that: If nothing happens outside the sovereign control of God, then there is no genuine evil; if everything truly does happen for a reason, then God's hands are rightly stained with the blood of every Jewish Holocaust victim and countless Africans who have died because of starvation and malnutrition.

Because God is hyper-relationally involved with the world and is dynamic, rather than distant and immobile, history is marked by changeability, leading to real alternative possibilities, leading to the presence of evil. The idea that the events of life can change is largely understood in light of God-given human libertarian freedom: a free, active God crafted beings after His own Image as free, active beings that engage in give-and-take relationships with their Creator and others. The Bible itself seems to insist in this freedom when it holds people responsible for their actions, something not easily accounted for by modern-day classic theists. Furthermore, we see this intersection where God experiences change most evident in the activity of prayer.

"In prayer," says Clark Pinnock, "God treats us as subjects not objects and a real dialogue takes place. God could act alone in ruling the world but wants to work in consultation. It is not His way to unilaterally decide everything. He treats us as partners in a two-way conversation and wants our input." [51] God is intimately connected to humans in relationship and exercises a general sovereignty that allows for a variety of outcomes in the world, and the God of the Bible responds to the real needs and requests of humans through prayer. Just think, God changes His mind in response to the interactive relationship of individuals and intervenes in response to these relationships to execute His ultimate goals. Prayer influences God because He wants a genuine relationship with us! This contrasts drastically with the classical understanding of God that prepackages history as predetermined and set, while portraying God as a programmer of code for the Machine of Time.

As A.W. Tozer once said, "A right conception of God is basic, not only to systematic theology, but to practical living as well." Ultimately that is what this conversation is about: flesh and blood humans encountering a real, existential God who dips down into the stories of individuals. While some fear a relational view of God dances to close to the edges of reasonable orthodoxy, it is that unreasonable dancing that will, hopefully, move classical theists from a "Sinners in the Hands of An Angry God" depiction closer to a hyper-relational Lover. Instead of viewing God as a wrathful housemaid who is just waiting to fling a freshly found spider into the licking flames of hell, may we take cues from a view that paints God as a loving Creator who crafted beings after His own Image with real freedom and beckons them to real partnership, yet respects human choice and risks rejection. May we appreciate the vibrant portrait of a God who loves and beckons people from their broken, destructive choices, while still carrying out His ultimate plans for cosmic re-creation. In the end, maybe Western culture is emerging into post-Christendom not because of the God it finds in the Bible, but the one it comes across in the Holy Sepulchers (read: churches) on street corners each Sunday morning. Maybe that is why an entire generation is skipping town, because of the god we are offering people, because of the God we say Jesus expresses.

The Fullest Expression of God

As Wolfhart Pannenberg says in his *Systematic Theology*, only through Jesus is it made known who or what God is. No better do we see the God described in the last several pages than in the person of Jesus Christ. The hyper-relational Lover of a more relational view of God is entirely evident in divine-human Jesus who came to love humans to Life through His death on the cross.

In Chapter 1 of his letter to the Church of Colossae, the apostle Paul wrote about this divine-human Jesus and His act of rescue on the cross. In describing how we have rescue from the dominion of darkness and forgiveness from our rebellion and sin, Paul also described the true nature of this rescuer. Just listen to the cadence of this majestic poem as Paul described the reality of the divine-human Jesus of Nazareth:

> For He is the visible representation of the invisible God,
>   the first born of the whole of Creation.
> For in Him everything in the Heavens and on the Earth
>   were created,
>   the visible things and the invisible things,
>   whether thrones, or dominions, or rulers,
>   or authorities,
>   everything through Him and for Him have been created.

And He Himself is before all things
   and all things are held together in Him,
And He Himself is the head of the Body, the Church.
Who is the beginning,
   the first born out of the dead,
      in order that He Himself might become foremost
      in everything,
   because in Him all God's fulness resolved to take up residence
in Him and through Him to reconcile all things to Himself,
   making peace through His blood of the cross,
     through Him, whether things which are on the Earth
     or things which are in the Heavens.

"He is the visible representation of the invisible God. God in all His fulness resolved to take up residence in Him." These two stanzas communicate everything about the divine-human paradox of Jesus: while Jesus was fully human, He fully expressed God, and is God. So when we the Church seek to bring God to the world, Jesus is who we are to bring. If you are searching for God and desire to know who God is and know His character, Jesus of Nazareth is the one on whom you are to fix your eyes. Through Jesus you know and meet God. Through the Gospels we meet the (un)offensive Jesus.

The (un)Offensive Jesus

In beginning to retell the Story found in the Gospels within the Holy Scriptures, I am again reminded of the unsafe, yet very good Aslan. Similarly, Jesus is very, very good. He is also very, very unsafe. Everyone who met this good, unsafe, (un)offensive Jesus was not left unchanged. It was impossible to stay the same in the midst of His destabilizing presence, to not walk away changed. While Jesus is good and (un)offensive, He is certainly not safe!

He is good and (un)offensive, because He is God. But that very deity also made/makes Him unsafe. He is good and (un)offensive, because He is also very human. Like His deity, He is unsafe because He is very human.

The story the Gospels tell and the Jesus they show is a God-Man who is throughly good, (un)offensive, inviting, hospitable, loving, and caring, yet also very unsafe. He is unsafe, because of His exclusive teachings and demanding Way. Each person who comes across the God-Man Jesus found in the Holy Scriptures must wrestle with the good, (un)offensive, yet unsafe Jesus that he or she encounters on the journey toward Life. It is a journey that co-mingles the divine and human, a dance in which deity twirls with humanity.

We first glimpse this dance in Luke 4, when Jesus announces to His Jewish community that He is the Messiah, the One whom the prophets testified, the One whom they had been waiting for generations. After being beckoned into the desert where He endured temptation by the Enemy, Jesus returned to the town in which He grew and developed. The scene is quite amazing, really: He walked into the synagogue that He had attended for years and sat down with all the other teachers and learned men; upon sitting and waiting He made His move: Jesus stood up to read, took the day's scroll of the prophet Isaiah from the scribe, unrolled it and read the following words:

> The Spirit of the Lord is on me,
>> because he has anointed me
>> to preach good news to the poor.
> He has sent me to proclaim freedom for the prisoners
>> and recovery of sight for the blind,
> to release the oppressed,
>> to proclaim the year of the Lord's favor. [52]

Then He handed the scroll back and sat down. With the eyes of heaven and earth fixed upon Him, Jesus said, "Today this scripture is fulfilled in your hearing. I am the Anointed One sent to the marginalized to tell them the good news of the in-breaking presence of God's hopeful Reign. I am the One the Father has sent to proclaim freedom for the physically and spiritually imprisoned. I have come to re-create the eyes of the blind, to recover their sight. The Father has sent me to release the oppressed and proclaim the Year of the Lord's Favor."

This is the mission of the very divine, very human Jesus.

Jesus said He was anointed and sent to "preach good news to the poor." Poor here is much more holistic, not simply economic or even spiritual poverty. The *poor* described by Luke includes everyone who for any number of socio-religious reasons are marginalized and dismissed to positions outside the boundaries of God's people. In the Mediterranean world economic status wasn't the only determiner of low class status. And the Father sent Jesus to those people, to preach the good, hopeful, (un)offensive news that the gates to His Kingdom are flung wide open, for all people, even the socially spit upon.

Next, the very human and very divine Jesus was sent to heal. Obviously healing people from diseases and illnesses, and even raising people from the dead, was a huge part of Jesus' ministry. The announcement that Jesus was anointed to bring recovery of sight to the blind is clearly an issue of physical healing. This announcement, though, indicates that Jesus also meant it as a metaphor for the eyes of the world being enlightened, receiving revelation, and experiencing salvation. Through the anointed Jesus, the scales on the eyes of the spiritually blind would fall off to provide understanding of God's rescue and the hope of Life.

Finally, Jesus declared that He was sent on mission "to proclaim for the captives release; to send forth the oppressed in release." Here, the mission is repeated twice. Note the repetition of the word "release." Using "release" twice draws special attention to this word as a characteristic activity of Jesus' ministry and mission. Throughout his Gospel, Luke develops this theme of "release" in three ways: Release means forgiveness, that is "release/forgiveness from sins" signaling a restoration to relationship with God and entrance into His community; release made available through Jesus is set in opposition to the binding powers of Satan, so Jesus proclaims healing, wholeness, and freedom from the binding forces of darkness that have their hold on people and society; a final use of release by Luke is a "release from debts" which relates to the Hebrew Scriptures Jubilee legislation— the freeing of slaves, cancellation of debts, fallowing of the land, and return of all land to its original distribution under Moses. This theme is certainly emphasized in the ending when Jesus says He came "to proclaim the year of the Lord's favor."

Everywhere the good, (un)offensive Jesus went, good news flowed to the socially marginalized, individuals were rescued, and people found healing and re-creation. In short: the Year of the Lord's Favor had dawned and the very human, very divine Jesus was the person through which this favor was spreading. The Gospels are writ large with this divine-human Jesus spreading hope and wholeness and release to every corner of the Judean-Galilean countryside. I encourage you to sit in the Gospels (Matthew, Mark, Luke, and John) for an entire year to get to know this (un)offensive Jesus. Throughout these four books, Jesus' mission, life, teachings, and Way are defined by what we have just read and discovered in Luke 4. Story after story is marked by the good news of the Kingdom of Heaven being proclaimed to the marginalized, healing and restoration, and physical and spiritual release.

One such story that incorporates these elements is in the Book of Luke, Chapter 8. I have found this story incredibly helpful in my life journey, especially my journey with Jesus. As I rewrite and reread these words, I still marvel at the very good, (un)offensive Jesus found in this story, the very good, (un)offensive Jesus in which so many people have found rescue and re-creation. Don't we all crave rescue and re-creation, especially in the dark moments of our life when the affects of rebellion come crushing in around us? In those moments, I myself have been comforted and restored by the divine, loving, gentle, caring, (un)offensive Jesus that Luke offers us here in Chapter 8, the same good, (un)offensive Jesus available to every person.

"Don't Fear, Just Believe!"

There are times in our lives when we can move mountains, when our faith is so strong and big and mighty that we face Mt. Everest in the same way we face an ant hill on a stroll through the forest: with one big "stomp" and smother of the shoe! But there are days and weeks (years?) when mustard seeds frighten us to death, sending us to the sweet comfort of the refuge that is our bed.

At the end of 2006 I was in such a state. My life and identity were in shambles. I had lost a second job after being kicked out of ministry and was questioning my existence and reason for being on this earth. To top it off, I rear-ended a guy three days before Christmas *and* spent the holiday alone away from my family. Talk about the depths of despair!

Though I was exceedingly provided for beyond what I could have asked or imagined, I had super trouble having faith in a hopeful, prosperous, and good future; I could hardly see through the chaos of the moment and dream of a land flowing with milk and honey.

A passage which brought great comfort was Luke 8. An amazing story of divine-human Jesus' compassion, kindness and power is presented by Luke. The story provided me with the glimmer of hope I needed to make it to another day, let alone another year. Here is that beautiful story:

> Now when Jesus returned, a crowd welcomed Him, for they were all expecting Him. Then a man named Jairus, a ruler of the synagogue, came and fell at Jesus' feet, pleading with Him to come to his house because his only daughter, a girl of about twelve, was dying.
>
> As Jesus was on His way, the crowds almost crushed Him. And a woman was there who had been subject to bleeding for twelve years, and she had spent all she had on doctors but no one could heal her. She came up behind Him and touched the edge of His cloak, and immediately her bleeding stopped.
>
> "Who touched me?" Jesus asked.
>
> When they all denied it, Peter said, "Master, the people are crowding and pressing against you."

But Jesus said, "Someone touched me; I know that power has gone out from me."

Then the woman, seeing that she could not go unnoticed, came trembling and fell at his feet. In the presence of all the people, she told why she had touched him and how she had been instantly healed. Then he said to her, "Daughter, your faith has healed you. Go in peace."

While Jesus was still speaking, someone came from the house of Jairus, the synagogue ruler. "Your daughter is dead," he said. "Don't bother the teacher any more."

Hearing this, Jesus said to Jairus, "Don't be afraid; just believe, and she will be healed."

When He arrived at the house of Jairus, He did not let anyone go in with Him except Peter, John and James, and the child's father and mother. Meanwhile, all the people were wailing and mourning for her. "Stop wailing," Jesus said. "She is not dead but asleep."

They laughed at Him, knowing that she was dead. But He took her by the hand and said, "My child, get up!" Her spirit returned, and at once she stood up. Then Jesus told them to give her something to eat. Her parents were astonished, but He ordered them not to tell anyone what had happened. [53]

My concern in this section is not the story of the woman, though there is much to talk about here, too. I marvel at the story of Jairus, a synagogue leader and father who came to Jesus with great expectations only to have them crushed, and later restored.

At the beginning of this narrative, you see a man who is part of a system that was diametrically opposed to Jesus and His teachings. Jesus was the competition and a threat to the power structures of the Judean religious order. The rulers of this religious system tried everything to discredit and take Him out, efforts which later culminated in Jesus' kangaroo court conviction and crucifixion.

In the midst of Jairus' personal chaos, his powerful and political persuasions vanished. Instead, he came to Jesus and postured himself in a humble, respectful position by pleading at Jesus' feet on the dusty, grimy ground. He knew deep down who Jesus was and what He could do, and neither his title as ruler nor association with the Jewish elite stopped him from seeking Jesus' help and power.

What created this chaos? The story says Jairus' twelve year-old daughter was dying. So here is a powerful, religious elite who comes to Jesus not as synagogue ruler, but as a father; Jairus is a father beset by stress, worry, pain, fear, and sorrow over the potential of his little girl being taken from him by disease and death.

I find it interesting that there is never any dialogue in the story. Maybe there was an exchange of words, but the narrative shows Jesus continuing about his business (what ever that was at the time) and moseying on through the crowd without dropping anything or immediately coming to Jairus' aid.

How many times does it feel the same for us? I remember sobbing in bed one night in December 2006 and feeling like the darkness was positively going to engulf me, all the while hearing not one word from my supposed Redeemer and Rock! I get the feeling that was how Jairus might have felt. I get the sense that he is humbling himself, maybe he's all dressed up in his synagogue ruler doodads, complete with robes and jewelry, and stooping down before Jesus begging Him to rush to the rescue of his dying little princess. Jesus hears him and acknowledges him, and may show some sorrow for his situation, but continues on His way without the rush or concern that the urgency of the situation deserved.

Then the unthinkable happens!

Jesus stops to investigate a woman who has been hemorrhaging for years. As Jesus is walking through the crowd, this woman believes in who Jesus is and what He can do, and she reasons that even if she just touches the threads on His garment she will be healed. And she is. Then Jesus stops to see what happened.

I can only imaging what Jairus is thinking here. The disciples think He's weird for asking "who touched me" since they were wading through a Red Sea of a crowd. Here is Jairus, who I get a sense is almost dragging Jesus along to get Him to see his daughter and tend to his chaos. Then Jesus stops to seek out the person who touched Him in a sea of people! I'd be pretty frustrated if I were him. I'd be pacing and mumbling under my breath and wringing my hands and trying to push Jesus along with my thoughts to get Him to tend to *my* chaos *right now*!

As Jesus is talking with the woman, one of Jairus' aids comes to bring an update on his daughter's condition: death. Jairus may have thought, "She died while Jesus was taking his own sweet time and asking silly questions. My little princess is gone and the one person who could have done something is just standing here in the middle of the market street having a conversation with a bloody peasant woman instead of rushing to my house to tend to my chaos!"

Then Jesus breaks through the darkness with these words:

"Do not fear, just believe."

Jesus grabs Jairus' shoulders, looks him in the face and tells him, with the same voice and divine authority that calmed the Sea of Galilee and summoned a dead Lazarus back into this reality, to not fear what has just happened in the moment. Instead, Jesus calls on Jairus to continue in the same belief that brought him to His feet in the first place. "Jairus, do not be afraid, just believe, continue believing that I am capable and willing to heal your daughter and it will be so."

Finally, Jesus goes with Jairus to his home. When He gets there people are wailing and mourning at the loss of this girl. Jesus' reply? "Stop it!" I don't image it as a callous, heartless response, but rather a truth-infused, gracious response. He goes on to say, "She is not dead but simply asleep." Sometimes we need the grieving Jesus that we find at the house of Lazarus, and sometimes we need the truthful Jesus to tell us that it's going to be OK. It isn't as bad as you think, and the moment isn't even what you think it is. Jesus steps in and (re)defines the situation for these people by breathing truth into their moment of despair and sorrow: "There isn't death here, simply life waiting to be reawakened through my word and my power."

The people's response? Laughter and doubt. Typical isn't it? I know it was for me in my "dark night of soul." When Jesus reminded me of the words he breathed into me after I was kicked out of ministry, when it was confirmed through other people and circumstances, when Jesus reminded me countless times in silence and solitude that he was drawing me into a season of training and preparation, I laughed and doubted.

But the doubt didn't stop Jesus from working and moving in Jairus' moment. Even when the crowd lacked faith, and even when Jairus' faith was as runny as chicken broth, Jesus cried, "My child, get up! Come back to life, my child. Wake from your slumber, run back to the arms of your daddy and mommy, for I am the Giver of Life, I restore what has been lost."

And that's what divine Jesus is saying to you, too.

These words "My child, get up" are even more powerful because they open wide Jesus' intentions toward us: the good, (un)offensive Jesus longs to draw us into life out from the Valley of Death itself through His hopeful gospel Story.

So, my friend, when you are in the depths of despair, when your soul is dark in the blankness of the night as you drift through the Valley of the Shadow of Death, may you not fear. When you claw in the darkness and try to grasp faith, only to find it whistling through your fingers, may you believe that mustard seeds still move mountains and may you rejoice even in the itsy-bitsy seed that rolls around in your palm. When you feel the creepy claws of death gripping you to the point of suffocation, may you rest in the knowledge that the very divine Jesus is the Giver of Life and He *will* call out to you, by name, and speak "Arise, my Daughter, arise my Son, to new Life!"

Though we find in Jesus the Anointed One who is fully divine and sent by the Father to break the chains of spiritual and social oppression by providing release and freedom and ultimately healing, restoration, resurrection, and re-creation, we also find a very human Jesus. Right along side the divine Jesus who still miraculously raises dead daughters and restores the blind and lame, we have a High Priest who understands our lives, who lived life in full solidarity with us as the God-with-us-God and the very human Jesus.

The Very Human Jesus

We see the very human Jesus at His most fragile (and perhaps best) state on His march toward the cross and resurrection in the Garden of Gethsemane. Here we see the full display of Jesus' humanity, the full display of the suffering Jesus who stood as our ally unto the very end, enduring the shame, humiliation, and ravishment of the cross for every person on the planet.

To begin to understand the Garden experience of the very human Jesus we look to *The Heidelberg Catechism*. The *Catechism* asks this questions about Jesus' experience of suffering in the Garden and subsequent decent into hell:

> *Question:* Why is there added (to the Apostles Creed): He descended into Hell?

> *Answer:* That in my severest Tribulations I may be assured that Christ my Lord has redeemed me from hellish anxieties and torment by the unspeakable anguish, pains, and terrors which he suffered in his soul both on the Cross and before.

Think about that: in our severest of hurts and the most chaotic moments of our life we can be assured that our Savior, Jesus Christ, has redeemed us from hellish anxieties and torments by the unspeakable anguish and pain and terror which He experienced and suffered on the cross, and *before*.

Gethsemane shows us the "before" of Jesus' sufferings.

Because Jesus suffered both before and on the cross, He can have solidarity with humanity. In other words, Jesus is our ally in *full*. We have a very human ally in the very, very human Jesus. Yes, Jesus is fully God. God fully revealed Himself in the person of Jesus Christ and He is God. But Jesus is also fully human. Often we forget this part. We make Jesus out to be a Superhero, someone with Superhuman powers who is shielded from our normal experience of life, who never stubbed His toe, got a cold, or had smelly arm pits. Jesus seems more like Superman than the very human, (un)offensive Jesus of the Gospels!

The Gospel writers, however, were never truer to Jesus than when they avoided the temptation to paint Jesus as a hero who was superior to negative emotions, or as a courageous martyr above fear. Throughout the whole of Jesus' life and ministry we witness up close a very human Jesus who experiences all life has to offer. At the beginning of His ministry He was brought into the desert to experience temptation; He became enraged at the money changers who turned His Father's House into a den of thieves; at the death of His good friend Lazarus, Jesus wept after He was overcome with the emotional chaos of the situation; and you see Him having compassion for people while also becoming irritated at times with the disciples. In the New Testament we see a very human Jesus don't we? Gethsemane teaches Jesus' *full* humanity as well as any text in Scripture.

For some people emphasizing Jesus' humanity is scary. They think that by embracing this very human Jesus we will somehow take away from His divinity, that we will loose the very divine Jesus in the process of embracing a very human Jesus. But think about this: if Jesus had not been truly and very human—meaning had Jesus not been an entire human being without a body like ours or emotions and a mind like ours, nor experienced everything life has to offer—could He really have been our entire and utter representative before God on the cross?

As one commentator says, "take Jesus' humanity away and you take away humanity's salvation." 54

If you take Jesus' humanity away, you take away humanity's rescue.

Embracing a very human Jesus is incredibly important and the great contribution of Gethsemane is to teach Jesus' utter and loyal humanity. Because Jesus was fully human, because He's our utter and loyal ally, He fully experienced everything life has to offer. Jesus can sympathize with our own weakness and temptation and the chaos of our lives. Because of His humanity, Jesus understands what we go through because He Himself has gone through life and conquered it through His loyal obedience and the resurrection.

They went to a place called Gethsemane, and Jesus said to His disciples, "Sit here while I pray." He took Peter, James and John along with Him, and He began to be deeply distressed and troubled. "My soul is overwhelmed with sorrow to the point of death," He said to them. "Stay here and keep watch."

Going a little farther, He fell to the ground and prayed that if possible the hour might pass from Him. "Abba, Father," he said, "everything is possible for you. Take this cup from me. Yet not what I will, but what you will."

Then He returned to his disciples and found them sleeping. "Simon," He said to Peter, "are you asleep? Could you not keep watch for one hour? Watch and pray so that you will not fall into temptation. The spirit is willing, but the body is weak."

Once more He went away and prayed the same thing. When He came back, He again found them sleeping, because their eyes were heavy. They did not know what to say to Him.

Returning the third time, He said to them, "Are you still sleeping and resting? Enough! The hour has come. Look, the Son of Man is betrayed into the hands of sinners. Rise! Let us go! Here comes my betrayer!" [55]

After their pre-Passover meal Jesus and the disciples retreated to a garden in the Mount of Olives called *Gethsemane.* It was an olive garden and a common meeting place for the disciples, which was why Judas easily found them later in the narrative. After sharing a meal with His friends Jesus takes them and retreats to a familiar place to wrestle with this march to resurrection and the inevitable cross beforehand. Once He arrived at this familiar place, Jesus grabbed His three closest allies, Peter, James, and John to comfort Him in His deep emotional experience.

The emotional turmoil of the very human Jesus begins to unfold. In front of His three close friends, He begins to completely unravel emotionally and psychologically.

Key to this whole episode are three important Greek words:

Ekthombeomai—utterly distressed; *"He began to be deeply distressed"* communicates that Jesus begins to become deeply and profoundly shocked at that events that were about to unfold over His entire Being.

Adaymonein—*"He began to be deeply...troubled,"* which means Jesus was in much distress. It is a very strong Greek term for *much trouble and distress* and means severe depression. So as Jesus anticipated the event of the cross, He began to dive into a severe depression with mental anguish and distress.

Perilupos—This word means, "Being stretched to his emotional limits." Mark 14:34 is then translated: "My soul, the very core of my innermost Being is being stretched to its emotional limits to the point of death." Jesus is literally saying, "I feel so bad I could die!"

How many of us have felt the same way? How many of us have felt the creepy crawly claws of fear and chaos and distress wrap themselves around our soul to the point of utter despair, to the point of wanting to die? I think many of us have experienced what Spanish poet and Roman Catholic mystic Saint John of the Cross called "the dark night of the soul," which has become an expression used to describe a metaphor for loneliness and desolation at certain points in our lives.

The very human Jesus experienced that loneliness and desolation, experienced the dark night of the soul.

But why? Why was the Son of God so distressed and stretched to His emotional limits that He wanted to just dissolve and fade away?

Going a little farther, He fell to the ground and prayed that if possible the hour might pass from him.

"Abba, Father," He said, "everything is possible for you. Take this cup from me. Yet not what I will, but what you will."

Jesus left His friends behind to meet with and confront His Father. He fell flat on His face, a physical position that tells of His deep spiritual and emotional condition. Then he cried out, "Take this cup from me!"

Embedded in this "cup" metaphor is deep, biblical language for God's judgment, wrath and punishment on sin and wickedness. A cup in the Scriptures often symbolizes the stored up wrath and punishment of God that is waiting to be poured or given to someone or something.

In this case it was Jesus.

On this march toward the cross and resurrection, you have the very human Jesus sat and prayed in the garden, anticipating the receipt of the cup of God brimming with the full wrath and punishment stored up for all humanity because of our deliberate rebellion.

Now the mental depression and inner anguish and deep emotional shock now begin to set in.

And Jesus begins to waver.

"Please take this cup from me!"

Jesus in some way wanted out. We can only guess what's going through His mind, but in naked honesty before the Father the very human Jesus is asked for an out, for a "get out of jail free" card. He asked His Father if there was some other way, any other way besides the cup, besides the cross.

"Yet not what I want, but what you want!"

The Book of Hebrews says, "even though He was a Son, He learned obedience from what He suffered, and once made perfect, became the source of eternal salvation for all who obey him..."[56] Jesus' acceptance, though, is not like William Wallace's at the end of Braveheart, who simply resigned himself to death and martyrdom. The portrait here contrasts with a portrayal of martyrs who gladly went to their death. Here the very human Jesus of Gethsemane accepts the Father's will not with a "stoic" indifference, but with a mental as well as physical agony, which will reach its horrifying climax with His cry from the cross, "My God my God why have you rejected and forsaken me?!"

On the other hand, His prayer for this cup removal, for the removal of God's wrath and judgment from Him, was not simply a resigned, "Oh well, your will be done...do what you will." No, no rather Jesus told the Father the honest truth about His present emotional and existential condition: He says, "If possible, please take this cup away!" But then He prayed with equal passion, "But the main thing I want is not what I want; yes indeed it is what you want!"

Mark, in his gospel, says that He did this two more times: Jesus returned to his friends who abandoned Him and then back to His Father who abandoned Him, too. He asked the Father out of His depression and agony to take the cup away, but in the midst of His suffering and agony, Jesus learned obedience.

On His march to the resurrection He obeyed by going to the cross.

He drank the cup dry!

For the Church, for those who have placed their trust in Jesus Christ and have given Him their lives and story, the thrill is that when Jesus *did* drink the cup of divine wrath, judgment, and punishment it all *did* indeed go away! Because Jesus drank the cup of divine wrath entirely, there is rescue and no more judgment or condemnation for those who are in Christ Jesus. When Jesus obeyed His Father by going to the cross and drank the cup of divine punishment of human sin, He performed nothing less than universal rescue for the entire world.

For *us* that is the hope: even when we are in the midst of the Dark Night of the Soul, when we are surrounded by chaos, when our inner most Being is stretched to its emotional limit, to the point of death, there is hope. Our hope is in the rescue and resurrection provided by Jesus.

Look at how this drama ends:

> Returning the third time, He said to them, "Are you still sleeping and resting? Enough! The hour has come. Look, the Son of Man is betrayed into the hands of sinners. Rise! Let us go! Here comes my betrayer!"

In the distance, in the darkness that engulfed His entire being, Jesus saw what appeared to be little lightning bugs dancing on the horizon. Those lightning bugs became little flames attached to torches attached to a band of Roman soldiers and Jewish leaders led by one of His friends, even a disciple. They were moving closer and closer towards Jesus and His disciples. He saw it coming. He saw the flood gates about to burst wide open to set in motion the events, the very events that He was agonizing over, over which He was so distraught, depressed, and terrorized in the garden.

And He wanted to run.

He said: "Guys, let's go. Let's get out of here. Here is my betrayer. It's about to happen!"

"Rise! Let's go!"

But then something happened:

He stayed.

He obeyed the Father and He stayed.

He stayed for me.

He stayed for you.

And because He stayed, we have forgiveness and rescue and re-creation.

This isn't what the world sees, though. This isn't the Jesus the Church often shows, and especially the Jesus people see. Somehow we've missed the very human Jesus who came as the Anointed One to bring the hope of the Kingdom, healing and restoration, and release and freedom. The Jesus we see in the garden and with Jairus has somehow left the buildings of thousands of Churches. Somehow the Church has lost Her way, Her moorings to mission and identity as the show-er of the good, (un)offensive Jesus and teller of His hopeful Story. In his landmark book on the Church, Chuck Colson casts a convincing, hopeful vision for the Body of Christ. Throughout his book, *Being the Body*, Dr. Colson explores who the Church is and how She is the manifestation of God's hope for and presence of Jesus in the world. During this exploration, he also laid down a scathing indictment: the Church has lost Her effectiveness and must recapture Her biblical identity.

He is right.

The twenty-first century American Church's fascination with crafting slick worship events (complete with fog machines and rock-star quality light shows), building $93 million facilities (complete with a bookstore, cafeteria, gym, and Starbucks) [57] and fighting petty, alienating "culture wars" (complete with fear-mongering political attack ads) has seriously warped the Bride's understanding of Her identity, mission, and presence. As we saw in Chapter 2, She is failing to show Jesus and tell His hopeful Story well. But how exactly do we recapture our identity as a good Jesus-Show-er and Story-Teller? This is where we pick up the journey in the next chapter.

Chapter 4
showing Jesus well

In describing the great task of the Church in our postmodern post-Christendom world, Ghandi's words are like Paul Revere announcing the arrival of the British Red Coats: "I like your Christ. I do not like your Christians. They are so unlike your Christ."

They are so unlike your Christ.

This needs to change. Period.

A freshman at a local college in my area voiced the same frustrations. Rachel grew up in a West Michigan church and is frustrated by the same hypocrisy that plagues American Christianity to which Ghandi reacted. "Christians sort of say, 'Monday through Saturday are my days to do what I want, but Sunday I have to buckle down.' Christians say one thing and do another. They do not live out the teachings and Way of Jesus. Why would someone want to be like Jesus if we act the way we do?" She's right: why would someone want to follow the Jesus we Christians often show, a Jesus that is often unlike Jesus Christ of Nazareth?

As followers of Jesus, we are called to reflect, show, and be Him to the world around us. As God incarnated Himself in the world as a human, so are we to incarnate the God-Human Jesus Christ in the world around us.

Those who claim the mantle of the "offensive gospel" are usually the first to blame because of their poor show efforts. When I asked my friend Mykha'el to respond to the accusation that "the gospel is offensive" he immediately said, "People are offensive." He continued by saying, "Christians are highly offensive and I have been deeply offended by many Christians." In answer to my question, "How do you think the Church shows Jesus?" Mykha'el said, "They don't! Instead they present a very oppressive religion that does not bring freedom, but condemnation. Jesus talked about Pharisees placing heavy burdens on people, but the Church (especially the conservative variety) does this. It's emotional masochism!" These comments are from someone who has grown up in the Church, who is a deeply passionate follower of Christ. According to Mykha'el, Jesus' community is not showing Him well.

My Jesus-follower friends, Ben and Cameron, and their atheist friend Taylor had similar things to say. In answer to the same question, "How do you think the Church shows Jesus?" consider this dialogue around the table of a local sandwich shop:

> *Cameron*: Part of it is people make mistakes. Christians should strive to be perfect but know that you can't be. We also need to be more accepting. Instead of telling people about our faith, we need to live it. To make a good witness is to be at shalom constantly.

> *Taylor*: I would like that much better!

> *Ben*: We just need to strive to show Jesus' unconditional love.

> *Taylor*: I dated a kid named Tom once, and his dad was an alcoholic. I was never at his house when his dad was not drunk. Tom is an atheist, too, and refused to go to church one Easter. His family and

dad forced him to go and threatened him if he didn't go to church with them. The whole thing, his dad's alcoholism and the Easter drama, seemed so *unChristian*! His dad was unChristian not only because he was an alcoholic, but that he would force Tom to believe.

I think Ghandi and these friends of mine have grasped something significant with their observations. For whatever reason, the world is not seeing the Jesus we find in the Gospels in the individual lives and collective communities of Christ. Since this book is not meant to simply rip on the American Church, I want to cast a vision for showing a better Jesus than the one the American Church is showing, than the one Mykha'el, Ben, Cameron, Taylor, and Rachel have seen growing up in West Michigan.

In short, followers of Jesus are called to incarnate Christ, to be Jesus to the world around them, to embody, demonstrate, and proclaim the Way of Jesus within their own individual communities.

In the same way Michael Jordan lived and breathed basketball, so to are we to live and breath the Way of Jesus. Just as John Coltrane and Miles Davis *were* Jazz, so too are we to *be* Jesus. To live and breath the Way of Jesus, be Jesus to the world around us, and show Jesus well, we must first embody the teachings of Jesus and the Way of the Kingdom of Heaven. After embodiment comes demonstration, a living out of the Way we've stored up in our heart and mind. Then, only after we have embodied and demonstrated Jesus do we have the right to proclaim Him and His Way to those people whom we have developed relationships.

Embody. Demonstrate. Proclaim.

This is how we can show Jesus and tell His Story well.

Embody Jesus' Teachings

Before Jesus sends His disciples on mission to demonstrate the new Reign of God, He sits them down for a little hillside chitchat on the Kingdom of Heaven. On a hill in Galilee, Jesus gathers around Him those whom He has chosen and called to carry forth His mission. He taught them about their new commitments.

These instructions were to those who already responded to Jesus' proclamation to come follow Him. Now these followers needed to learn what life in the Kingdom of Heaven was really about.

These teachings describe a calling to a radically new lifestyle in conscious distinction from the norms of the rest of society. They were to be an alternative society, a "Christian counterculture."

Jesus isn't simply laying down ethical standards, though. Instead, He explained to these new disciples what it looks like to embody the specific demands of the Kingdom of Heaven. These demands do not easily translate into practical day-to-day morality. Jesus isn't giving so much a philosophical discourse on ethics, but rather delivering a *Messianic Manifesto*. He set out the unique demands and revolutionary insights of the one who claimed an absolute authority over other people and whose word, like the word of God, determined the destiny of these men.

As we, the twenty-first century Church, think about showing Jesus well, we are called to think differently about what it means to be human and demonstrate that difference to the world around us. First, however, we must embody the teachings and Way of Jesus regarding this new Reign of God. The values and mores of that Reign must become part of our very nature if we are to demonstrate the Way of Jesus and show Him well.

Jesus' *Messianic Manifesto* in Matthew 5-7 is where we begin to understand what it means to embody the Kingdom and Way of Jesus; this is where we learn how to live as God intended us to live at the start of creation. Only after the disciples learned about the values of the Kingdom did Jesus then send them out to demonstrate the fullness of the new Reign.

The same must be true for us.

As you read through Jesus' *Messianic Manifesto*, consider these questions to help you being thinking about how to embody Jesus' teachings and Way in anticipation of demonstrating a new, more real way of being human:

- What is the internal mind/heart shift I must *embody*?
- What is the corresponding external action I am called to *demonstrate*?

• How would demonstrating these embodied teachings and Way bring rescue and re-creation in the world around me? How could demonstrating these embodied teachings repair the "vandalism of shalom" sin/rebellion have brought to the world?

Jesus' *Manifesto*, Matthew 5-7

Now when He saw the crowds, He went up on a mountainside and sat down. His disciples came to Him, and He began to teach them saying:
   "Blessed are the poor in spirit,
      for theirs is the kingdom of heaven.
   Blessed are those who mourn,
      for they will be comforted.
   Blessed are the meek,
      for they will inherit the earth.
   Blessed are those who hunger and thirst for righteousness,
      for they will be filled.
   Blessed are the merciful,
      for they will be shown mercy.
   Blessed are the pure in heart,
      for they will see God.
   Blessed are the peacemakers,
      for they will be called sons of God.
   Blessed are those who are persecuted because of righteousness,
      for theirs is the kingdom of heaven.

Blessed are you when people insult you, persecute you and falsely say all kinds of evil against you because of me. Rejoice and be glad, because great is your reward in heaven, for in the same way they persecuted the prophets who were before you.
   You are the salt of the earth. But if the salt loses its saltiness, how can it be made salty again? It is no longer good for anything, except to be thrown out and

trampled by men. You are the light of the world. A city on a hill cannot be hidden. Neither do people light a lamp and put it under a bowl. Instead they put it on its stand, and it gives light to everyone in the house. In the same way, let your light shine before men, that they may see your good deeds and praise your Father in heaven.

Do not think that I have come to abolish the Law or the Prophets; I have not come to abolish them but to fulfill them. I tell you the truth, until heaven and earth disappear, not the smallest letter, not the least stroke of a pen, will by any means disappear from the Law until everything is accomplished. Anyone who breaks one of the least of these commandments and teaches others to do the same will be called least in the kingdom of heaven, but whoever practices and teaches these commands will be called great in the kingdom of heaven. For I tell you that unless your righteousness surpasses that of the Pharisees and the teachers of the law, you will certainly not enter the kingdom of heaven.

You have heard that it was said to the people long ago, 'Do not murder, and anyone who murders will be subject to judgment.' But I tell you that anyone who is angry with his brother will be subject to judgment. Again, anyone who says to his brother, 'Raca,' is answerable to the Sanhedrin. But anyone who says, 'You fool!' will be in danger of the fire of hell. Therefore, if you are offering your gift at the altar and there remember that your brother has something against you, leave your gift there in front of the altar. First go and be reconciled to your brother; then come and offer your gift. Settle matters quickly with your adversary who is taking you to court. Do it while you are still with him on the way, or he may hand you over to the judge, and the judge may hand you over to the officer, and you may be thrown into prison. I tell you the truth, you will not get out until you have paid the last penny.

You have heard that it was said, 'Do not commit adultery.' But I tell you that anyone who looks at a woman lustfully has already committed adultery with her in his heart. If your right eye causes you to sin, gouge it out and throw it away. It is better for you to lose one part of your body than for your whole body to be thrown into hell. And if your right hand causes you to sin, cut it off and throw it away. It is better for you to lose one part of your body than for your whole body to go into hell. It has been said, 'Anyone who divorces his wife must give her a certificate of divorce.' But I tell you that *anyone who divorces his wife, except for marital unfaithfulness, causes her to become an adulteress, and anyone who marries the divorced woman commits adultery.*

Again, you have heard that it was said to the people long ago, 'Do not break your oath, but keep the oaths you have made to the Lord.' But I tell you, Do not swear at all: either by heaven, for it is God's throne; or by the earth, for it is his footstool; or by Jerusalem, for it is the city of the Great King. And do not swear by your head, for you cannot make even one hair white or black. Simply let your 'Yes' be 'Yes,' and your 'No,' 'No'; anything beyond this comes from the evil one.

You have heard that it was said, 'Eye for eye, and tooth for tooth.' But I tell you, Do not resist an evil person. If someone strikes you on the right cheek, turn to him the other also. And if someone wants to sue you and take your tunic, let him have your cloak as well. If someone forces you to go one mile, go with him two miles. Give to the one who asks you, and do not turn away from the one who wants to borrow from you.

You have heard that it was said, 'Love your neighbor and hate your enemy.' But I tell you: Love your enemies and pray for those who persecute you, that you may be sons of your Father in heaven. He causes his sun to rise on the evil and the good, and sends rain on the righteous and the unrighteous. If you love those who love you, what reward will you get? Are not even the tax collectors doing that? And if you greet only your brothers, what are you doing more than others? Do not even pagans do that? Be perfect, therefore, as your heavenly Father is perfect. Be careful not to do your 'acts of righteousness' before men, to be seen by them. If you do, you will have no reward from your Father in heaven.

So when you give to the needy, do not announce it with trumpets, as the hypocrites do in the synagogues and on the streets, to be honored by men. I tell you the truth, they have received their reward in full. But when you give to the needy, do not let your left hand know what your right hand is doing, so that your giving may be in secret. Then your Father, who sees what is done in secret, will reward you.

And when you pray, do not be like the hypocrites, for they love to pray standing in the synagogues and on the street corners to be seen by men. I tell you the truth, they have received their reward in full. But when you pray, go into your room, close the door and pray to your Father, who is unseen. Then your Father, who sees what is done in secret, will reward you. And when you pray, do not keep on babbling like pagans, for they think they will be heard because of their many words. Do not be like them, for your Father knows what you need before you ask him.

This, then, is how you should pray:

> *'Our Father in heaven,*
> *hallowed be your name,*
> *your kingdom come,*
> *your will be done*
> *on earth as it is in heaven.*
> *Give us today our daily bread.*
> *Forgive us our debts,*
> *as we also have forgiven our debtors.*
> *And lead us not into temptation,*
> *but deliver us from the evil one.'*

For if you forgive men when they sin against you, your heavenly Father will also forgive you. But if you do not forgive men their sins, your Father will not forgive your sins.

When you fast, do not look somber as the hypocrites do, for they disfigure their faces to show men they are fasting. I tell you the truth, they have received their reward in full. But when you fast, put oil on your head and wash your face, so that it will not be obvious to men that you are fasting, but only to your Father, who is unseen; and your Father, who sees what is done in secret, will reward you.

Do not store up for yourselves treasures on earth, where moth and rust destroy, and where thieves break in and steal. But store up for yourselves treasures in heaven, where moth and rust do not destroy, and where thieves do not break in and steal. For where your treasure is, there your heart will be also. The eye is the lamp of the body. If your eyes are good, your whole body will be full of light. But if your eyes are bad, your whole body will be full of darkness. If then the light within you is darkness, how great is that darkness! No one can serve two masters. Either he will hate the one and love the other, or he will be devoted to the one and despise the other. You cannot serve both God and Money.

Therefore I tell you, do not worry about your life, what you will eat or drink; or about your body, what you will wear. Is not life more important than food, and the body more important than clothes? Look at the birds of the air; they do not sow or reap or store away in barns, and yet your heavenly Father feeds them. Are you not much more valuable than they? Who of you by worrying can add a single hour to his life?

And why do you worry about clothes? See how the lilies of the field grow. They do not labor or spin. Yet I tell you that not even Solomon in all his splendor was dressed like one of these. If that is how God clothes the grass of the field, which is here today and tomorrow is thrown into the fire, will he not much more clothe you, O you of little faith? So do not worry, saying, 'What shall we eat?' or 'What shall we drink?' or 'What shall we wear?' For the pagans run after all these things, and your heavenly Father knows that you need them. But seek first his kingdom and his righteousness, and all these things will be given to you as well. Therefore do not worry about tomorrow, for tomorrow will worry about itself. Each day has enough trouble of its own.

Do not judge, or you too will be judged. For in the same way you judge others, you will be judged, and with the measure you use, it will be measured to you. Why do you look at the speck of sawdust in your brother's eye and pay no attention to the plank in your own eye? How can you say to your brother, 'Let me take the speck out of your eye,' when all the time there is a plank in your own eye? You hypocrite, first take the plank out of your own eye, and then you will see clearly to remove the speck from your brother's eye.

Do not give dogs what is sacred; do not throw your pearls to pigs. If you do, they may trample them under their feet, and then turn and tear you to pieces.

Ask and it will be given to you; seek and you will find; knock and the door will be opened to you. For everyone who asks receives; he who seeks finds; and to him who knocks, the door will be opened. Which of you, if his son asks for bread, will give him a stone? Or if he asks for a fish, will give him a snake? If you, then, though you are evil, know how to give good gifts to your children, how much more will your Father in heaven give good gifts to those who ask him! So in everything, do to others what you would have them do to you, for this sums up the Law and the Prophets.

Enter through the narrow gate. For wide is the gate and broad is the road that leads to destruction, and many enter through it. But small is the gate and narrow the road that leads to life, and only a few find it.

Watch out for false prophets. They come to you in sheep's clothing, but inwardly they are ferocious wolves. By their fruit you will recognize them. Do people pick grapes from thorn bushes, or figs from thistles? Likewise every good tree bears good fruit, but a bad tree bears bad fruit. A good tree cannot bear bad fruit, and a bad tree cannot bear good fruit. Every tree that does not bear good fruit is cut down and thrown into the fire. Thus, by their fruit you will recognize them. Not everyone who says to me, 'Lord, Lord,' will enter the kingdom of heaven, but only he who does the will of my Father who is in heaven. Many will say to me on that day, 'Lord, Lord, did we not prophesy in your name, and in your name drive out demons and perform many miracles?' Then I will tell them plainly, 'I never knew you. Away from me, you evildoers!'

Therefore everyone who hears these words of mine and puts them into practice is like a wise man who built his house on the rock. The rain came down, the streams rose, and the winds blew and beat against that house; yet it did not fall, because it had its foundation on the rock. But everyone who hears these words of mine and does not put them into practice is like a foolish man who built his house on sand. The rain came down, the streams rose, and the winds blew and beat against that house, and it fell with a great crash."

When Jesus had finished saying these things, the crowds were amazed at His teaching, because He taught as one who had authority, and not as their teachers of the law.

How about you? What do you think? How do you feel? Are you amazed at His teachings? Are you beginning to understand the gravity and weight, joy and beauty of this new Reign, this new original Way of being human?

The Way of Jesus and mission of His community of followers doesn't end with simply reading text on paper, though. Embodying His teachings and Way in our heart and mind is only the beginning. For Jesus, unless that embodiment translates into demonstration, our so-called 'following' is fake. Following Jesus begins with learning the Way of the Kingdom through the teachings of Jesus with full anticipation that the learning will lead to living.

Showing Jesus well begins first with embodiment in our own individual lives. Then, as we participate as member of Jesus' community, we are called to collectively live incarnationally in the world around us by being the eyes, feet, ears, and hands of Jesus.

Demonstrate Jesus' Rhythm of Life

What does it mean to live incarnationally?

In short, it means that we are to be Jesus to the world around us, to do "Jesus acts" in our suburban neighborhoods and urban communities.

Following Jesus first requires an internal shift in our mind and heart; first we are called to retrain our thoughts, feelings, will, and body in cooperation with God's Spirit by learning and adopting the values and way of God's Reign through Jesus. We are called to *embody* the Way of Jesus before we *demonstrate* it.

As I previously mentioned, Jesus' *Messianic Manifesto* of Matthew 5-7, as well as the entirety of His teachings, isn't simply a set of ethical standards. This *Manifesto* is a description of what it looks like to embody the specific demands and Way of the Kingdoms of Heaven, to think in conscious, radical distinction from the norms of the Way of Self and Rhythm of this World.

Jesus-followers are an alternative society, a "Christian counterculture." They need to demonstrate that alternative to the world around them.

That demonstration begins by *noticing* and *going*.

But whom are we to notice? To whom are we to go?

We already saw in the previous chapter how the prophecy of Isaiah as found in Luke 4 completely framed Jesus' understanding of His own mission in the world. In Luke we see whom Jesus was sent to notice: the poor, prisoners/captives, blind, and oppressed. This "noticing" is demonstrated in full at Jesus' table in the next chapter in Luke 5. While the Pharisees and scribes were concerned with the maintenance of clear boundaries between groups, between clean and unclean, Jew and Gentile, righteous and sinner, Jesus broke down those boundaries by noticing and going. After noticing Levi, Jesus goes to Levi to call him to join His movement, to follow. Levi repents and responds to Jesus' announcement, and then Jesus joins Levi by going to his own community to dine with some of Levi's friends.

Now this was no backyard barbeque. My guess is that it was probably closer to a college kegger party given the type of people who were labeled "sinners" and considering the life out of which Levi came. Through Jesus' table practice and teaching, He demonstrates through words and deeds the enlargement of the boundaries of God's people. Jesus noticed the sinner Levi, went to him and announces the good news of God, and called him to repent. Jesus then went with Levi to his community to re-announce the Kingdom and call his friends to repentance, as well.

There is no better place to be schooled in the art of *noticing* and *going*, however, than in the story of Zacchaeus. Jesus demonstrates in full whom we are to notice and to whom we are to go. Read this amazing story of *noticing* and *going* in Luke 19:

> Jesus entered Jericho and was passing through. A man was there by the name of Zacchaeus; he was a chief tax collector and was wealthy. He wanted to see who Jesus was, but being a short man he could not, because of the crowd. So he ran ahead and climbed a sycamore-fig tree to see him, since Jesus was coming that way.
>
> When Jesus reached the spot, he looked up and said to him, "Zacchaeus, come down immediately. I must stay at your house today." So he came down at once and welcomed him gladly.

All the people saw this and began to mutter, "He has gone to be the guest of a 'sinner.'"

But Zacchaeus stood up and said to the Lord, "Look, Lord! Here and now I give half of my possessions to the poor, and if I have cheated anybody out of anything, I will pay back four times the amount."

Jesus said to him, "Today salvation has come to this house, because this man, too, is a son of Abraham. For the Son of Man came to seek and to save what was lost." [58]

Note the surrounding stories that precede this one in Chapter 18: a widow, blind beggar, toll collector, and children; all people of low social status. Then the Zacchaeus story follows the Rich Young Ruler who claims to keep the commands and appears clean/righteous while Zacchaeus is a full-blown sinner. Straight away we have an amazing comparison between Zacchaeus and a whole host of other lowly people, and a contrast between a seemingly righteous man and big time rebel. Zacchaeus belonged to a circle of persons almost universally despised. Luke's introduction of this man as a toll collector identifies him as a person given to dishonesty, abuse of authority, and in the wider Greco-Roman world a person of low status. Even if he was wealthy, it wasn't "landed wealth" (by birth) but money obtained in a way that would not have qualified him for an enviable status. So even as a "ruler" and "wealthy," Luke portrays him as a "toll collector" and "sinner."

And Zacchaeus was a short man!

It isn't simply that he couldn't see over the crowd; rather, the crowd deliberately created a boundary and obstacle for Zacchaeus. They refused him the privilege of seeing Jesus as He passed. Zacchaeus was a person of lowly status in Jericho and was painted as a member of the other low class people in the previous chapter, along with a widow, a toll collector, children, and blind beggar.

But Jesus notices him and goes to him and pursues him. He wants to "stay at his house," which is an illusion to hospitality. Jesus' mutual pursuit of Zacchaeus would indicate to him that Jesus hoped, in the context of a shared meal, to forge a relationship with Zacchaeus in which they were united around the good news of the Kingdom of Heaven.

Contrast this pursuit with the reactions of everyone else, disciples included: grumbling, name calling, boundaries, marginalization. Despite the boundary making and marginalization of everyone else, Jesus brings rescue to Zacchaeus' household. Zacchaeus then joins Jesus in demonstrating the Kingdom to others. He reaches out by giving part of his wealth back to those whom he took advantage and to others who were marginalized. For Luke, almsgiving is neither charity in the modern sense nor an ascetic ideal. Rather, it meant making friends with those who could not give back and giving without expectation of return. Unlike the Rich Ruler, Zacchaeus does not use his wealth to secure honor and friends. Instead, he is a social outcast who puts his possessions in the service of the needy and for the sake of justice. Such a person would indeed be eager to welcome Jesus and, anointed by the Spirit, bring "good news to the poor."

By Jesus' simple act of *noticing* and *going*, He brought rescue and re-creation for a man shoved to the margins of society and gripped by greed. "Being Jesus" doesn't stop there, however, for the Way of Christ also involves deliberately *serving* by being Jesus' hands, by doing acts of neighbor-love to the world in which we find ourselves. No better place do we find a discussion of neighbor-love than in Jesus' conversation with a teacher of the Law.

Let's consider this fascinating dialogue:

On one occasion an expert in the law stood up to test Jesus. "Teacher," he asked, "what must I do to inherit eternal life?"

"What is written in the Law?" He replied. "How do you read it?"

He answered: "'Love the Lord your God with all your heart and with all your soul and with all your strength and with all your mind'; and, 'Love your neighbor as yourself.'"

"You have answered correctly," Jesus replied. "Do this and you will live."
But he wanted to justify himself, so he asked Jesus, "And who is my neighbor?"

In reply Jesus said: "A man was going down from Jerusalem to Jericho, when he fell into the hands of robbers. They stripped him of his clothes, beat him and went away, leaving him half dead. A priest happened to be going down the same road, and when he saw the man, he passed by on the other side. So too, a Levite, when he came to the place and saw him, passed by on the other side. But a Samaritan, as he traveled, came where the man was; and when he saw him, he took pity on him. He went to him and bandaged his wounds, pouring on oil and wine. Then he put the man on his own donkey, took him to an inn and took care of him. The next day he took out two silver coins and gave them to the innkeeper. 'Look after him,' he said, 'and when I return, I will reimburse you for any extra expense you may have.'

"Which of these three do you think was a neighbor to the man who fell into the hands of robbers?"

The expert in the law replied, "The one who had mercy on him."

Jesus told him, "Go and do likewise." [59]

The central issue in this amazing story for Jesus is the practice of God's words and Jesus' teachings. We see this especially evident in the deliberate repetition and placement of the verb "to do":

Lawyer: What must I *do?*
Jesus: Do this...
Neighbor Dialogue Story

Jesus: who *did* neighbor love?
Lawyer: the one who *did* mercy.
Jesus: Go and *do* likewise…

Hearing God's words and understanding them correctly is authenticated in doing. Late this Fall a friend of mine is attending a conference put on by the *Society of Biblical Literature*. The society is a "secular" association of professors and scholars who do nothing more than study the Bible. Most all of them who attend are scholars in their own fields of biblical studies and experts on large portions of the Holy Scriptures. These people know a lot about the Bible, but not everyone *knows* it. Not everyone has given themselves over to its poetry and prose and made a total commitment to the person and Story of the Scriptures. Not everyone is *living* and *doing* the Text.

Jesus makes it clear that a person's practices reveal his or her character and true nature, which flow from a personal response to Jesus and His Story; love of neighbor flows out of a radical love of and devotion to God revealed in Jesus.

The Lawyer in this story knew about God and His Law very well. He quoted from Deuteronomy 6:4, the *Shema*, the fulcrum upon which all Jewish spirituality rested, and he quoted from the Book of Leviticus. So he knew very well the need to do neighbor-love. In Leviticus 19:18, love of neighbor is a loving posture of the heart expressed in tangible behavior, which of course reflects Jesus' own mission and teachings: First, we are called to love God, which includes allegiance to Him as Lord and obedience to His Way; then as He calls us to love God, we are to love others. It is one thing to interpret God's Law correctly and believe it, but an entirely different thing to demonstrate it. This is Jesus' challenge to the Lawyer.

As the Story unfolds, the Lawyer wises up and responds, in classic Jewish form, with a question of his own: "Jesus, who exactly is my neighbor?"

This is not simply "to whom do I show love?" but rather an attempt to identify those whom he *should* love so he knows exactly whom he doesn't have to love. It's a border-making question. He is asking, "Jesus describe the person whom I am to love...so I know all the people to whom I don't have to show love."

In Second Temple Judaism, the neighbor-love of Leviticus 19:18 was interpreted as love for fellow Israelites and maybe the resident aliens who embraced covenant with Yahweh. It absolutely did not assume that those dwelling with them in their territory qualified as neighbor. What the Lawyer is asking as a first Century Jew is, "How far should my love reach?" What he is asking is, "Jesus, tell me exactly where the border is around me so I know whom exactly I am to love."

In response, Jesus asks the only relevant question at the end of the story: Who *acted* as a neighbor? Who *did* neighbor-love?

What's interesting in Jesus' telling of the Good Samaritan story is that He completely subverts the Lawyer's question. He leaves the identity of the wounded man a complete mystery. So the "who question" is a complete non-issue for Jesus. What's even more brilliant is that Jesus has the Samaritan—a man from a people group who were universally hated and despised by all Jews—do God's Law by doing neighbor-love. Brilliant! Jesus nullifies the very interpretation of the Law that led to the question in the first place through this subversive story. Jesus asks the man, "Who did neighbor-love?" because that's the only issue that matters to Jesus: doing neighbor-love to *all* people.

For Luke, neighbor-love is care for one who is a social outcast, which is the heart of Luke's picture of Jesus throughout his Gospel. What's more: loving God is demonstrated in loving our neighbor. The Greek word for *neighbor* literally means "someone in close proximity to another; a fellow human being." Neighbor-love truly knows no boundaries.

Doing Neighbor-Love

How might practically showing Jesus look in our communities? One friend of mine, Tim, has taken Jesus' example of noticing, going, and serving very seriously. He started a new monastic community in inner city Grand Rapids with some other friends from his college. The entire mission of these committed young adults is to be the presence of Jesus by loving their neighbors in the Way of Christ in a marginalized neighborhood in Grand Rapids. Throughout the week they invite people over for meals, share their lives with their neighbors, and find ways to simply and purely love those around them as Jesus has called them to do. Dawnielle, a friend in Washington, D.C., moved into an all Hispanic apartment with two other women to intentionally love others in the Way of Jesus. Through shared meals, hospitality, and teaching english as a second language to their neighbors, they have had countless opportunities to practically notice, go to, and service those whom society normally ignores.

Some of you might be thinking, "Showing and doing and noticing and serving is great and all, but what is that really accomplishing? When do you get to the gospel?" I thought this same thing when I went on a mission trip a few summers ago. In August 2005, the ministry for which I worked took eight government workers on a mission trip to Romania to work in a missionary orphanage and practically serve the poor in a village in North Eastern Romania. One of the things I struggled with as I went on this trip was, "Are we really going to accomplish anything? So we're going to go and play with some kids and deliver food to people, but what are we going to really accomplish?" What a typical American question! So often we're concerned with *producing* that we forget what God has really called us to: to be available and faithful to His call to do acts of love.

On this trip to Romania, God taught me that what we are called to do as followers of Jesus is love the world around us with the same furious, creepy love of God by "gospeling" within our own little worlds. We are called to incarnate the good news of the rescue and re-creation of the Kingdom of Heaven through Jesus Christ by deliberately doing acts of love. Just as the affects of the good news of the Kingdom of Heaven spread throughout Judea and Galilee through the wandering presence of Jesus, so to is the rescuing and re-creating affects of the gospel to spread throughout our own communities by being the presence of Christ ourselves.

A few months ago my friends Ben and Cameron did this very thing by loving on some of the most un-loved people in their high school. Towards the end of their senior year, they approached me with the idea of having an appreciation dinner at our church for the lunch ladies of their high school. They wanted to love on the ladies who served them for four years by providing a dinner at our church. I positively melted! So one evening, all thirteen lunch ladies came to our church to enjoy a four-course meal cooked by some of the ladies of the church. Some of us men dressed up in white shirts, black pants, black bow-ties, and black aprons and served them meals at decorated tables. We pulled out all the stops and had a great time serving a group of people who are generally thought of as one rung higher than the janitors on the high school social ladder.

Needless to say, the ladies were blown away by the thought and care that went into the night. One lady, who has worked at the high school serving food for 30 years, said she had never been appreciated like this for her work. In fact, each year the staff of the high school are honored with an all-staff luncheon, all them except the lunch ladies. What's more: these thirteen women not only cook for the high school (about 1700 kids), but also for the elementary students as well (another 800). Each day these women cook for some 2500 kids, all with nary a word of appreciate from the students or the administration.

Then along came two teenagers trying their best to follow Jesus better and show and share the love of Christ with those who are neither appreciated nor cared for. That's just like Jesus himself, isn't it? Jesus noticed those who were on the margins of society, went to those who were the least in the world, and flooded their lives with love, attention, and care.

I learned an important lesson that evening: the Church does not have to put on a production and reach massive amounts of people to live out the way of Jesus. The Church need only love. That's what Ben and Cameron taught me that night, and I'm a better soon-to-be-pastor for it.

As followers and show-ers of Jesus, we are called to love all fellow human beings that are in close proximity to us with the same furious, creepy love that God showed us through Jesus Christ, regardless of the "who." We are not, however, called to be Jesus on our own. Even Jesus didn't go on mission without help. He Himself realized, "The Son can do nothing by Himself; He can do only what He sees the Father doing, because whatever the Father does the Son also does. For the Father loves the Son and shows Him all He does." [60] Since Jesus was sent by the

Father, He was intimately aware that He could not act independent of the Father. Since we are sent by Jesus neither can we act independently of Him or the Spirit He sent to empower us.

Showing in Christ

How exactly are we Christians to live incarnationally, to show Jesus well by being His presence in the world around us? That seems like a pretty tall order! In John Chapter 15, Jesus paints a beautiful portrait of the intimate connection His followers need in order to live as a sent people. In this passage, Jesus uses the metaphor of a vine to drive a discussion of the fruitfulness (or fruitlessness) of His disciples. He is the True Vine and says, "Remain in me, and I will remain in you. No branch can bear fruit by itself; it must remain in the vine. Neither can you bear fruit unless you remain in me. I am the vine; you are the branches. If a man remains in me and I in him, he will bear much fruit; apart from me you can do nothing." [61]

Jesus explicitly links our fruitfulness as be-ers and show-ers of Himself not to human achievement, but to simply abiding in Him. Our demonstration of Jesus to the world around us is dependent upon our intimate connection to Jesus. As He says, no branch is able to bear fruit on it's own. A branch must remain attached to the vine for the life-giving, fruit-producing sustenance it needs to be a fruit-bearing branch. The same is true of His followers. We are called to "remain" in Jesus to do the specific things Jesus has called us to do. If we do remain in Him, Jesus promises that we will produce "much fruit." In fact, "apart from [Jesus] you can do nothing."

How does it look to remain and abide in Christ? One commentator says that 'abide' (another word used in this passage for 'remain') is the regular maintenance of an unbroken connection and speaks of the necessity of a constant active relationship between the follower and His Lord. [62] That connection and relationship is cultivated when the words of Jesus Christ remain in us. As Jesus says in verse 7, "If you remain in me and my words remain in you, ask whatever you wish, and it will be given you." [63] When we sit before the feet of Jesus, learn from His teachings, and then embody them in our hearts and minds, we maintain our connection to the True Vine. Likewise, when we obey Jesus' command to love we remain in and abide with Christ. John 15:10-13 says, "If you obey my commands, you will remain in my love, just as I have obeyed my Father's commands and remain in his love. I have told you this so that my joy may be in you and that your joy may be complete. My command is this: Love each other as I have loved you. Greater love has no one than this, that he lay down his life for his friends."

Apart from abiding in Jesus by obeying and feeding off His teachings, Jesus provided a Helper to empower us to do the things He called us to do. Before Jesus ascended to the right hand of the Father He reiterated His promise of sending another Counselor: "You will receive power when the Holy Spirit comes on you; and you will be my witness in Jerusalem, and in Judea and Samaria, and to the ends of the earth." [64] Before His death, Jesus told the disciples that He would ask the Father to send another Counselor to be with them. In fact, unless Jesus went away, the Counselor wouldn't have come. It was for their good that Jesus went away so He could send the Counselor to empower them to demonstrate His Way and be Him to the world. [65] That day finally came at the time of Pentecost.

During the day of Pentecost, the Book of Acts explains that the disciples were all together in one place and suddenly what sounded like a violent rushing wind from heaven came and filled the entire room in which they were sitting. Then, everyone saw what appeared to be dancing tongues of fire in the air that eventually rested upon the disciples. In the Holy Scriptures, the presence of fire usually signified the presence of God. In the Book of Exodus, for instance, God went before the Children of Israel in the desert in a cloud of fire. Here in this room somewhere in Jerusalem, the tongues were filled with the promised Counselor, the Holy Spirit. Once the tongues of fire rested upon the disciples, they spoke in other tongues as the *Spirit enabled them.* This enabling continues throughout this fascinating book as the movement of God blossomed and the disciples live-out their commission to embody, demonstrate, and proclaim Jesus and His Story.

Similarly, we have been empowered by the Holy Spirit to embody, demonstrate, and proclaim the Way of Christ and Reign of God throughout the world. As Paul says, it is God Himself who works within us to will and act according to His Rhythm of Life; it is the Spirit of God who helps us obey the teachings of Jesus, demonstrate His Kingdom, and proclaim the rescue and re-creation made possible through His death and resurrection. [66] If we Christian truly desire to show Jesus well to the world around us, we need to be intimately connected to the very person we long to show and fully rely upon the power of the Counselor He sent on our behalf. It is through Jesus and the Holy Spirit that we will be able to incarnate Jesus to the world. As Matthew 28:19-20 reveals, because all authority and heaven has been given to Jesus, He has sent us to demonstrate and proclaim His Way and Kingdom to the world. We are not alone, however, because this passage closes by reassuring, "And surely I am with you always to the very end of the age." [67] The loving, gentle, caring, powerful Jesus Himself is with us in full as we show Him to the world. Let us, then, remain in Jesus and rely upon the Spirit as we bring to the world the wonderful Jesus who beckons all humans to follow Him into His alternative, countercultural Rhythm.

Not only are we the Church called to show good, (un)offensive Jesus well, we are called to proclaim and tell His Story well, too; not only are we humans called to follow good, (un)offensive Jesus, we are called to totally commit ourselves to His Story. That's the topic of part two: telling Jesus' hopeful Story.

Part Two

Story-Tell

"What is the Story we tell;
what is the Story people hear?"

Chapter 5
a story among stories

Postmodernism.

For some, it's the god Molech come in the wispy flesh of ideas to consume the children of every Western nation. Gulp!

For others, it's simply the pool in which they've swam from birth.

Love it or hate it, every Western nation must grapple with the postmodern condition. While that may be true, what is postmodernism and how does it affect spirituality? How does this cultural shift relate to the Church and telling of God's Story of Rescue, a Story among stories?

Over the past four decades, our culture has been emerging beyond modernism into postmodernism (*post-* simply means 'beyond' not 'anti'). Some believe we already are a postmodern culture, while others insist we are still emerging. Regardless, our contemporary American society is reacting to and emerging beyond modernism, which is what postmodernism is: a reaction to modernism and an effort to move beyond this philosophical explanation of reality.

Without going into great detail of the philosophical distinctions, pure modernism (the period between 1600 to 1960, especially the years after the Enlightenment project of the 19th century) held to a single, universal worldview and moral standard, a belief that all knowledge is good and certain, truth is absolute, individualism is valued, and thinking, learning, and beliefs should be determined systematically and logically. Postmodernism, however, insists that there is no single universal worldview, all truth is not absolute, community is valued over individualism, and thinking, learning, and beliefs can be determined nonlinearly.

Postmoderns (those intellectuals birthed out of the 1960s counterculture revolution and beyond) react severely to dominant groups imposing a single worldview and life story (called a metanarrative). They have witnessed the tragic consequences of various groups throughout history using certainty and metanarratives to bring destruction upon the world through grand, sweeping story claims. These metanarratives range from the Fascism of Nazi Germany, to Communism in the former Soviet Union, to Christians suppressing different people groups like slaves and women using the metanarrative of the Bible. Obviously, the fact that Christianity is lumped in with evil, dictatorial beliefs is unfortunate, but the biblical metanarrative (also called worldview) is considered just as oppressive as these other stories. As a result, diverse spiritual experiences and stories are accepted, celebrated, and embraced.

While most believe the transition into a fully postmodern, post-Christendom era has not fully culminated, American society is leaping into a world beyond the values and worldview of modernism, and even more significantly beyond Christianity. Much of the culture no longer understands nor accepts Christianity and Her Story as being true, real, or valuable. At worst, Christianity is perceived as a metanarrative used to oppress Blacks, women, Native Americans, and other non-Western nations. At best, Christianity is one other alternative story among stories in the spiritual smorgasbord of modern society and completely irrelevant to twenty-first century living.

"O.K." you may be thinking, "This is all well and good, but what are we followers of Jesus to do in the face of so much skepticism and hostility? How can we embrace our Story with conviction and share it among so many other stories?"

To tell God's Story of Rescue well in our emerging postmodern, post-Christian culture, the Church needs a crash course in postmodern thought. She needs to understand what it means to be a postmodern, post-Christian person, because this is the culture in which we find ourselves. The Church has always had to embed Herself within particular cultures, even those ambivalent and hostile to Her mission. This is nothing new. Since Christianity has been the dominate voice and story within Western culture for nearly a thousand years, we're in unknown, difficult territory, even in our own backyard!

Sure we understand the logic of contextualizing Jesus and His hopeful Story for non-Western nations, like Zambia, Papua New Guinea, and Thailand. But New York City, Iowa, and Seattle? Showing and telling Jesus and His Story in postmodern, post-Christian terms and expressions is difficult for many Christians to understand, much less accept.

Such contextualization is 100% necessary, however, given the seismic shift of our American culture and demands of Jesus' own commission to the Church to disciple all people, Papua New Guinean and postmodern alike. My goal in this chapter is to help the Church better understand Her context and provide some help to telling God's Story of Rescue to postmoderns.

While studying modern and postmodern political thought in my undergraduate classes, I discovered three dominate themes to the postmodern condition: an exposure of agendas, biases, and presuppositions in interpreting what is real about life; the denial of a single reality-defining story, while encouraging the promotion and celebration of all world stories; and finally the disrobing of Institutions of Power that use power and knowledge to control people and force them to conform to their version of what is normal. Before the Church considers how to retell God's (un)offensive Story of Rescue, it is essential that we first understand the context in which we are telling that Story. If you are not a

Christian, it would be equally valuable to understand how postmodernism conditions you to reject this Story as the only real story in a sea of alternatives.

While, many Christians fear all things postmodern and run for the hills at the mention of the word, it is a fear rooted in profound misreading and misinterpretations. If the Church is to tell and apply the Story of Jesus well, though, it must understand and engage these important prophets on their own terms, realizing that philosophy influences culture and is not completely void of any helpful instruction. Sit tight for a roller-coaster ride through postmodernity!

Interpreting and Living the Text

Jacques Derrida is the first of three thinkers that have heavily influenced our emerging postmodern context. To many Christians, Jacque Derrida is part of the unholy Trinity of postmodernists, with Jean-François Lyotard and Michael Foucault being the other two. Derrida is considered the father of French deconstruction, a method for rethinking long held beliefs and intellectual assumptions. One of his primary contributions to modern philosophy is his often repeated phrase: "there is nothing outside the text." Last summer, I began reading through his fascinating book, *Writing and Difference*, a collection of essays in which Derrida engages the themes of language, the act of writing and codifying thought, the relationship of words and meaning, and the important topic of textual interpretation, which led to his famous phrase on texts. This later idea has great bearing on Christian spirituality and the retelling of God's Story of Rescue.

In this phrase, "There is nothing outside the text," Derrida is saying that interpretation is an inescapable part of being human and experiencing the world. For Derrida, texts and writings do not simply stand between us and the world, rather the world itself is sort of a Text that needs to be interpreted; "there is no reality that is not always already interpreted through the mediating lens of language." [68]   This stands over and against the modern thinker Jean Jacque Rousseau's notion that we simply read a text without thought or interpretation and approach the world "as it is" without any outside force influencing our interpretation and experience.

This Rousseauian naivete is addressed by Derrida when he proclaims "there is nothing outside the text." For Derrida, no realm of pure reading exists beyond the realm of textual interpretation. In other words, people do not simply read a book or experience life without bringing something to the table, without bringing the art of interpretation with them on their journey. We do not simply step out of our skins and abandon language and interpretation to step into a world without language or a state where interpretation is not necessary. No, the event (and daily events) of interpretation is part of being human and experiencing the world.

Consider a cup of coffee to illustrate this understanding of textual and life interpretation. When I see a cup in front of me and use it to get coffee to satisfy my morning caffeine obsession, I am not simply experiencing drinking a cup of coffee as a brute fact. Whether consciously or not, I am actively interpreting the thing in front of me as an object that will hold hot liquid, not fall apart in my hand when I pick it up, and help cure my insatiable need for caffeine and pounding morning headache. So in this simple example, the cup is a Text of sorts to interpret as I experience my morning.

The same is true for the rest of our experience of life: life is interpretation all the way down, whether of the substance of life itself or the words on a page, like the Story of the Holy Scriptures.

In his essay entitled "Force and Significance," Derrida alludes to this notion of text and interpretation, especially as texts themselves interpret the one "Text" of the world. He writes:

> To write is not only to conceive the Leibnizian book as an impossible possibility. Impossible possibility, the limit explicitly names by Mallarme. To Verlaine: "I will go even further and say: the Book, for I am convinced that there is only One, and that it has [unwittingly] been attempted by every writer, even by Geniuses." "...revealing that, in general, all books contain the amalgamation of a certain number of age-old truths; that actually there is only One book on earth, that it is the law of the earth, the earth's true Bible." *The*

difference between individual works is simply the difference between individual interpretations of one try and established text, which are proposed in a mighty gathering of those ages we call civilized or literary. [69] (emphasis mine)

According to Derrida, individually written texts are merely interpretations of the one Text that defines reality; there is only one Text, and this Text is distributed throughout all books. For some people this is frightening, because they assume this leads to an "anything goes" worldview, devolving into relativism. Rather than reducing interpretation to relativism, this understanding does a few things: 1) it owns up to the very real part of the human condition to figure out this thing called life, and in fact there is a "Thing" to figure out; 2) everyone brings interpretations to the "Thing" in an attempt to understand the Text of reality; 3) because we are finite, the event of textual interpretation is finite, riddled with agendas, and subjective. We are not God, but are instead broken humans. We all bring something to the table when we try to interpret, and those interpretations are subjective because we are interpreting from a particular point-of-view. In my reading of Derrida, there does not seem to be doubt about the Text itself, but rather doubt in the individual and communal events of textual interpretation and our ability to simply and purely interpret anything without external influence.

Part of the Derridian fascination is his insight that we all interpret and that multiple interpretations exist and arise out of multiple communities. In the face of a plurality of texts (i.e. Buddhism, Islam, New Age, etc...) interpreting The Text, the challenge to the Church is to be the Text-made-flesh. While we may have disagreements about interpreting the Text, the Church needs to far more humble with interpreting the Bible and focus on living out the Text of Jesus. Not simply with pen and paper, but through the (re)breaking of body and (re)shedding of blood by denying ourselves, taking up the boards of execution, and following Jesus into the way of sacrificial love. Only after we embody the Holy Scriptures will we have the right to proclaim that the Story of Jesus is what is real about Life, even in the face of a plurality of stories, even in the face of Jean-François Lyotard's critique.

An Incredulity Toward Reality-Defining Stories

"I define postmodern as incredulity toward metanarratives."

This is the famous saying by Jean-François Lyotard that has caused much heartburn among professing Christians for his supposed rejection of "Big Stories." While postmodernism is a (healthy) skepticism and suspicion toward grand, sweeping Big Stories, Christians need not fear. As the logic goes, since postmodern thought is an incredulity toward reality-explaining stories and the Christian faith is informed by the stories of the Holy Scripture, we must reject, wholesale, any postmodern sensibilities, because it pits a "storied" belief system against an entirely a/narrative worldview. As James K. A. Smith describes in *Who's Afraid of Postmodernism*, however, "orthodox Christian faith actually requires that we, too, stop believing in metanarratives." [70] We now turn our attention to this notion of grand stories in the intersection of postmodern thought and Christian spirituality.

First, we must note that Lyotard has been largely misunderstood by Christian and non-Christian alike. "Incredulity toward metanarratives" does not mean that postmodernism rejects "Big Stories," but that it rejects the *manner* in which those stories legitimize themselves. In other words, it isn't the stories themselves that are the problem, but the way they are told (and to a degree why they are told). "For Lyotard, metanarratives are a distinctly modern phenomenon: they are stories that not only tell a grand story, but claim to be able to legitimate or prove the story's claim by an appeal to universal reason." [71] The appeal to rationalistic, scientific knowledge supposedly legitimates them as universal narratives.

The tension between modernity and postmodernity revolves around the issue of legitimation: Modernity appeals to science and a universal, autonomous rationalism to legitimate its claims on reality and truth, which is set over against narratives that seek not to prove claims, but proclaim them within a specific story. Postmodernism on the other hand, critiques these universal stories by unveiling the irony of their legitimization: while science dismisses myths and fables, scientific "stories" *themselves* are rooted in a narrative; the narrative of science is rooted in a story that appeals to a universal, rational, scientific criteria that supposedly stands outside any particular "language game," thus guaranteeing universal truth. Yet the postmodernist understands that all scientists are themselves believers; every modernist sits within a particular "story of reality," just like every Christian.

"What characterizes the postmodern condition, then, is not a rejection of grand stories in terms of scope or in the sense of epic claims, but rather an unveiling that all knowledge is rooted in some narrative or myth. The result, however, is what Lyotard describes as a 'problem of legitimation' since what we thought were universal criteria have been unveiled as just one game among many." [72] In other words, all claims to universal truth (including and especially Christian claims to absolute truth) are reduced to one "language game" among many, one story among stories. These games and stories are conditioned by their own sets of cultural and historical rules. Thus, there is almost no consensus in the postmodern community, because there are a multitude of competing myths, language games, and stories.

In the midst of a plurality of stories is it really the task of the Body of Christ to insist belief in our Story, or are we simply called to bear witness to its poetry and prose? Since we do exist in a multicultural, pluralist society, do we have the right to impose our Story on others, or are we simply called to draw others into our own Story? Isn't that what God is doing anyway, beckoning and wooing and drawing people into His Story?

I am not suggesting we abandon our Story or give up sharing it. Obviously, we are called by Jesus to share His Story of rescue and re-creation. That isn't the issue. What is the issue is how we are telling the Story, what we are saying as we tell it, and (maybe most importantly) how the world perceives that storytelling. As Lyotard explains, part of the postmodern condition is an inherent skepticism of stories and their underlying agendas, power plays, and commitments.

The idea of competing stories was at the forefront of controversy a few years ago with the book, and subsequent movie, release of *The Da Vinci Code*. Much to the fright of the Christian community, Dan Brown, a great storyteller, decided to tell an alternative story of the person of Jesus, a very different story than the one told by historic Christian orthodoxy. To be sure, it was pure fiction, but in the eyes of the world it seemed to be more compelling and legitimate than the

Story told by the Church. While the Christian community developed a severe case of apoplexy, I and many others wondered why so many people were drawn more to this alternative story of Jesus told by a non-Christian author than to the one often told by the Church? Thanks to Lyotard, the Church can understand the world's reaction to the substance and style of our storytelling.

The Dan Brown *Da Vinci* flap was not Dan's fault nor was it an indictment against the forces of secular humanism. In light Lyotard's analysis of our postmodern condition, the book and movie exposed some problems with the Bride of Jesus' story telling: in many ways She is not telling a compelling story nor is the way She legitimizes Herself and that Story very helpful. If postmoderns perceive metanarratives and the Church's storytelling as an agenda driven by power-plays, why do we think the world will listen to and believe our use of knowledge to legitimize ourselves? As previously mentioned, one of the flaws Lyotard brilliantly exposed was the false use of reason to claim a universality, when in reality those "universal" claims are merely one other language game among many, one Story among stories. If this is true, why do we think continuing to assert facts about our faith will have any sway over a skeptical postmodern world?

How we Christians tell the Story and what we say in its telling is extremely important; the way we "legitimize" Christian spirituality among a plurality of spiritual stories is crucial. May the Church return to a bold proclamation of the Creation–Rebellion–Rescue–Re-Creation Story, rooted in the sweeping redemptive narrative of the Holy Scriptures themselves. May the Church's weekly act of Narrative Reenactment (read: Sunday worship) hospitably invite a transcendence-sapped world to join us in mysteriously experiencing God's Story. May the church proclaim that Story not simply with words, but with actions by incarnationally living the Way of Jesus to show a hurting, broken, desperate world that our Story is real and legitimate. And may we shed all agendas and powerful persuasions to simply "be Jesus" to a world skeptical of our prejudices and commitments, something with which Foucault will help.

Let's see how.

Disrobing Institutions of Power

Finally, as we consider the postmodern condition in which we retell God's Story of Rescue, we need to consider Michael Foucault, the master institutional deconstructor. He is famous for his often quoted phrase: "power is knowledge." Yes, you read that correctly. Not, *knowledge is power*, but *power is knowledge*. Let me explain.

Much of Foucault's philosophical work was in the area of institutional deconstruction and revealed the inextricable link between power and knowledge; knowledge is not a neutrally determined "thing," but is discovered and formed within networks of power—social, political, economic, and...religious.

In his book, James K. A. Smith uses the example of the film *One Flew over the Cuckoo's Nest* to highlight how institutional systems use power to shape people through reason and knowledge into what they perceive as what is normal. This film recounts the struggle of the System in its attempt to repair the protagonist, R. P. McMurphy, and his resistance to its power. In the end, the System of Power triumphs over the individual, culminating in McMurphy's forced lobotomy, which leaves him a near lifeless, obedient shell.

"One Flew over the Cuckoo's Nest leaves us just where we would expect from a work dating from the 1960s: with a deep suspicion of institutions, institutional power, and the control they exert over us." [73] Michael Foucault led the charge in cultivating a "deep hermeneutic of suspicion" that marks our postmodern culture's relationship to Institutions of Power, including and especially the institution of the Church. His contribution, though, follows in the footsteps of another renegade figure that gives Christians as much heartburn: Fredrick Nietzsche, a pre-postmodern if there ever was one.

In my undergraduate studies, I read almost all of Nietzsche and was utterly fascinated by his prophetic prose. His famous "God is dead" saying from his "Parable of the Madman" in *The Gay Science* was never meant as a prescriptive course of action, but rather as a descriptive tool: he was describing the God-is-dead state of Western Europe and wondered aloud why they were ordering their society and morals as if God still mattered/existed. From there, Nietzsche took Western civilization on a roller-coaster ride through the deconstruction and reconstruction of morality outside of God. Through his work, *On The Genealogy of Morals,* he described all moral and ethical claims as nothing more than "will to power" and begged his readers to rise above powerful institutions (especially the Church) to become the ultimate moral being: the *ubermencsh* (translated "over man," though I don't believe he thought anyone could truly reach that state but him.)

Like Nietzsche the genealogist, Foucault traces the lineage of secret biases and powerful prejudices that lay submerged beneath institutional truth claims, especially those ideas deemed "moral" or "normal" by Institutions of Power., like Christianity According to Foucault, nothing that is "true" is innocently and purely discovered. Instead, what those institutions (State and Religious) deem normal and moral are covertly motivated by various interests of power, interests Foucault seeks to completely unmask for all the world to see. Foucault is an archaeologist who digs beneath the surface of what masquerades as Objective Truth to expose the Mechanisms of Power at work below the surface.

Thus, the disciplinary society, as addressed by Foucault in his book *Discipline and Punishment,* molds individuals into what it wants them to be: passive, productive consumers who are obedient to the State. We are projects in need of reengineering and repair, and the State is more than ready to squish us like Play-dough through its own mold. We are all like the residents of the mental ward being supervised and controlled, watched over and dominated by structures of surveillance and discipline by our society's Institutions of Power. Those structures can be actual State institutions or other structures of society.

Throughout his *Discipline and Punishment,* Foucault unpacks why the matrix of discipline and punishment exist in the first place: to repair the delinquent, the abnormal. If the penitentiary system is intended for the delinquent, then society has decided what is normal. No longer is the target of reform a person or a criminal. Instead, they exist to reengineer the "abnormal." The creation of this "abnormality" is the heart of Foucault's prophecy: Institutions of Power aimed at normalization. "Normal" is determined by various rational, societal Institutions of Power. It is precisely these powers of normalization that concern Foucault. As a classic, Enlightenment liberal (ideological, not political), Foucault places a premium on the self-ruling, sovereign, rational person. The "individual rational man" is to be uncontrolled and uncoerced, especially by institutions. Thus, Foucault's critique is decidedly anti-institutional and entirely concerned with the autonomous rational man.

Foucault's critique has birthed the deep hermeneutic of suspicion of institutions that characterizes our postmodern culture. For postmoderns, any institution that tries to control belief and behavior is viewed as repressive and domineering. In fact, there is a deep sense that institutions are structures of domination. One of the primary institutions that has felt the full weight of this anti-institutionalism is the Church. A recent cultural piece that milked Foucault's philosophy for all it's worth was the recently released and bemoaned movie *The Golden Compass*.

When I first heard about the movie I was excited to see it because I knew it had an agenda: the series of books upon which the movie is based was written by an atheist, Philip Pullman, who wanted to expose the deep harm done to society by Institutions of Power. The movie was a pointed condemnation of what the author perceives as the most heinous of all mechanisms and institutions of normalcy: Christianity. Though this is one perspective on Christianity, I think it is fairly reflective of how many in our culture perceive the institution of the Church.

In the movie, an imperialesque organization called *The Magisterium* (which, apparently, is a technical ecclesiastical term in the Roman Catholic Church referring to the teaching authority of the church) is bent on snatching adolescent children's daemons (which in the movie actually represents their soul) to prevent them from experiencing/enjoying "dust" (which by all accounts represents "sin" and especially the sexual kind). The primary religious Institution of Power's entire mission is to control humans (especially children) and prevent them from experiencing what is deemed abnormal. In the process, the Institution of Power destroys their souls, leaving them lifeless and impotent. The Institution of Power judges what is normal (and thus abnormal), develops a mechanism of normalization (which is a sort of factory in the middle of what appears to be

Siberia surrounded by utter darkness), and executes that mechanism to radically transform people into *their* version of what is normal, and thus truthful.

Do you see what's going on here? According to the perspective of this man (and by all accounts many within culture) the entire mission of the Church is to arbitrarily and rationally decide what is normal (especially power-plays within the Church itself), develop powerful mechanisms of normalization to wrestle the human will in subjection to those opinions of normalcy, and intentionally employ those mechanisms, all the while denying people self-autonomy and individual freedom.

Take the issue of gay marriage, for instance. I realize I am fighting with fire in mentioning this example, but I think it is an important anecdote. Many Americans, young outsiders especially, have viewed the Church's efforts at judging and preventing this "alternative lifestyle" to be nothing more than a Foucauldian power play. They believe this Institution of Power has decided on its own what is normal (defining "normal" marriage as heterosexual from institutional tradition and interpretation), developed a mechanism of normalization (political action groups that try to prevent gay marriage or other groups that try and "repair" homosexuality), and execute that mechanism to transform an entire group of people into *their* version of what is normal (antigay marriage ballot initiatives and gay reparative therapy). In offering up this example, I myself am not making commentary on the Church's efforts at maintaining heterosexuality as normative. I am simply offering a current example from culture to help the Church understand how our culture perceives our "truth telling" efforts.

To some extent both Pullman and Foucault are right: Church Inc., often uses its power as a weapon, gavel, and hammer to further its powerful aims. Throughout history the Church has used its power to declare "God Wills It!" in the Crusades, Inquisitions, Witch Trials, abomination of Slavery, and even contemporary Antigay Marriage Constitutional Amendment efforts. At many turns throughout Her life, Church Inc. has flexed its institutional muscle to declare what is normal and abnormal for a society, usually with disastrous consequences.

This is what our postmodern culture sees when they picture the Church in the form of Christianity: A Warring Despot hell-bent on using any powerful means necessary to bring all people and people-groups in subjection to *their* version of normalcy. If you ask 10 random people on the street tomorrow what they think of Christianity you'll get the words "judgmental," "bigoted," "controlling," and other similar words to define the Church, all words laced with *power is knowledge.*

What is the Church to do in the face of this reputation? How can we move beyond Church Inc. and truly be the Body of Christ to a lost, hopeless, broken, and hurting world? We need to return to the example Jesus gave us in the gospels: incarnational living. We are called to be Jesus to the world around us, rather than be Christians. Let us become servants to the world instead of an Institution of Power; the basin and the towel must be our instruments of choice, rather than the sword and shield. Let us simply point people to the God-with-us-God who enfleshed Himself as a human being, rather than to the institution of Church, Inc. We must show an alternative way of living by following the alternative Way of Jesus, rather than mirror all the other institutions of our world. We must tell a better, more hopeful Story of this Rescuer than we've been telling, a Story that is more reflective of God's Story of Rescue itself.

People are skeptical and cynical about the Church, and we have little to blame but ourselves. Of course, there are fantastic things that the Church is doing around the world and in individual communities, but the fact remains: the system of the Church has left a sour taste in the mouths of our postmodern, post-Christian culture. The only way to move beyond these impressions is to embed ourselves in our communities, become indigenous, intentionally live out the way of Jesus among our various relationships, and retell Jesus' hopeful Story and message well. It's the only way to reach and fight the skepticism of our postmodern, post-Christian world. But as we retell this story amidst a skeptical postmodern culture, let us also remember that there is a Story to tell. While postmodernism insists that our Story is merely one among many, we know that we can know the one true Story, because God has deliberately revealed it to all humans.

Revelation and the Ongoing Act of Revealing

In contrast to the postmodern insistence that we really cannot know anything, I want to make something very clear before we launch into God's Story of Rescue. Listen to these ancient words from the ancient Book of Deuteronomy in chapter 29:

> The secret things belong to the LORD our God, but the things revealed belong to us and to our children forever, that we may follow all the words of this law. [74]

During a period in my life when I began to seriously wrestle with the things of God, I began to doubt and question our ability to know anything about Him and His Reality. After delving into theology and the writings of some great Christian thinkers, I began to wonder whether we could know anything about God with certainty, especially in the face of hundreds of denominational versions of truth and a myriad of cultural stories.

Then one evening I believe God gave me some words from Himself for me and others. He spoke the above verse from Deuteronomy as a reminder that we can know things about God and His reality. What was even more amazing was a single sentence that God spoke to me that countered "I think therefore I am" and affected me as much as "salvation by grace through faith" affected Martin Luther:

God revealed, therefore I can know.

Think about that.

We can know things, because God the Creator has both revealed Himself to us and revealed things about His reality.

The Modern Era (philosophical, not technological) was defined as the Age of Reason, in part, because of a cleverly concocted phrase by René Descartes: *cogito ergo sum*, "I think therefore I am." In the face of the epistemological (how we know and arrive at understanding what is real) conundrum of doubt and certainty, modern thinkers tried to eliminate, or lessen the damage of, these twin threats in two ways: 1) they elevated the mind and reason through the scientific method; and

2) centered knowing squarely in the individual. The only thing Man could be certain of was himself and his ability to reason with his own mind. From the position of the Self, through engaging his mind and reason, he could know everything outside himself; knowledge begins with the individual's mind, and works itself outward by means of the scientific method.

Postmoderns, however, reject a mind/reason-centered explanation of our ability to know, because outside stimuli can influence our mind and the tools our mind uses to understand the world (smell, taste, sight, sound, touch) are fallible. This realization cast doubt on a persons ability to know purely through his own mind and reason. In postmodern ideology, Man isn't removed from the equation, because his reason is replaced by his experience. While doubt is actually elevated in the process, we can know because we can feel and experience. In the face of this individualized experience, truth is again relegated to the individual. No one, transcendent, knowable truth story can exist, because my personal experience dictates and defines the truth of that story.

Unlike moderns and postmoderns, however, we Christians begin with God. We begin with a Creator who created with purpose, meaning, and design. He did not create just for the fun of it. He created our reality on purpose, with purpose. Also, He purposefully created humans to exist with Himself in an eternal relationship defined by mutual love. Thus, if God created this reality with purpose, it must be possible (and I would say extremely probable) that He purposefully revealed Himself to that creation. In designing humans on purpose, for a purpose, God would've had to have revealed Himself on purpose to share His purpose. Therefore, God has revealed things to humanity.

I believe the nature of revelation should be understood as divine self-disclosure. God, through His own will, decided to purposefully unveil Himself to humanity. These God-revealed things belong to humans, allowing them to understand what is real about God and His works. We understand what is real about God and His works through two sources: General Revelation and Special Revelation.

In General Revelation God discloses Himself to all of humanity through the created order in three purposeful acts of unveiling: 1) nature; 2) an internal, created awareness of the Divine; 3) and the participation of God in history. Through all He created in the natural world, Man can both know of and about God. Humanity also has access to this knowledge through an internal awareness of an "Other" that is beyond and above themselves. Lastly, God's purposeful participation in history reveals a Creator who is intimately involved in the affairs of His creation through deliberate acts of disclosure, human involvement, and redemption.

Despite God's purposeful act of self-disclosure, though, humans struggle to properly understand God and His works. Though humans are crafted after the Image of God and have a limited understanding of Him, that created Image is broken because of sin; because humans have consciously chosen the Way of Self over against the Way of God, humans misread God's self-disclosure through nature, human conscience, and history. Even though we can see that there is an Other that is above and outside ourselves through creation and have an innate sense of the divine, and even though we all strive to make sense of this Wholly Other, our brokenness prevents us from understanding God entirely.

God solved this through Special Revelation by becoming a human to fully reveal Himself to humanity in the person of Jesus Christ and breathing into life a Text that stands as witness to Himself and His works.

While God's transcendence is disclosed through General Revelation and reveals a Creator who is above His creation, Special Revelation helps us understand God as a creator who is intimately involved with His creation, a God of immanence. This second instance of divine unveiling corrects the distorted and misunderstood views of God that broken humans experience as the result of sin. Because humans are holistically broken, we need a more complete unveiling to understand God and His works. This second act of disclosure more fully unveils God in view of His partial disclosure through creation; God is more fully unveiled through the Holy Scriptures and Jesus Christ.

Through the climax of Special Revelation, God and His reality is fully unveiled through Jesus Christ of Nazareth. Ultimately, the fullest expression of what is real about God's nature, character, intentions, desires, and works are entirely revealed through the person of Jesus. All of these are only properly understood by observing, understanding, and listening to Him. Though we textually understand God and His works through the Holy Scriptures, even this valuable dimension of revelation must be interpreted through the teachings, person, and Way of Jesus Christ.

One additional act of immanent unveiling is through the sacred writings of the children of Israel and apostles of Jesus. These collections of writings in their respective testaments are compiled in a Sacred Text we call the Bible. While it is not God's ultimate act of self-disclosure, the Holy Scriptures are the standard by which we measure our understanding of God and His works. I believe the textual unveiling found in the Holy Scriptures is well preserved, proves and authenticates itself, and truthfully contains everything God desired to communicate to humans in writing about Himself and His works. Through this textual self-disclosure God beckons humans to relationship and worship, calls them to live according to a Way of Life, and restores them to the way He intended them to be at the beginning of creation. The Sacred Text of God was primarily written by God through the full participation of human writers under the guidance of their Jewish spiritual traditions, culture, and specific contexts.

God's textual self-disclosure, as found in the Holy Scriptures, is marked by six distinctions: Authority, Power, Unity, Sufficiency, Perspicuity, and Contemporaneity. The Text is authoritative on how to restore humanity and creation to God, and what it means to live restored in these relationships. It unveils the power of God to restore the God-Man relationship and creation to the way He intended them to be at the beginning of creation. The Holy Scripture is an ancient document of great unity that reveals God's one continuous Story from beginning to end. To properly understand God a reader and listener of this particular divine self-disclosure must sit in this grand, unified Redemptive Narrative, which includes four Acts: Creation, Rebellion, Rescue, and Re-Creation. The Scriptures sufficiently testify to everything we need to understand how the God-Man relationship and creation is restored, and how to properly relate to God and others. God's Holy Text is perspicuous, meaning the message of restoration that it carries is clear and can be plainly and simply understood by all humans. Finally the Holy Scriptures apply to contemporary problems and provides contemporary solutions, because while God was speaking to specific people at particular times, He was speaking through the prophets and apostles to those people with us in mind.

Again, the things revealed to humans are found in the biblical narrative, a collection of ancient stories, poems, and letters inspired by God to reveal Himself and His purpose to humans, on purpose. Because God revealed Himself to humans on purpose, we can know, not with certainty, but with confidence that the good, hopeful Story that truly is (un)offensive.

Let us explore, then, how we should tell and understand this good, hopeful, (un)offensive Story of Rescue. This Story begins with *creation*, explains our brokenness due to human *rebellion*, reveals a *rescue* from God through Jesus Christ alone, to provide *re-creation* for the entire world to restore us to the way the Creator intended His very good creation to be at the beginning. The next four chapters explains the hopeful details of these exciting acts of the (un)offensive gospel of Jesus.

Chapter 6
our creation

Blankness.

Like a canvas waiting for colors and forms to bubble up out of the imagination of an artist, so too was the earth. The Holy Scriptures say it was "formless and void." And the Spirit of the Creator hovered over this blankness to breathe a symphony of diverse chords, rhythms, beings, and forms into existence.

This is the beginning act of God's Story of Rescue.

The creation event was a purposeful act of God to bring into existence a reality for His glory, reflection, and interaction, a reality that was formed from nothing; the universe and all that exists therein was created on purpose with purpose by the Creator. This act of creation was a real time-space event that set the universe and all its processes in motion through the will and word of God. In this chapter, I will not argue whether that creative act occurred over a period of six literal twenty-four hour days or through an evolutionary process of millennia. For my money, I don't see why God would have needed six days—or several million years for that matter—to accomplish His creative act. I and others feel the Genesis narrative was simply a tribal repetition of our collective origin, rather than a play-by-play script of the events of those first few days. As such, I will treat this narrative like myth, a true account of reality set to story to tell how we came to exist, God's original purpose for that creation, and how God's Story began.

If you are like some Christians, though, you begin God's gospel Story with sin and the Fall through Genesis 3 or the need to escape the Fall and this Fall-marked world by going to heaven. Have you ever noticed this? As I mentioned earlier, One of the most well known tools for sharing the gospel begins with sin by emphasizing our screwed-upness. Another well known method begins with heaven. On the one hand, the world is so screwed-up that we better be sure we're not going to a *more* screwed-up place (hell). On the other hand, we are so screwed-up and in need of help that we do not even realize our screwed-upness and our need for rescue apart from God, if we are lucky enough to be among the 'chosen elect,' the elite. Both understandings and explanations of Jesus' gospel message either begin with sin or heaven.

Do people really need to be told they sin, though? Do people really not realize they do things which they should not do, that the way they live is not the way it's supposed to be? Are people really wondering about life after death or are they wondering more about life *before* death? Are people simply concerned about some magical world in outer space down the road, or do they instead long to figure-out life right now in *this* time and space? While explaining our rebellion and need for rescue from its consequences is necessary, both are not the beginning nor the point of the Story. Both of these beginnings transform Jesus' good news into a message that's either drained of love and compassion or completely unappealing.

Why? Because both views start in the middle of the Story.

While I do believe in everlasting life and appreciate the concern that individuals understand they rebel against a Holy God, this is where I depart: I do not believe humans are so screwed up that they do not realize things are not the way they are supposed to be nor do I believe getting to heaven is the purpose of

Jesus' good, hopeful message. If eternity is grafted into the very core of all humans by the very fact they are crafted after God, wouldn't it make sense that they would intuitively know that there is a Wholly Other that is beyond them and a Story that is bigger than their own, while desperately longing for another world to burst forth through the seams of this good, but terribly screwed-up one? I think most people in their most honest and desperate moments are right here: they realize that things are not the way they are supposed to be, that *they* are not the way they are supposed to be.

What's more: if Jesus' teachings and ministry were entirely concerned with living now, if He thought mini acts of re-creation (e.g. healing the blind and lame, restoring the social dignity of the marginalized) were important enough now before a final re-creation, then shouldn't we Christians tell a Story that is entirely concerned with living and re-creating now with the promise of life after "life after death" built-in?

As in on *this* earth?

In *this* lifetime?

People who believe the human story starts with Genesis 3 would say "no." They can't. If our Story starts with the "Fall" and our screwed-upness, then humans are fundamentally sinful and cannot possibly demand or desire anything else but sin and any other Way but the Rhythm of this World. If this world is not our home and we're just a passin' through, to quote a famous hymn, then the point really *is* heaven. If the world is evil and bad, and if the point is to fly away to glory some glad mornin' when this life is o'er, then escaping out of *here* to a home on God's celestial shore (heaven) out *there*, in outer space away from earth, is the point.

But if the human story begins in Genesis 1 and 2, then it is, well, a whole other story! In this Story humans were created good. They were creatures crafted after their Creator and were by nature Eikons, Image-Bearers of the divine. Accordingly, we truly are earthlings and this good, yet broken world, really is our home. Genesis 1 and 2 paints a portrait of how the human story began, what that Story is fundamentally, and where God wants to return the human story. If the human story begins with Genesis 2, then humans are not fundamentally sinful nor are we fundamentally sinners. Instead, we are fundamentally Image-Bearers of the Creator; fundamentally we are beings that are created to reflect and *do* bear the reflection and Image of God, an albeit faded, crack one. Furthermore, God created a good world and called us to be co-creators with Himself to steward, explore, and enjoy the very good earth right now in this lifetime and into eternity.

To be sure, the Scriptures do teach that humans sin; we choose the Way of Self over against the Way of God. All humans are born with the capacity and desire to do sinful things, any front page of the newspaper will attest to this. But humans are cracked Eikons, meaning they are broken Image-Bearers of God and in need of rescue and re-creation.[75] They also exist in a world that is, in the words of C.S. Lewis, controlled by Deep Magic, a real and present evil power that dulls the senses to fully understanding God and His reality, while enticing people to do things they know deep down just isn't the way life is supposed to be lived. Jesus said this when He revealed that human hearts are blinded by the darkness of this world.

So while humans do things that are sinful, humans are also profoundly influenced by the Deep Magic of the world.

But you ask, "What the heck does any of this have to do with the gospel being offensive or (un)offensive?" I won't finish the argument in this chapter, but this is how I see it: the (un)offensive gospel of Jesus is about what God is taking all of creation back to: the way He intended it to be at creation. According to the beginning of that Story, human nature is not *fundamentally* sinful, though we do sin, but fundamentally Image-Bearers of God. I'd say that's a very different Story than the message typically told! We should understand humans as Image-Bearers of God who are cracked and in need of rescue and re-creation, both of which God Himself provided.

We need to be restored to the way we were originally intended to be, the way all of "this" was created at the beginning. And how were we originally crafted? As beings crafted by a Creator after His own Image and Likeness. This vision of restoration to the way things were at the beginning starts not with our sin, but with who we were as integrated, whole beings crafted after God Himself.

The Way It Was Supposed To Be

Have you ever disconnected from the modern world and hiked a forested mountain or attempted to wrestle a massive serpentine river? When I lived in Northern Virginia, every summer I would make it a point to hike the great Shenandoah Mountain and immerse myself in God's creation. I would usually hike up 3,000 feet and five miles or so to a *Little House on the Prairie* type cabin to not only reconnect with myself after modern society wrecked my innards, but also to reconnect with a world my distant ancestors (Adam and Eve) forsook.

I've found that marching alone headlong into the wilds of a mountain satiates that lingering hunger we all have for the way it was before it all collapsed, the way it was supposed to be at the beginning. That hunger for what was is somehow met by reconnecting to creation.

I remember on one excursion into the Shenandoah I came across a deer. I was reaching the summit of one of the peaks of the Mountain and the trail I was walking was fairly narrow and allowed little room for escape, either up or down. Suddenly, there was Bambie! We just stood staring at each other: Beast staring down Man, Man staring down Beast. Mostly I stood still because I didn't want the deer to charge me if I made a quick, wrong move. Part of me, though, just stood there marveling at the majesty of the creature in front of me, longing to run up to it and ride it up and down the mountain. I longed for a taste of what it might've been like when deer and human rode together, when lion laid down with lamb.

That's the picture I get from the Genesis narrative of the beginning of our earth: perfect *shalom*. Not simply "peace," which is what people think of when they hear *shalom*, but pure wholeness. Experiencing a creation that is completely integrated and undefiled. You get a fleeting glimpse into this lost state of reality when you wade through nature because it is undefiled by humans. Nature simply exists. It is whole. When you step into this wholeness, you are immediately humbled at how things are outside of human touch and you long to return to a place of such naked, pure innocence. To return to the way things were when creator crafted creation. To return to a creation that, in the words of the creator,

was *goooood*.

141

Creation was supposed to be good. It wasn't good because creation itself simply sprang into existence. It was good because God made it that way. He intended creation to be good and in the end, after humans were formed, God said it was all *very good*. That was before humans screwed things up, though.

The first narrative account of creation presents a very logical, step-by-step process of bringing this whole complicated thing called creation into existence. The narrative presents God as *Elohim* who is completely in control and above and outside the world. He is the Picasso above his canvas. He is Mozart above the keys. He is Michelangelo outside the unformed slab of marble before David emerged. In chapter one God completely forms creation, directing the flow of forms and functions like a Maestro guiding the ebb and flow of an orchestra. Every note and form was exactly the way God wanted it. And the way it was, was *good*.

At the start, from the *tohu wabohu*, the "emptiness and chaos" of the blankness of our un-created universe, God breathed light into existence. An array of colors beamed across the blankness and burst forth like a grand Forth of July celebration on the Mall in Washington, D.C. Out of the symphony of colors God separated the light from the dark, declaring what was light *day* and what was dark *night*. God looked upon this initial handwork, sat back and declared it *good*. That was Day One.

Then, across the canvas of light and darkness came a vault that separated water from water—the sky. Amidst the array of light and dark God spread out from what had already been formed the great expanse of the sky called *heavens*, separating water above from water below. Day Two, complete and *good*.

On Day Three, the Creator gathered the waters beneath the heavens so that dry land would appear. God named that dryness *earth* and the wetness *seas* and it was so. Afterwards, God marveled at its beauty, the innocence of the undefiled earth and seas, but He knew even in the just-formed state more artistry was needed. Out of the breath of *Elohim* came lush green grass, seed-yielding plants of every kind, and magnificent fruit trees to feed that which would later burst forth on earth's stage. End of Day Three, a *good* day, indeed.

Next, erupted from the great expanse of the sky above the earth lights of every kind. The Creator was very thoughtful with these lights for He painted two great luminaries, one to rule and light the day, which was the sun, and one lesser light to rule the night, including the moon and stars. How thoughtful! God also decided that these two great lights would help the eventual inhabitants keep track of the seasons, days, and years. He thought of everything! When He retired His brush for the day, God turned around and saw all that He painted was beautiful and *good*.

Now that things were just right, now that the Creator had crafted the perfect environment for living things, He beckoned forth creatures from every corner of the earth and heavens. From the depths of the seas bubbled out the most magnificent sea creatures imaginable! Out of the heavens flew birds of great variety and creativity. Great harmonic chords streamed throughout the seas and heavens as creatures took the stage to inhabit *Elohim's good* creation. After the symphony died down a bit, God blessed the sealy and heavenly creatures saying, "Be fruitful and multiply and fill the water in the seas and let the fowl multiply in the earth." That was Day Five, another *good* day.

After God's show of creative ambition in the sea and sky, the Creator turned His attention toward the earth itself. Onto the surface of the Earth stormed beasts of every kind. He made every kind of wild animal, crawly thing, and beast that you could dream of. *Elohim* topped His last performance in every way imaginable. An array of colors and sounds collided from all earth's corners as sea creatures, heavenly fowl, and land animals played their part in *Elohim's* grand performance, all reflecting the majesty, glory, and creativity of their Creator. He looked across the spectrum of all He had created thus far and saw it was all *good*.

Then a hush fell across the entire expanse of Creation.

An anticipation began to well-up within the belly of earth, for all was not yet created. Just when Creation thought all had been formed, *Elohim* dipped His hand into the earth.

What was He doing? wondered Creation.

Beady little eyes from every corner watched in eager expectation. Wings flapped as they hovered over the Earth in wait. The wild beasts could hardly contain themselves and stomped in anticipation for the curiosity *Elohim* was causing. At just the right moment, when everything thought they would burst with excitement for God's final act

it happened:

The Hand of *Elohim* retreated from earth to reveal a being not yet seen before, yet all too familiar.

On the surface of earth laid a being that God called *Human*. It was in its own unique category, yet it mirrored the Creator that brought it into existence.

Out of the dust of Earth, the Creator crafted a creature after Himself. He molded the Human out of the soil in His Image and Likeness.

And *bleeeew*.

The Creator bent down and blew His own breath into the nostrils of the Human. After the Human received the Breath of Life from God Himself, the Human became a living creature.

God looked at all He had accomplished, at all He had created, from light to heavens and seas to earth, from plants to fowl and sea creatures to wild beasts, and at last the Image of God—the Human Being.

After the last work of art in His wonderful environment had been crafted, God decided that all He had done was *very good*.

Then, after He completed His creative tasks, God ceased from all painting and sculpting. On Day Seven God blessed the Day and hallowed it, because on that Day He set aside His brush and sculpting wheel after He created all He intended to create. After God crafted everything He intended to craft, He rested.

This is our collective Story, the way it was supposed to be at the beginning.

The way we became human.

The way we became Image-Bearers of our Creator.

Image-Bearers of Our Creator

And God said, "Let us make a Human in our image, by our likeness, to hold sway over the fish of the sea and the fowl of the heavens, and the cattle and the wild beasts and all created things that crawl upon the earth.

And God created the Human in His Image, in the Image of God He created Him, Male and Female He created Them. [76]

We, you and I, are created after the Image and Likeness of God Himself; creature was crafted to reflect the Creator.

Let that sink in for a moment.

Sit and ponder the grandness and majesty of the reality that humans are Images of God. We are created in God's likeness and still bear His reflection.

In understanding ourselves apart from General Creation, we should be understood by the term *Eikon*, a Greek word that means "Image-Bearer." Human beings are the culmination of God's purposeful act of creation and are crafted after the Image of God. This "reflection of the Creator" was originally created to enjoy, worship, and love Him forever in an eternal relationship with Him defined by mutual love. As human beings made in the Image of God, we are set apart from the rest of creation in every way, not simply because we have a soul, but rather because we are fashioned after God Himself.

As Image-Bearers, humans were placed on earth as God's sovereign emblem, God's representative and agent in the world with the authority and power. As these Agents of the Divine, we were crafted to share in His rule and administration of earth's resources and creatures. In fact, the creation of the human after God's Image and Likeness and vocation is modeled on the nature and actions of God Himself in Genesis 1.

Read the words of this ancient Hebrew poem that describes the nature of human beings:

When I consider the work of your heavens,
  the work of your fingers,
the moon and the stars,
  which you set in place,
what is man that you are mindful of him,
  the son of man that you care for him?
You set him a little lower than the heavenly beings
and crowned him with glory and honor.
You made him ruler over the works of your hands;
  you put everything under his feet:
all flocks and herds,
  and the beasts of the filed,
the birds of the air,
  and the fish of the sea,
  all that swim the paths of the seas. [77]

As the Psalmist ends his poem, "O Lord, our Lord, how majestic is your name in all the earth!" [78] Amen and Amen!

The Creator crafted the Human after Himself and crowned them with glory and honor. As the flow and cadence of the creation narrative suggests, we are the pinnacle of the created order, the crowing achievement of God's creative ambition. As J. Richard Middleton suggests in his book, *The Liberating Image*, humans have been given royal and godlike status in the world to rule and enjoy it as God's representatives. [79] In fact, the creation in Genesis 1 is not complete (or very good) until God creates humanity on the Sixth Day as His Image-Bearers to represent and mediate God's Divine presence on earth; it isn't until the human is created to exercise power on God's behalf on earth that the Creator exclaims His creation, "Very good!" Middleton goes on to say that humans are like God in exercising royal power on earth; the Divine Ruler delegated to humans a share of His rule of the earth. [80] This depiction of humans as ruling Eikons of God in the creation story in Genesis is incredibly consistent with the ancient Near Eastern use of statues and images to represent the rule and reign of kings within Mesopotamia.

During the "shock and awe" military campaign of the United States in the middle of 2003, you will probably remember the scene of American soldiers draping an American flag over the head of one of several hundred Saddam Hussein statues that dotted Iraqi cities and countryside. Along with these statues, Saddam also placed hundreds of murals and paintings of himself to remind people that he was the sovereign ruler in power, and to mark his territory as ruler.

The same was true for several Mesopotamian kingdoms during the time the Book of Genesis was written. The Genesis creation story mirrors the practice of ancient Near Eastern rulers establishing images or statues of themselves in lands they conquered where they were physically absent to serve as symbols of their rule over those lands. [81]   Like the rulers of Mesopotamia who erected statues to represent the ruler's presence and authority, there is a legitimate parallel to the creation of humans as the Image of God in Genesis to similarly represent the rule and reign of God on earth. Just as these earthly rulers acted on behalf of their gods as representatives and intermediaries on earth, so too do humans act as Image-Bearers of the one true God. We humans act as divine representatives of God in creation.

According to Middelton, the similarities between these ancient Near Eastern ideas from Mesopotamia and the Genesis narrative are striking: "The description of ancient Near Eastern rulers as the image of a god, when understood as an integral component of Mesopotamian royal ideology, provides the most plausible set of parallels for interpreting *imago Dei* (Image of God) in Genesis 1. If such texts—or ideology behind them—influenced the biblical *imago Dei*, this suggests that humanity is dignified with a status and role vis-à-vis the nonhuman creation that is analogous to the status and role of rulers in the ancient Near East vis-à-vis their subjects." [82]   In other words, it is very likely that the author of the creation narrative in Genesis was crafting a tribal story to explain human origins in relationship to Yahweh and function in relationship to other known ancient ideological understandings. As divinely crafted statues of the Creator, humans are given the responsibility and called to represent the rule and reign of the Creator among His creation. As Eikons, fundamentally we reflect the character and attributes of God and are functionally His representatives here on earth.

How cool is that?

Fundamentally Eikons

Now we come full circle: If humans were crafted after God as Eikons, then they bear a (albeit faded) reflection of Him. If we bear that cracked, faded reflection, then fundamentally we are reflectors of the Creator, our worth and dignity flow directly from God Himself, deep down we know God exists, and we know there is a Story bigger than our own and another Rhythm to which we should dance. While sin distorts all four, God through rescue in Jesus desires to re-create all humans to the way they were intended to be at the beginning of creation: Eikons in complete *shalom* (wholeness) that exist in an eternal relationship with God and properly relate to themselves, others, and the world.

What a completely different beginning! Rather than all of humanity being screwed (sorry, but that's the way it is usually portrayed!), God wants to restore all people to the way they were intended to be. There *is* a better way of being human. The way humans are was not intended when God crafted us after Himself.

We are not the way we were supposed to be!

But there is hope. We can be made clean. Wholeness and restoration and life *is* possible because God deep down wants to bring all individuals back to how they were intended before rebellion.

Throughout the entire ministry of Jesus you see a Man who spent three years wading through the cracked stories of Eikons and declaring the "kingdom has invaded your story" through deliberate acts of re-creation: the Samaritan woman's social and human dignity was restored; the blind man's eyes were re-created to their created function; a demon possessed boy found spiritual and physical re-creation; the dignity and spiritual worth of those outside religious borders ("sinners" as the teachers of the Law would say) were restored as participants in relationship with God. The list goes on and on. For three years, Jesus restored people to the way they were intended to be as beautifully crafted Eikons in relationship with the creation and in relationship with their Creator. For three years, Jesus proclaimed the dawn of God's re-creative movement to bring the whole created order back to His original good creation; He showed special interest in cracked Eikons.

This is where we must *begin* God's Story of Rescue. Paul writes in 2 Corinthians 5 that we Christians have been given the ministry of restoration, we are called to partner with God's movement to restore Eikons to the way they were intended to be at creation, not merely to get sinners to heaven when they die! Unless the Church begins the (un)offensive gospel of Jesus at Creation, however, then getting sinners saved and into heaven becomes the point, which distorts the Story and our mission.

The (un)offensive gospel of Jesus begins with Creation, not sin or heaven. So must we.

If humans are not the way they were intended to be at creation, if all of us are not the way we were meant to be, how are we to understand our nature? We've sinned and do sin and there is no way around that, is there?

Yes, and no! While sin and sinning are part of the human condition and is described so in God's Sacred Text to humans, I believe we need to re-understand the sin idea to be rebellion: Eikons rebelled against God and His Rhythm and they still rebel against both.

I think this notion of rebellion is much more proper because it places the idea of sin and sinning squarely in its relational reality, rather than simply being a legal one. The (un)offensive understanding of the gospel of Jesus recognizes sin as relational rejection, rather than simply violating a code of conduct, which relates to our originally created state as Eikons of God. The question is: *who* have we offended more than *what* have we done? That bring us to the next act in God's Story of Rescue: our rebellion.

Chapter 7
our rebellion

Let me introduce you to Detron Mack.

For over a year I saw Detron every morning on Capitol Hill as I met with congressional staffers for spiritual mentoring. Every morning he greeted me with his smile and warm personality—the kind of warmth that's just a tad bit perky for 7:30 a.m.—and served me and my friends tasty breakfast sandwiches. He really was a stellar guy!

I remember my coworker, Lisa, telling me one afternoon that as she was walking past the sandwich shop where he worked, he yelled out her name and came barreling down Pennsylvania Avenue to give her a big hug. People stared. They stared because he was black and she was white; he was a lowly sandwich maker and she a high class Ms. Professional. Lisa didn't care, though. Like me, she loved Detron's enthusiasm for life and infectious happiness.

This all changed one weekend, though.

One hot summer weekend, Detron Mack died of gunshot wounds on the streets of South East, Washington, D.C. Detron was in the wrong place at the wrong time and was caught in the cross fire of a drive-by shooting. This joyful man's life was sliced in half by small metal objects whizzing through the air like hornets through a summer field. (If you know anything about South East, D.C., you know that death, injustice, and suffering are all too familiar forces on the streets and alleyways a hop, skip, and a jump beyond the Capitol Building. The irony is stifling!)

In an instant evil, rebellion, and death snuffed out the life of Detron, blasting his family and friends.

I found out about this unfortunate weekend of violence the next Monday when I walked into the sandwich shop with a friend for my morning sandwich and coffee. I felt the mood was unusually stiff and somber. When I asked where Detron was, the place fell apart. People explained the weekend events and expressed their grief over the loss of their friend and their frustration with the ongoing violence in their urban neighborhoods. They gave me a newspaper clipping of his death notice and invited me to the funeral the next day. (Actually, it was from a local, indy neighborhood paper. The Washington Post isn't really interested in the deaths of black sandwich-makers from the South East.) Lisa, another coworker, and I attended the funeral of Detron, an experience I will never forget.

The funeral was in a little Pentecostal church in the heart of South East, D.C. on a very hot, sticky July day, and we almost got lost trying to find the place because it was in a world we never visited. When we finally did arrive, we assumed our place in the processional line to view the body and to give our condolences to his mom. She was a sweet old lady who was visibly scarred by the injustice, poverty, and violence that engulfed her community, that robbed her of her son.

Over and over she told us how she couldn't believe her baby was gone. We explained who we were, pastors of sorts on Capitol Hill, and how we appreciated her son's infectious spirit and joyous presence when he served us each week at the sandwich shop. Detron's mom said he loved his job. She then went on to talk about how he was involved in the lives of young people in his community, nurturing them as a father to keep them clean and to clean up the users and gangbangers in the neighborhoods of the South East. None of us knew this and we got a sense from his mom and the others that we had stood in the presence of royalty, a royalty not based on what Detron did or who he worked for, but who he was and how he lived.

Evil and rebellion and death, however, snuffed out the life of this Duke of South East, Washington, D.C.

The most disturbing moment of this whole 24 hour episode came at the end of the viewing. At the end, the family, Detron's sister, mother (he had no father), and aunts stood and stared at their murdered Duke. They stared and sobbed at the sight of the shell of their son, brother, and nephew laying in the modest coffin.

Then the wailing began.

I can honestly say I have never heard sounds come from any human being like the sounds I heard that afternoon. From the depths of their being the mother and sister raged against the evil and rebellion and death that struck Detron. Joining with the cries of this family, the anthem of a legion of Heavenly Beings echoed off the stained glass of this church screaming:

Death is not the way it's supposed to be!

All of creation is not the way it's supposed to be because of the real choices of rebellious, broken humans.

Though we are broken, though all of creation has been vandalized by our choices, it was not originally like this. God didn't originally create a broken, vandalized creation. No, He created a *good* creation and *very good* humans. You wouldn't know this, though, with the way God's Story of Rescue is often told. Many insist with an offensive gospel that the Story must begin with the screwed-upness of humans, rather than with the goodness of God's original design. Because the fundamentals of humanity are wrong, the Story is wrong, too.

This brings us to act two of God's Story of Rescue.

The Fundamentals of Humanity

As I've already written, I often hear Christians claiming the gospel is offensive, especially when their efforts at converting others go awry. Christians almost use the offensive gospel as an excuse to alleviate any guilt or responsibility. They insist that the world isn't rejecting them, but Jesus and His good news. They insist people are so screwed-up and depraved that the gospel is like what kryptonite is to Superman: utterly crippling and repulsive to the senses.

Besides framing the gospel as "offensive" to excuse their behavior, it seems their belief is rooted in something much more unfortunate: some Christians actually believe Jesus and His message are fundamentally offensive. The reason these Christians believe this is because they've gotten the Story wrong, or at least its parts are not understood properly and are moved in the wrong place.

I want to push a bit against this popular notion and say that Jesus and His good news are entirely (un)offensive. Jesus and His good news are (un)offensive, not offensive. Rather than being unhelpful, unhealing, and repulsive, the life and teachings of Jesus point toward "good news" that is wholesome, healing, and attractive. Throughout Jesus' ministry people clung to Him, they loved being around Him and sought Him out to find personal healing and re-creation. Whether that re-creation was social, economical, physical, or spiritual, everything for which people longed was found in encountering Jesus the Christ of Nazareth.

We miss this when we get the Story wrong. The reason the Story is wrongly told and understood is because we start in the wrong place. Rather than beginning with creation, as God's Story of Rescue begins, many Christians start the Story with sin. Jesus' hopeful message doesn't begins with our screwed-upness, but with the way humans and the rest of creation were originally intended. Human nature is not *fundamentally* sinful, though we do sin. We are fundamentally Eikons of God. I'd say that's very different from the offensive message typically told. We should understand humans as Image-Bearers of God who are cracked and in need of rescue and re-creation. We need to be restored to the way we were originally intended to be, the way all of "this" was created at the beginning.

Why *are* things so screwed-up? Why aren't we the way we are supposed to be? We do sin. How, then, does sin play into God's Story? This brings us to Act Two in the Divine Story of Rescue: rebellion. Rather than understanding human nature in traditional terms that places sin at the center of God's Story, we should re-understand humans as rebellious and broken Eikons, rather than hopeless sinners.

Let me make something clear at this point: with all the talk about rebellion, I am not trying to downplay human participation in sin. Sin and sinning are part of the human condition, described as such in God's Sacred Text to people called the Bible. While I believe sin is now part of creation and humanity, I believe we need to re-understand the sin idea as rebellion. Eikons rebelled against God and His Rhythm and continue to rebel against both.

The problem with traditional ideas of sin is that those ideas are mainly legal and relate to a more legal understanding of atonement (how sin is forgiven by God). Many Christians who hold to a penal substitutionary theory of atonement begin with sin in their version of the gospel because, as they say, humans are fundamentally sinful. People have violated and broken a moral, legal code of God which requires a substitute for God's wrathful judgment. The substitute was ultimately provided by Jesus who replaced the "violator" in God's Cloudy Courtroom and was sent away to die by Bailiff St. Peter. That death paid the penalty for humans (usually an elite few, like the Christian, their family, and their friends) which bought for them a place in God's Cosmic Castle.

I'm being playful in my description of penal substitutionary atonement, of course. I do appreciate this view as a tool for understanding how God forgives our sin. The problem with this theory of atonement is that it assumes sin is more of a legal problem, a violation-of-a-code-of-conduct problem. Sin, however, is much more relational. While people do violate God's instructions for how we are to live as humans with God and others, those violations center on our failure to love both God and people. This is why the word rebellion is a better description for how we relate to God's Rhythm of Life.

155

Relational vs. Legal

For too long sin has been understood in mostly legal terms: we humans have broken a sort of law or code that was established by God, resulting in chaos and division. I wonder what this framing does to the Story we tell, a framing that doesn't take into account the relational nature of sin and rebellion.

Instead, sin should be re-understood in more relational terms, rather than strictly legal one. Since God's Rhythm of Life is more relational than legal, sin is a relational problem, not simply a legal problem. Jesus summed up this Rhythm this way: love God with all your heart and with all your mind and with all your strength; love those around you as you love yourself. While God does outline how we are to live in relationship to Him, others, and the rest of creation, sin is not loving God and not loving other people. In order to sin, you must do so in the context of relationships, either with God or others.

Again, sin is relational.

Sin is un-love

You may protest, "What about the Law?" What about Judge Roy Moore's Ten Commandments? *Clearly* we violate some sort of Theistic Code of Conduct!

Sorry, the Law was given *after* God's people were already in relationship with Him. While covenants in our mind have a contractual ring to them, in the ancient Near East they were far more relational. The Law was not a code of conduct, per se, but an outline of how the Children of Israel were to live as a people set apart for relationship with God. Even then, all ten commands are themselves relational: the first four laws relate to loving and relating properly to God; the last six concern our proper relationship with other people.

Obedience to the Law did not get them into the Covenant nor ultimately repaire what humans had broken. Instead, obedience to the Law came in response to that newly formed Covenant and renewed *relationship*; obedience and not sinning were required to stay in and maintain and cultivate the relationship that God had freely provided. [83] They were already in relationship with God because He chose them. God then explained to them how they were to relate to God and others in loving relationship. In its most basic sense even the Law was entirely relational and a violation of the Law (sin) was an act of un-love.

At the foundation of the world we were created to exist in an eternal relationship with God and live according to a certain Pattern, a certain Rhythm. At our creation we were designed to exist in an eternal dance with God and move according to His Rhythm. But we chose to dance our own dance, we chose to move according to a foreign Rhythm. We abandoned God and chose to pattern the steps of our life after the Rhythm of Self, resulting in a complete unraveling of God's good creation, a Great Rupture in the fabric of reality itself.

The Great Rupture

The rebellion that plunged all of creation into brokenness resulted in what French lay theologian Jacques Ellul called, "The Great Rupture." [84] When Mama Eve and Papa Adam chose to pursue their own Way by seeking *knowledge* about Good and Evil, when they pursued their own Rhythm of Life over against the Way and Rhythm of God,

something tragic happened.

A Great Rupture occurred in the "soul" of reality.

Shalom was vandalized.

Not only our relationship with God ruptured, but our relationships with each other did, too. Now not only do we not love God as we ought, we do not love other humans as we were originally designed. Even though we were made for each other, made to live together, and created to find our meaning and purpose not simply in ourselves but in one another, we find doing so incredibly difficult. Every generation in every part of the globe has experienced a Crusade, the Conquistadors, Trails of Tears, Holocaust, Rwanda, and Darfur. On every part of the globe The Great Rupture is evident in broken, oppressed relationships between tribes and nations, between friends and family.

I think most of us intuitively know this, though. Just look around you: isn't it pretty obvious that things aren't the way they are supposed to be? Many of our postmodern poets think so. While most of the top forty pop-culture songs usually celebrate the screwed-up things we humans do, many also bemoan the evil that has stolen into our world. Consider these words from the American instrumental post-rock band *Explosions in the Sky*:

> This great evil: where's it come from?
> How'd it steal into the world?
> What seed, what root did it grow from?
> Who's doing this?
> Who's killing us, robbing us of life and light,
>   mocking us with the sight of what we mighta known?
> Does our ruin benefit the earth,
>   aid the grass to grow and the sun to shine?
> Is this darkness in you, too?
> Have you passed through this night?

What an intuitive group! They seem to realize just how much creation has ruptured, just how much *we've* rupture. But as they ask: Where has this great evil come from? Why are things the way they are? Why are *we* the way we are?

As we saw in our creation, everything was originally complete, whole, and *very good*. Creation was complete and pure *shalom* reigned, which isn't simply peace, but wholeness and integration. *Shalom* is the way things ought to be.

The first humans rebelled, however. Certainly they were drawn, beckoned, and wooed into rebellion, but they rebelled, nonetheless. The thing about any rebellion is that it is always directed toward a *relationship*. Whether toward our parents, spouses, friends, or government, a "someone" is rejected; a relationship is severed.

The same is true for sin: it's always committed against and directed toward God. We cannot understand sin apart from reference to God, nor can we understand *shalom* apart from vandalism of the way God originally intended things to be. As Cornelius Plantinga says in his masterful book, *Not the Way It's Supposed to Be*, "God hates Sin not just because it violates his law, but more substantively, because it violates *shalom*, because it breaks peace, because it interferes with the way things are supposed to be. God is for shalom and therefore against sin." [85]

In short, sin is deliberate vandalism of *shalom*, vandalism of the way it's supposed to be between God and human, between human and human.

Sin is un-love.

Therefore, every time we partner with Sin, we scream a big "Yes!" to the vandalism of *shalom*. We say we want "More!" of the way things aren't supposed to be and "Less!" to the way things ought to be. When we sin we reject relationships, primarily with God our Creator, but also with His Image-Bearers, other people. By sinning, we ourselves affirm the Event of the Great Rupture, and perpetuate the continued ravishment of relationships and the wholeness of God's original creation.

Let me say that again: when you and I sin, we both affirm the original act of rebellion that shattered all of this, and we scream a big "Yes!" to the continued vandalism of shalom, the destruction of others and rebellion against God.

How devastating, indeed!

Because of the Great Rupture, because of the vandalism of shalom, I believe the consequences of human rebellion are exhaustive and holistic, infecting every crevice of creation. Human rebellion caused a rippled effect beyond humans to all creation, which now groans for ultimate restoration under the weight of sin.

Human Culture is fallen and polluted by sin. While human society is capable of producing much good, such as art and science, it is still undeniably broken and incapable of restoring itself to the way God intended it to be. While Francis Fukuyama declared, "the end of history" in his similarly titled book—claiming modern Western society had reached its crowning achievements economically, politically, technologically, societally, and culturally—9/11 destroyed such hope in Modern Man's efforts at self-salvation through the utopian Enlightenment Project. While human society insists we can save and repair ourselves, the evil that slammed into New York that September day reminded us all just how weak we really are.

Likewise, I believe the Earth itself and the animal kingdom are damaged by the pollution of sin and human rebellion. Through this pollution natural evils occur and animals are affected so that they eat each other, resulting in deaths not intended to be. Creation is broken, too, resulting in famine, massive earthquakes, tsunamis, and drought. No part of creation's original *shalom* has not been disrupted. As the apostle Paul writes, every corner and crevice of creation groans in anticipation of rescue. [86]

In short, the rebellion of humans at the beginning of creation shattered the *shalom* of all reality, vandalizing and polluting it to death. Consequently, all of creation groans under the weight of sin, while humans are especially cracked because of our willful rebellion.

Rebellious, Cracked Eikons of God

By "cracked," I don't simply mean we murder, steal, and cheat on our partners. Of course we do these things. Broken humans also cultivate deep hatred for one another, cheat on their taxes, and lust after other humans. We tell awful, vicious lies and rumors about our neighbors and coworkers. Out of a heart of pride, we cut each other off on our way to work and raise our fingers in admiration of each others driving habits. We bring up past mistakes in heated arguments with friends or family members to gain the upper-hand in an argument or rub salt into old wounds. Let's face it: we can be pretty awful toward other people! Everyday we all do mini-acts of denial toward God and His Way, all while rebelling against both.

Let me illustrate just how broken we are with a personal story.

After I left ministry on Capitol Hill in the summer of 2006 I needed a break from the intense political world before I went to seminary, so I took a job with a national upscale department store to recuperate from four years in the government. Because I love the creativity of fashion, I gravitated toward the men's fashion department. I ended-up getting a wonderful job in Men's Furnishings selling $150 shirts, $200 ties, and $1800 suits. It was a great gig!

In fact, it was so great and I did so well that I was on a fast track toward management. Somehow, this thoroughly salesmanship-handicapped individual quickly rose to number three in department sales. The number one in my department was number one in the company, selling $2.5 million the year prior. The second person in sales had been in the business for years and sold several hundred thousand dollars the year before. Then there was me. Somehow I managed to sell fairly well and develop a good relationship with the store director, which almost translated into an assistant management position.

I say almost, because the day before I was going to be promoted I was called down to Human Resources. I thought I was going to fill out some paperwork for the promotion. Instead, I was asked to step into a room for a little chitchat with the head of Loss Prevention and an internal investigator.

Before I continue, let me give you some helpful information: if you are ever asked into a meeting with Loss Prevention and an internal investigator, it isn't going to be very pretty!

So I stepped into the room, sat down, and they begin talking about the different things they investigate. Theft. Company policy violations. Abuse. Harassment. I sat there trying to appear as calm and cool as possible, all the while reeling inside.

Then they came to me and my issue:

Commission Fraud.

In this company sales people are paid on commission, which was based on sales minus returns. At this particular national department store, they basically had no return policy and generally accepted items that were years old even without a receipt, providing the means to cheat the system. If someone returned an item and we could not determine when they bought it, we could zero-out our employee number to make the transaction. My new friends revealed surveillance photos of me returning items, receipt in tote, while zeroing-out my employee number. They accused me of deliberately violating the commission policy.

They were right.

I stole from the company by deliberately failing to honestly account for my returns. (By the way, this little act of honest self-disclosure won't get me in trouble anymore. I've already made my recompense!)

Worst of all: I lied about it.

To the face of the man who pushed for my promotion, I lied about the acts and pulled out all the stops to try to manipulate him and the conversation to keep my job. The thing is, I almost had him. I was *this* close to convincing him it was all a mistake, all a silly misunderstanding, and keeping my job, while skipping toward my promotion.

I'm glad he did the right thing and fired me.

I deserved it.

I vandalized *shalom*, again, by rebelling against God and His Way. I ravished my relationships with this company and my store director. I screamed a big "Yes!" to Mama Eve's and Papa Adam's original rebellion by stealing and then lying about it.

The same is true for us all.

Through every mini act of denial, we all continue to vandalize *shalom*, ravish our relationships, shout a big "Woo Hoo!" to Adam's and Eve's rebellion, and sin against God and His Way.

While humans are still fundamentally Eikons of God, they are also thoroughly broken, rebellious, and shaped by sin. In the words of Scot McKnight "humans are both brilliant and bad." [87] Through Adam's initial rebellion we continue to rebel against God and His Way. As cracked Eikons, we are desperate for holistic restoration, a restoration we are incapable of providing on our own.

I think people inherently know that's the case, that things are not the way they are meant to be, that we are broken. If Eternity is grafted into the very being of all humans by the very fact they are crafted after God, wouldn't it make sense that they would inherently know that there is an Other who is beyond them, a Story that is bigger than their stories, and long for another world—no *need* another world—to burst forth through the seams of this good, but terribly screwed-up one? If this is what people long for, a new world and a new life, then wouldn't people embrace them both if they were offered to them? Do Christians *really* need to remind the world they sin, or should we rather offer from the start a vision of the way things were supposed to be? Should we really start with sin and rebellion as we retell God's Story of Rescue, or should we present to the world the hope of rescue and re-creation to the divine intent found in Genesis 1 and 2?

This is why I love the Gospels: they are a collection of stories of real-life cracked and screwed-up people who encounter the very divine and very human Jesus. Through this encounter, they find the rescue and re-creation they've been longing for all their lives, because Jesus offers them Life in all of its fullness. In the last chapter I wrote that throughout the ministry of Jesus we see a Man who spent three years wading through the cracked stories of Eikons and declaring the "kingdom has invaded your story!" He confronted their rebellion and the affects of rebellion with Life. And when people walked away from that encounter they were re-created. Now what is offensive about that?

Who is the Jesus we are showing people, what is the Story we are telling?

Are we confronting rebellion with life, rescue, and re-creation? Or are we confronting rebellion with more rebellion, with the sulfuric scent of death?

Even though we are broken, humans are not without hope. We celebrate the Season of Advent and Christmas for this very reason. Each time we celebrate the invasion of the God-with-us-God in the person of Jesus, we remember and declare the hope of rescue and re-creation for all of creation from the results of rebellion. Nestled in the scream coming from the swaddling-clothed Babe is the cry, "I can save you!" not "You are sinners who are screwed!" When the host of angels burst forth into the same time-space reality of the shepherds, they proclaimed wholeness and *shalom* to all of humanity, upon whom God's love and affection still rests despite the rebellion.

While rebellion brought Jesus here to earth, it was not the point of His message. Rescue is at the center of His invasion and re-creation is His banner. That is a good, (un)offensive gospel for us broken Eikons. And that good gospel should affect how we explain and respond to tragedy and evil.

163

Responding to Tragedy and Evil

Before we move to the next Act in God's Story of Rescue, I want to say a few words about how we should respond to the results of rebellion that seem to surround us at every turn. Much was made throughout the blogosphere of the comments by Christian leader and pastor John Piper in response to the Minnesota bridge collapse in August 2007. From Christians to atheists and everyone in between, Piper seemed to have left a sour taste in people's mouths. I think this one episode is representative of the Church's ongoing problem with responding to the results of rebellion: tragedy and evil.

As I already mentioned, after I found out about his comment I decided to write a blog post response, both to deconstruct his post and to flesh out my own understanding of God's sovereignty in the face of the affects of rebellion. I think I made some good headway and had some great responses from people there and elsewhere over those ideas. But one thing was missing, which was noticed by a few people: I provided little to the topic of how to help people amidst pain and how we should respond and react to tragedy and evil.

Hopefully, this will provide a response and will help some people think through this weighty, needed discussion. In short, how we respond to the effects of rebellion as followers in the Way of Jesus should flow from this understanding:

Love is greater than Evil.

My response to the immense evil and tragedy that engulfs our lives and the world thanks to human rebellion is that Love is more powerful and far greater than the power of Evil. In fact, Evil has been defeated and stripped if its eternal power by Love through the real time-space event of the cross. The Church is called to embody and proclaim the power of the cross by living in the Way of Jesus and spreading His hopeful message of rescue and re-creation.

Now let's be clear: Evil still exists in the world. Things are still not the way they were intended to be. People contract horrible diseases, natural disasters wipe out entire towns, entire people groups are systematically slaughtered, children die. The list goes on. As the apostle Paul helps us understand, there are real, deep, dark, magical powers that undergird the real-life tragedies that plague humanity. So absolute Evil exists and has made its reign on the earth from the near start of creation.

But something curious happened about 2000 years ago: invasion.

The Creator invaded creation to stage the single greatest, most important rescue operation. God became human and made His dwelling among us, full of love. As the fullest definition and demonstration of God, Jesus came to this earth to show a new way of living—the way of the Kingdom of Heaven, a way defined by loving God and loving others—all the while defeating evil, sin, and death through the cross.

While Jesus showed us a new and better way of being human by loving the world around Him, the fullest expression of that love was displayed on the cross where evil and death and rebellion were defeated. Jesus willingly endured the cross to defeat the powers of decay and death that touch the lives of all humans. To restore the entire creation to the way it was intended to be from the beginning, God lived and died.

As 1 John 3:16 says, "We know what love is because Jesus Christ laid down his life for us." That is what we as His followers are called to do: Love the world around us with the furious, sacrificial Love of God.

How does that look as we enter into moments of tragedy and evil? As Jesus loved, so we love. Since we are called to be Jesus to the world around us, I take seriously His call for us to do greater things than He did in the world. What did He do while He was on earth? Jesus loved people by restoring them emotionally, socially, physically, spiritually, and materially.

The woman at the well experienced social restoration by a loving Jesus in the face of a life held in tragic bondage. The leper's dignity and health were restored by a loving God in the face of a physical evil. A Roman official's family was restored in the face of the tragedy of a dead little daughter, through another act by a loving Yeshua. Ultimately, the powers of this world, who wallow in evil and tragedy and death were vanquished through the subversive death of God; God sacrificed God to kill death and restore creation to the way He originally intended it to be.

Jesus acted by confronting Evil with Love.

Even while He taught about the Kingdom, those teachings were always accompanied by acts of love that directly assaulted the effects of rebellion. Jesus called us to teach and be and show and explain His loving Way to a hurting, broken, sobbing, grieving, cracked world. In the face of pain and suffering, tragedy and evil, the world does not need another idea or teaching. No, the world needs people committed to simply and lovingly holding them while they hold the lifeless body of their child. The world needs people committed to doing acts of love to help rebuild lives devastated by natural disasters. The world needs people to listen to the stories of lives devastated by addiction and lovingly whisper to them that it really will be OK. The world needs people who speak prophetic words of love and restoration for the marginalized and socially spit upon.

The world needs lovers, not just teachers.

While teachers are important, they need to speak truthfully as lovers. Good teachers are good lovers.

The rhythm of Jesus' life was His love for the world, through his life and teachings and ultimately through the cross. If the way of Jesus was His love, then shouldn't that also be the Church's way, too? As Jesus fully participated in the gritty human drama, so also we must participate. As Jesus loved each person within their own narratives, confronting the pain, tragedy, alienation, and death with Love, so must we also do love to and for the great cloud of hurting witnesses that engulf us in our communities.

The world needs to know, understand, and feel the power of Love in the face of Evil and rebellion. Jesus defeated evil on the cross through the power of Love and He calls us to fully realize that same power by being Him to the world.

Because in the end:

Love wins.

In the next chapter, we will celebrate rescue even as we groan with creation about rebellion. May we fight rebellion in the lives of those around us by showing them a better Way of being human and by offering the hope of rescue and re-creation through Jesus. May we fight the systems and dark powers of evil that wage war against the Way of Jesus. Finally, may we fight rebellion in our own lives through the power of the Holy Spirit who provides us with power to dance with the Divine Community of Self-Giving Lovers according to God's Rhythm.

Chapter 8
our rescue

When I was about five years old, my family took a trip to a campground along Lake Michigan where my grandparents were camped in their big ol' trailer. Along the way we bought buckets of battered *Kentucky Fried Chicken* and tubs of mashed potatoes, coleslaw, and brownies for a grand picnic on the dunes of the Lake. It was a great family outing.

Great, until I almost drowned!

Like all five year olds, I decided to go exploring to see what buried treasure or washed up lake organisms I could find. Sometime along my romp in the sand I got a little too close to the lapping waves and one of them got me. To this day I remember bounding along the edge of sand and water one minute and gasping for breath the next.

In the process of almost drowning I even lost my piece of Trident spearmint gum my grandma gave me. Bummer!

Then something happened:

Rescue.

My parents, partly oblivious to what their ambitious five year old was doing, instantly launched into Superhero mode when they discovered I was floundering in the water. In an instant my dad ran down the beachhead, bounded into the water, and rescued me from the clutches of Poseidon.

The same is true for humanity; my story is humanity's collective story.

All of us are floundering in a sea of brokenness, bad choices, rebellion, evil, and chaos. All of us have gotten too close to the edge of the Garden, fully participating in every bite of the Tree of Good and Evil, choking on its pulp, drowning in its juices.

Then something happened:

Rescue.

God launched the greatest rescue operation in the history of humanity by becoming one of us. In an attempt to rescue His cracked Eikons, God invaded the world by becoming human in the person of Jesus Christ. This is where we pick up the exciting tale of God's Story of Rescue.

On to act three!

The God-with-us-God

Glory to God in the highest,
    and on earth shalom to all humans,
    on whom His favor rests!

These magnificent lines begin God's act of rescue; they proclaim the invasion of creation by the God-with-us-God, Jesus Christ. In this proclamation by the Heavenly Hosts recorded in the Book of Luke, the message of the angels is that the all powerful God seeks to bring *shalom* to earth and express His merciful will for all people. As we've already seen, *shalom* means wholeness and completeness. The Creator is declaring that the wholeness and completeness He offers is found in Jesus and available to all who receive His favor.

Finally, the moment Israel had been waiting for, the moment the whole *world* had been waiting for: God's act of rescue to put all of creation back together.

God's people knew that Yahweh intended to bring justice and shalom to earth, but the question was how, when, and through whom. These expectations were built upon a deep belief that the one true God does deeply care about human suffering, especially that of His own people. They trusted in God to send someone to help them again return from exile, like a Moses who brought liberation for Israel out of Egypt. This coming Messiah, then, would be similar to Moses and bring a final exodus for the Children of Israel, and ultimately for the entire world.

Embedded in this announcement, then, were the expectations of generations of humans. God's will and higher purpose is that all humanity, the whole entire earth, would experience His divine wholeness and salvation. God's rescue and re-creation were made possible through the invasion of God into the world through His Son Jesus Christ and made available to all who will eventually embrace Jesus as Lord.

The Book of John records just that: "The Word became flesh and made His dwelling among us. We have seen His glory, the glory of the One and Only, who came from the Father, full of grace and truth." [88] The Word, who is later identified as Jesus Christ, invaded the world and "tabernacled" among the Earth's people. Tabernacled. That is the Greek word used in the NIV as *made His dwelling.* The Jewish readers would have instantly remembered the provisions of God for the desert journey of His people after they were released from their Egyptian oppressors. In the Book of Exodus, God tells His people to, "make a sanctuary for Me, and I will dwell among them. Make this *tabernacle* and all its furnishings exactly like the pattern I will show you." [89] Just as God "tabernacled" with His people in the desert, and later in Solomon's Temple, so too was He "tabernacling" among all the world through His Son.

God enfleshed Himself as a real human being to make His dwelling among us. Creator became creation to rescue it from rebellion and death. By perfectly obeying the Way of the Creator when we had not, providing the final sacrifice, absorbing our punishment for our rebellion, and ultimately defeating the dark powers by triumphing over death itself on the cross and through the grave, Jesus rescued the world.

The Loving, Gentle, Caring Jesus

I have the amazing privilege of helping pastor a wonderful missional community outside of Grand Rapids, MI. After returning to the area where I grew up after I fled five years prior, I am certain God deliberately placed me in this community of people. God placed me there not so much for them but for me. I've learned so much about pastoring from these people, and about Jesus and His amazing Story. One of the people from whom I've tried to soak as much as I can is a very wise man by the name of Ray Minema.

Ray is an 84 year old Dutch man who immigrated to the United States after World War II. During the War, Ray was involved in the Dutch underground movement to free Jews from the evil, systematic slaughter of the Nazis. In fact, Ray knew Corrie Ten Boom, the famous Jewish refugee organizer who later wrote an autobiography on her anti-Nazi efforts called *The Hiding Place*. Ray has seen the face of evil and death in ways I can only touch at movie length. So whenever he speaks, I listen with great attention and savor every word like it was my last meal on earth.

This past year at our Maundy Thursday service, this great man stunned us all by rewriting and reading the Passion narrative of the Gospels in his own words. Here is a guy who nearly tasted death himself, and certainly smelled the sulfuric stench of evil wafting through the countryside of his beloved country, yet still continues to passionately pursue "the loving, gentle, caring Jesus" as Savior and Lord. So when this man spoke about the words of the most ironic evil event of the history of the world, I listened.

Because I could think of no better way to retell the moments leading up to the event of the cross, I want you to read the poetic words of this wonderful man, too. His words add a weight and texture I could never express in my own meager words. So with Ray's permission, this is the account of the last 24 hours of the loving, gentle, caring Jesus and event of the cross:

172

Jesus.
The loving,
gentle,
caring
and healing Preacher was worried and sorrowful.

After celebrating the Passover with His friends, they went out of the city unto the Mount of Olives into the Garden of Gethsemane. It was already early evening and actually time to retire, but Jesus told His friends to take a rest and He went on alone in that peaceful garden.

But Jesus felt no peace and prayed and pleaded with God His Father: "If it is at all possible take this cup away from me! But not my will but yours be done."

And God the Father heard His beloved Son's cry for help and sent an angel from heaven to comfort and encourage Jesus. Then Jesus went back to His friends and found them sleeping, unaware of the tragedy that was happening around them. Another sorrow for Jesus.

"Why could you not watch with Me, just for a little while?"

Jesus went away alone again and prayed for the safety of His friends. He knew what was going to happen that evening and the next day, and that their enemies were near while His friends were sleeping. At the same time a band of soldiers and high priest servants led by Judas had surrounded them, and Jesus was taken away to the chambers of the High Priest. There a gathering of hateful Pharisees were waiting for the captive Jesus. Another great sorrow for the loving, gentle, caring Jesus.

Jesus did not talk back at the false accusations except when the High Priest asked Him, "Do you claim to be the Son of God?"

"Yes," Jesus answered, "you're looking at Him!"

That was enough for them to condemn Jesus to death.

The next morning a Roman guard command took Jesus to the court of Pilate. After questioning Jesus, Pilate found no fault worthy of a death sentence. He had Jesus flogged and tortured with a crown of thorns pushed on His head. But the fanatic, hateful screaming crowd in front of Pilate's courts, threatening vengeance, made Pilate give in. He washed his hands in innocence and asked them what they wanted done with Jesus."

"Crucify Him! Crucify Him!"

The loving, gentle, caring Jesus was pushed to carry His heavy, rugged cross onto Golgotha and there Jesus was laid down on His cross, His arms stretched and held by the soldiers, while the iron spikes were hammered into and thru His hands and feet into the rugged cross. Then the cross was put upright with Jesus hanging from His torn hands and feet.

The loving, gentle, caring Jesus never complained or asked for mercy. He only prayed: "Father, forgive them, for they don't know what they are doing."

And the man next to Jesus was saved by grace. "Today you will be with me in paradise." Jesus seeing His mother with His friend John told them to be like mother and son.

Suddenly it became dark, very, very dark and silent. And then Jesus cried out in agony, "My God, my Father, why have you forsaken me? Why Father? Why Father, where are you? Why?"

Why?

For you

and for me.

What an amazing, powerful retelling of our loving, gentle, caring Rescuer! Just think: Jesus endured the entire event of the cross (the torture, the abandonment, the physical agony, and spiritual rupture) for you and for me. He never complained or asked for mercy, for you and for me. God the Father forsook Jesus His Son, for you and for me. I think if anyone has the right to abandon God after the horrors of war he saw and endured, it is Ray. Yet, he knows that after the loving, gentle, caring Jesus what else is there? Where else is rescue?

Just as important: how are we to understand this rescue? Can we really pin down the nature of God's rescue with mere words? While Ray brilliantly described the events of the cross, we should also examine how Jesus' entire act of rescue saves us through his life, death, and resurrection.

The Victorious Obedient Substitute

At the risk of over simplifying Jesus' redemptive act, I believe Jesus is the *Victorious Obedient Substitute.* Through His life, Jesus obeyed God perfectly after the First Adam did not, demonstrating how we are to live as humans. Jesus' death paid the final penalty to God for rebellion on behalf of all humans through a final sacrifice, making it possible to restore humans to relationship with God. Through His resurrection, Jesus defeated the dark powers to liberate all humanity from Satan's control and to free us from the bondage of evil and sin and the consequence of both: death.

This is how we can view the atoning event of the cross.

Through Jesus' life, His baptism commissioned Him for ministry and empowered Him by the Holy Spirit to retrace Adam's steps, to defeat the dark powers, and to restore the God-Man relationship through His sacrifice. He perfectly obeyed God's moral law throughout His life, resisting the temptation to sin unlike Adam who gave in and disobeyed God's Way. With His words and deeds Jesus taught humanity how to obey the will of God while defeating evil in the process. Through Jesus' incarnation, humanity receives a new head, a new source and origin that is unfallen, pure, healthy, victorious and immortal. In his incarnation the very human Jesus assumed a solidarity through His existential life that gives all humans hope for redemption. The incarnation itself and Jesus' entire *life* is redemptive.

St. Irenaeus gave us this perspective of the atonement through his recapitulation theory. In this understanding of God's act of rescue, Jesus Christ provides redemption by going through the entire scope of human life and at each juncture reverses the effects of rebellion and disobedience of Adam. Whereas the first Adam disobeyed God and rebelled, thus introducing evil, corruption and death, Jesus as the Second Adam perfectly obeyed God and lifted humanity up to a higher state than even Adam experienced before he rebelled. [90] Irenaeus took many of his cues from Paul in Romans 5. In this chapter of his masterful treatise on the gospel of Jesus, Paul explains how sin and death entered into the world through one person, Adam. Consequently, through Adam's initial rebellion, humans are born polluted by sin, receive a distorted nature, and continue to rebel against God and His Way, resulting in death. That pollution influences the free choices of all humans to choose relationship with God and follow in His Way. We are guilty of sin when we choose to disobey God and vandalize shalom.

Paul continues by saying:

> Just as the result of one trespass was condemnation for all men, so also the result of one act of righteousness was justification that bring life for all men. For just as through the disobedience of one man the many were made sinners, so also through the obedience of one man the many will be made righteous. [91]

For Irenaeus, the real center of Jesus' redemptive life came in the wilderness when Jesus was tempted by Satan before He began His ministry. When Satan came to Eve and Adam in the lush Garden, they rebelled. Jesus, when confronted in the wasteland of the wilderness, triumphed through obedience. Jesus conquered Satan, not only for Himself but also for all of humanity. As we saw in Chapter 3, the very human Jesus learned obedience on His march toward resurrection by going to the cross and experiencing all it had to offer.

I like what Irenaeus gives us through this explanation. This perspective broadens Jesus' act of rescue from simply a "me-and-Jesus-thing" to a holistic humanity thing. What happened in the garden through Adam affected all of humanity; what Jesus did throughout His entire life (including the event of the cross) affected all of humanity. On His march toward resurrection as our rescuer, Jesus was first our utter and loyal ally who learned obedience throughout His entire life for the sake of all rebels. Humanity was dead in rebellion because Adam chose to consciously disobey God, and we affirm that initial act of rebellion with every mini-act of denial. Through every sin we scream "Yes!" to Adam's disobedient, rebellious act against God and His Way. Thankfully through the life and obedience of Jesus Christ, we can enter into a new humanity, a rescued humanity that is moving toward a final act of re-creation. Through Jesus' incarnation, Jesus lived as the fullest expression of a human that God intended and that Adam rebelled against. Jesus thus reversed sin, corruption, and evil, while ultimately providing re-creation as a restored Eikon of God.

This version of atonement, though, is only a glimpse of the entire act of rescue. Though Jesus was obedient throughout His life, thus retracing the first Adam's and humanity's steps of rebellion, the ultimate act of obedience came during the event of the cross. On the cross, all the depression, anxiety, and shock that engulfed Jesus in the garden in anticipation of what would unfold finds its prophetic fulfillment. While human defiance, rebellion, and disobedience needed to be confronted with humble obedience, the objective realities of evil, sin, and death also needed to be dealt with. These realities were defeated through Jesus' death on the cross, an event in which the full wrath and punishment brimming for humanity 's rebellion was drunk dry by our substitute Jesus.

Though Jesus' death on the cross has usually been the main focal point of God's redemptive act, being emphasized too much at the expense of the other facets of God's act of rescue, it is incredibly important, nevertheless. On the cross Jesus bore the punishment and guilt for all human rebellion, making peace between God and humans, leading to the adoption of people by God the Father as Sons and Daughters.

While Irenaeus' explanation of God's act of rescue emphasized the fusion of Jesus' divinity and humanity in the incarnation to reverse the evil, sin, and death introduced by Adam, the Protestant reformers and theologians rejected or neglected it in favor of a more legal and individualistic view of salvation, that is, personal reconciliation with God.[92] Consequently, a shift occurred from a communal, holistic understand to a more individualistic explanation of the extent to which God went to rescue humanity. This understanding of God's act of rescue is called penal substitutionary atonement and emphasizes the penalty Jesus paid during the event of the cross as our personal substitute.

While a hyper-emphasis on God's individual acts of rescue through Jesus' substitutional death is not warranted, we still need this facet to understand what happened at the event of the cross. In recent years some have labeled the penal substitution understanding of the cross event as "divine child abuse." [93] I find this characterization at best childish and uncharitable and at worse a failure to give due diligence to the biblical and theological realities of evil, sin, and death with which a holy God had to deal.

Penal substitution anchors reconciliation between humans and God in the sin-bearing work of Christ during the event of the cross during which the wrath of God was appeased. Those who hold to this version of God's act of rescue appeal to three theological themes: 1) the sinfulness and guilt of humanity; 2) the holiness of God; 3) the sacrifice of Christ. [94] First, this version emphasizes humans are utterly broken and in need of restoration and rescue; "all have sinned and fallen short of God's glory" and are unable to rescue themselves. Second, because the nature of sin is grasped in view of God's holiness, our rebellion is a deliberate assault against God and His character. Those who sin face judgment by this holy God for their unholy choices and unholy rhythm of life. Finally, penal substitutionary atonement reveals the need for a sacrifice to deal with our sin. It points toward the Jewish sacrificial system as evidence of God's requirement for a sacrifice so that rebellious humans could be forgiven by holy Yahweh. [95]

Romans 3:23-26 demonstrates much of the theological and biblical thrust for this version of atonement:

> All have sinned and fall short of the glory of God, and are justified freely by His grace through the redemption that came by Christ Jesus. God presented him as a sacrifice of atonement, through faith in His blood. He did this to demonstrate His justice, because in his forbearance He had left the sins committed beforehand unpunished— He did it to demonstrate His justice at the present time, so as to be just and the one who justifies those who have faith in Jesus.

Paul in Galatians 3:13 declares, "Christ redeemed us from the curse of the law by becoming a curse for us, for it is written: 'Cursed is everyone who is hung on a tree.'" As one author puts it, "The curse we deserve was borne by Christ. He became our substitute. The sinless One took upon Himself the curse of God that weighed us down. He freed us from God's curse 'by becoming a curse for us.' Christ took upon Himself the curse that we deserved. He paid our penalty. He saved us from the consequences of our sin." [96] I wholeheartedly agree! The event of the cross required Jesus to be a sacrificial substitute to pay the ultimate penalty for our willful rebellion. During this event, Jesus experienced the consequence of rebellion (death), while defeating evil, sin, and death by drinking dry the cup of God's wrath.

Some, however, object to this characterization of the event of the cross, because it makes God out to be a Person who must satisfy some sort of blood lust. Some wonder, "If God wants to forgive us, why doesn't He just do it? Why does He need to punish someone to the point of mutilation to make things better?" These types of objections fail to consider the real, objective problems of evil, sin, and death. All three realities were ushered into our time and space after the first Adam rebelled. After humans committed treason against the Reign and Way of God, reality ruptured.

Something terrible happened.

Because something happened to creation and because something resulted from that rupture, God needed to deal with those objective "somethings." Those "somethings" were evil, sin, and death. Before rebellion, evil, sin, and human death did not exist, they were not objective "somethings" that were part of our objective reality. Our lives as humans before rebellion did not in anyway consist of evil, sin and human death. That all changed, however, after Mama Eve and Papa Adam rebelled. After they chose the Way of Self over against the Way of God by committing relational rejection against God, something objectively happened. The "somethings" of evil and sin and human death that were not in existence before rebellion were now part of the fabric of reality.

If the objective realities of these three "somethings" did not exist before rebellion, and if God desired to restore creation to the way He intended it to be before rebellion, then doesn't it make sense that God would have to deal with those real "somethings?" If evil, sin, and human death resulted from rebellion and were not intended at creation, then there is no possible way God could ignore them. He could not give humans a "do over" or a mulligan for slicing a drive. In order for Him to stay true to His nature, God absolutely could not give humans a pass and not deal with the objective "somethings" of evil, sin, and death. If He intended to rescue and re-create through Jesus Christ, God needed to do something with all three "somethings."

Ironically, the very chapter in Romans that Irenaeus used to map out his view of atonement points toward the need for a substitute on behalf of humanity. Note these words of Paul in Romans 5:

> Just the right time, when we were still powerless, Christ died for the ungodly. Very rarely will anyone die for a righteous man, though for a good man someone might possibly dare to die. But God demonstrates his own love for us in this: While we were still sinners, Christ died for us.
>
> Since we have now been justified by his blood, how much more shall we be saved from God's wrath through him! For if, when we were God's enemies, we were reconciled to him through the death of his Son, how much more, having been reconciled, shall we be saved through his life! Not only is this so, but we also rejoice in God through our Lord Jesus Christ, through whom we have now received reconciliation. [97]

"Just at the right time, Christ died for the ungodly." Here there is a clear emphasis on the death of Jesus for humanity. As Paul explains, it is because Jesus' body was split open on the boards of execution and His blood drenched the soil beneath it that we will be saved from God's judgement. Because Jesus physically died and spiritually endured the full judgement and wrath of God that was stored up for humanity's rebellion, we have peace and reconciliation with God.

That is good, sweet news, indeed!

Through the event of the cross, Jesus took upon His entire being the wrath of a holy God for which we fully deserved. Because of our culpable vandalism of shalom, our rebellion and acts of un-love which deny the teachings and Way of Jesus and the very divine-human Being at the center of both, Jesus needed to die.

Through the event of the cross, the penalty for our rebellion (death) was accepted by the very divine and very human Jesus who was in solidarity with every ounce of our humanity in life. Jesus licked, bone dry, every ounce of wrath from the cup of death itself.

This perspective of the event of the cross and God's act of rescue is needed. We need this story of atonement to account for God's judgement, our forgiveness, and the three "somethings."

People who wholesale reject the penal substitution theory of God's act of rescue, however, usually believe the event of the cross either simply signified the subversion of Imperial powers or provided a moral example of love. On the one hand, Jesus is a revolutionary who confronted the earthly powers of Rome and Jerusalem by becoming weak and subverting their system of domination and violence. In the words of Shane Claiborne, a Christian social activist: "The cross is the culmination of all that the empire had to offer, where all the wrath of the world was poured out on God. And it is on the cross that we can see the ultimate power standoff. On the cross we can see what love looks like when it stares evil in the face." [98] While I generally appreciate Shane's Imperial perspective, the cross is not the culmination of all that *empire* had to offer, it isn't the focal point at which the wrath of *the world* was unleashed, and it is not simply a portrait of love.

The event of the cross is the culmination of the punishment for which we humans, as individuals and as a collective whole, were and are responsible because of our rebellion *against God*. It isn't that the Roman powers unleashed the full weight of Empire on this local upstart prophet as punishment for His rabble-rousery. Rather, we humans unleashed the full wrath of God upon the loving, gentle, caring Jesus because of our countless individual acts of un-love. Rome didn't kill Jesus. He willingly went to the cross to experience what we should have endured. Rome isn't responsible. We are. Rome didn't unleash *their* wrath upon Jesus at the cross. God unleashed *His* wrath and poured out *His* judgment upon the loving, gentle, caring Jesus as punishment for your rebellion and mine. At the cross, evil and sin and death are defeated, which ultimately is what provides the hope for resurrection and re-creation.

On the other hand, some suggest the Jesus Story and event of the cross is more about His powerful example and model of love than about God objectively dealing with the three "somethings" of evil, rebellion, and death. A recent postmodern Christian author essentially said this in his explanation of the Story of Jesus. In his book, *A Christianity Worth Believing*, Doug Pagitt dismisses the penal substitutionary aspect of atonement by claiming that, "The early evangelists recognized that they could help the Jesus story make sense if Jesus was seen as someone who was chosen to appease the wrath of God...the Gentiles thought of Jesus as saving them from the punishment that was due them. Jesus became the substitute, the stand-in. He was the special, divine, innocent one chosen by God to pay the price for sins of humanity. That's what the up-and-out, distant, vengeful God demanded." [99]

According to Doug, this isn't the God we see in the Holy Scriptures, but is instead a Greek impostor. Instead, the Jewish God of the Bible is like "a loving father figure, the down-and-in God who provided for the people and called them to join in with God's work in the world." Jesus wasn't a substitute on the cross that did something with evil, sin, and death for all humans, but was instead "their map, their guide to what true partnership with God looked like." [100] To what was Jesus the map, guide, and moral example? Love and peace.

> Jesus was not sent as the selected one to appease the anger of the Greek blood god. Jesus was sent to fulfill the promise of the Hebrew love God by ending human hostility. It was not the anger of God that Jesus came to end but the anger of people. The world God created is one of peace and harmony and integration. Through Jesus, all humanity is brought into that world. And that is the point of the resurrection.

When Jesus was resurrected from the dead, life won out. The power of God's love for humanity proved stronger than our capacity to hate one another. Jesus' death was about war, about violence, about destruction. But His resurrection was about peace, compassion, renewal.

Jesus is the core of Christianity because it is through Jesus we see the fullness of God's hopes for the world. [Jesus] shows us what it means to live in partnership with our creator. He leads us into what it means to be integrated with God. Jesus was resurrected with scars. The scars weren't simply a reminder of the past; they were the pathway to the future. They were there to show that the cause of death had been consumed. The hatred of death had been healed over by the love of God. The scars gave testimony to the power of death. Death gave Jesus its best shot; it laid it all on the line and accomplished its goal. But life overcame death. Love overcame hate. Peace over came war. The resurrection life needs death to remind us that the call to love our enemy not only means loving in the midst of scars but loving those who cause them. Because in Jesus, love wins.[101]

While I certainly affirm some aspects of Doug's understanding of God's act of rescue, like the defeat of death through resurrection and our ability to reconnect to God through Jesus, it isn't clear *how* the cause of death has been consumed and hatred of death has been healed over by the love of God. How exactly did that happen if the mechanism that ushered in death (sin and rebellion) was not atoned for, if the consequences that resulted from the "cause of death" (sin and rebellion) were not objectively dealt with in some way?

Unless something happened on the cross, we still have the three "somethings."

I am not at all persuaded that the cross was simply about ending *our* hate, war, violence, and destruction nor am I convinced Jesus is the center of Christian spirituality because he *shows* us through the example of His life and death how to partner and be integrated with God. It isn't that love and peace won out over hate and war, but that Jesus took upon Himself the punishment we deserved for our rebelliously hateful and waring actions, actions of un-love *primarily* directed toward God and His Rhythm of Life. Jesus isn't the center of Christianity because he shows us how to be integrated and partner with God, but rather because he drank dry the cup of wrath that was stored up for all humanity. Because of the three "somethings" of evil, sin, rebellion, and death, Jesus died upon that old rugged cross, not simply to show us how to end human hostility and hatred, but to take upon Himself the punishment we deserved for our hostile, hateful acts. Unless something happened to the objective realities of evil, rebellion, and death, humans are still screwed! Unless something was done with evil, sin, and death on the cross, ending human hostility and hatred is not possible. Thankfully, through the resurrection Jesus triumphed over all three, including the evil powers. Jesus endured the punishment we all deserved because of our willful vandalism of shalom and deliberate rebellion against God and His Rhythm of Life, providing rescue and defeating the dark powers of the world.

Finally, through resurrection Jesus triumphed over the dark powers, making a mockery of them, and revealed that the Father accepted His sacrifice on behalf of humans. We are raised to new life through His defeat of death, and declared and made righteous before God. This final perspective is commonly known as the *Christus Victor* theory of the atonement and centers on the truth that through the incarnation, life, death and, ultimately, resurrection of Christ, God defeated the powers of evil, providing freedom from rebellion and its consequence.

This dimension of God's work on the cross was brilliantly presented by C.S. Lewis in *The Lion, The Witch, and The Wardrobe.* In two scenes, Lewis masterfully illustrates the offering of Christ to the powers to appease the "dark magic," while ultimately defeating those powers through resurrection. The first scene shows Aslan (the Christ figure) willingly walking up the stairs to the ancient sacrificial altar to offer himself to the White Witch to atone for the lawbreaking Edmund and to appease the dark magic. The scene is quite traumatic: the beautiful mane of the Great Lion is humiliatingly sheared; he is bound and placed before the crowd, who act like Big Game Hunters gloating over a sacked lion in Africa; and finally Aslan is bludgeoned to death by the Witch and left to rot. The Powerful Lion was offered to the dark powers of the seen and unseen world to provide rescue for one small child. The same is true for us.

In the second scene we are left at the stone altar with grieving Susan and Lucy. As they retreat, the ground begins to shake and rumble. The altar cracks and Aslan momentarily disappears. Shortly thereafter, he reappears in fully restored glory as the resurrected Aslan back from the dead. After Susan and Lucy inquire about what happened, insisting that they saw the spike go through Aslan with their own eyes, the Great Lion reveals: "If the Witch new the true meaning of the sacrifice, she might have interpreted the deep magic differently. That when a willing victim who has committed no treachery is killed in a traitor's stead, the stone tablet will crack and even Death itself would turn backwards."

This is exactly what happened on the cross and through the grave: the loving, gentle, caring Jesus, who committed no acts of rebellion, willingly became a victim, while being slaughtered in the place of the collective rebels stead. Because the loving, gentle, caring Jesus was willingly slaughtered, even death itself was turned backwards through resurrection, providing the same incredible possibility for all of humanity. Through resurrection the consequence of rebellion (death) was sapped of its stinging power and the evil that reigned on earth was subverted and triumphed over. In fact, Christ disarmed these evil powers and authorities, making a public spectacle of them, triumphing over them by the cross through resurrection. And through both the altar and empty altar, our rebellion has been forgiven. We are indeed rescued and will be re-created through the same resurrection that brought Christ back from the grave.

Both artistic scenes from C.S. Lewis illustrate the extent to which Christ went to provide victory over the binding powers of evil, sin, and death for the entire world, for all humans. Paul speaks of this binding power throughout many of His letters: Romans 6 explains how all humans are slaves to the power of sin, which leads to death, while being able to set free from that power only through Christ's resurrection from the dead.[102] Likewise, Paul speaks of an evil power which compels us to do the things that we do not want to do and not do the things we know we should do.[103] Furthermore, our struggle, just like Christ's, is not against flesh and blood, but against the authorities and rulers and powers of this dark world and against the evil spiritual forces in the heavenly realm. [104] Other passages in the Holy Scriptures explain an entire reality that exists beyond our own to which humans were held captive, a reality that was confronted and defeated by Jesus Christ to provide freedom from evil, sin, and death for all people through His final sacrifice.

The Final Sacrifice

Before I began seminary in Fall 2007, I began working through the Book of Leviticus. As my fingers walked through this deeply cultic book (a book which reminds the reader of the ancient Jewish sacrificial system) I was struck by the idea of the sacrificial offering and the intricate and particular demands God placed in the sacrificial system. I became very intrigued by the idea of the physical sacrifice that God once demanded from us for our sins. I saw for the first time that it was the sacrificer who slaughtered the lamb/goat/bull for their own sins; the rebel presented a slaughtered sacrificial offering to the priest to sacrifice before the Lord. Through this self-involved slaughtering act, individuals had a physical representation and reminder of the consequences of their rebellion and offense to holy Yahweh.

Until this point in history, humanity did not know what it took to please God; creation had no direct knowledge of how to appease Creator. This is precisely why the sacrificial systems of various cultures escalated from simple gifts to horrific human sacrifice. Until God revealed to humans through the Holy Scriptures and the community of the Children of Israel His desires for appeasement, we were without knowledge of the means by which to atone for our rebellious actions toward the one true, holy God. So through the Levitical Text and Community of Israel, God communicated to the world the way in which we could be reconciled to Himself, in spite of our deliberate uprising against Him and His Way.

In some ways, the Church re-participates in the sacrifice of Jesus each time She gathers and celebrates the Holy Sacrament of Communion. After attending an Anglican church for a year and a half and regularly experiencing Holy Communion in that tradition, I came to appreciate the sacredness of this very communal experience. I grew up in a non-denominational church that "celebrated" communion four times a year, an experience that was incredibly individualistic, private, and detached from the original intent of Jesus providing this sacrament in the first place. Through this regular participation in the remembering act of Communion I gained a greater depth and appreciation for the once-for-all sacrifice of Jesus that the Book of Hebrews brilliantly addresses.

The Book of Hebrews is the one place in the New Testament that magically links the past with the present reality of Christ post-cross and post-resurrection. The Jewish Story, as told through the Hebrew Scriptures, is an unfinished Story that is always pointing forward toward a "something" beyond itself. Hebrews explains to the Jews of First Century Palestine why Jesus is the absolute climax and fulfillment of their Story of anticipation. This climax is manifest primarily in the sacrificial event of the cross, the final sacrifice for human rebellion that brought our rescue and current/future re-creation.

Note these words as the author explains the significance of the Great High Priest, Jesus, who offered Himself as the once-for-all sacrifice for rebellion:

> The law is only a shadow of the good things that are coming—not the realities themselves. For this reason it can never, by the same sacrifices repeated endlessly year after year, make perfect those who draw near to worship. If it could, would they not have stopped being offered? For the worshipers would have been cleansed once for all, and would no longer have felt guilty for their sins. But those sacrifices are an annual reminder of sins, because it is impossible for the blood of bulls and goats to take away sins.
>
> Therefore, when Christ came into the world, he said:
> "Sacrifice and offering you did not desire,

187

but a body you prepared for me;
>with burnt offerings and sin offerings
>you were not pleased.
Then I said, 'here I am—it is written about me
>>in the scroll—
>I have come to do your will, O God.'"

First he said, "Sacrifices and offerings, burnt offerings and sin offerings you did not desire, nor were you pleased with them" (although the law required them to be made). Then he said, "Here I am, I have come to do your will." He sets aside the first to establish the second. And by that will, we have been made holy through the sacrifice of the body of Jesus Christ once for all.

Day after day every priest stands and performs his religious duties; again and again he offers the same sacrifices, which can never take away sins. But when this priest had offered for all time one sacrifice for sins, he sat down at the right hand of God. Since that time he waits for his enemies to be made his footstool, because by one sacrifice he has made perfect forever those who are being made holy.

The Holy Spirit also testifies to us about this. First he says:
>"This is the covenant I will make with them
>>after that time, says the Lord.
>I will put my laws in their hearts,
>>and I will write them on their minds."

Then he adds:
>"Their sins and lawless acts
>I will remember no more."

And where these have been forgiven, there is no longer any sacrifice for sin.

First, we notice the incompleteness of the previous sacrificial system; the sacrifice of lambs, bulls, and goats was only a temporary fix for the ultimate sacrifice that God would take upon Himself: the offering of His very Self to atone for our rebellion. The author reveals that had Temple sacrifice been enough, had our own participation in the sacrificial system been enough and worked to bring a once-for-all "cleansing," the annual sacrifice would not have been needed. Since the blood of bulls and goats does not *take away sins*, it only provides for their forgiveness, another more permanent solution was needed. That permanency was provided in the invasion of the God-with-us-God in the person of Jesus Christ.

As we saw in Ray Minema's masterful piece, the loving, gentle, caring Jesus obeyed the Father by going to the cross. He said: "Here I am, I have come to do your will, O God." [105] As the Book of Hebrews reveals, the way in which God was appeased before, through the human effort of and participation in animal sacrifice, was completely set aside and actually replaced by the sacrifice of the body of Jesus. The previous human requirements of appeasement through offering have been vanquished through the butchered body of the Son of God

once and for all!

The remedy for which all people have been searching is available through the once-and-for-all sacrifice of God Himself through Jesus Christ. This finality is beautifully illustrated through the continued standing of the High Priest in constant offering versus the seated Jesus at the right hand of God. Hebrews says that day after day the High Priest continues to stand and perform his duties by offering and re-offering sacrifices to atone for rebellion and appease God's demands; acts which can never take away the results of rebellion: sin and death. But when *this* High Priest, Jesus Christ, offered for all time *one* sacrifice for our rebellion to provide eternal rescue and ultimate re-creation

He sat down!

Why? Because He declared on the very blood-soaked boards of execution that held His lifeless body that

it was finished!

It's over with.

No more sacrifice is needed.

We are no longer culpable for the vandalism of shalom.

We are no longer guilty for rebellion because of Jesus Christ.

Because God sacrificed Himself, we are no longer guilty!

Because of Jesus we have forgiveness.

Because of Jesus' sacrifice, God has made perfect those who are in the process of being made holy, who are being fully re-created.

Because of the event of the cross our sins and rebellious acts are no longer remembered by the very Creator whom we have rebelled against.

And because of the loving, gentle, caring Jesus no more sacrifice is needed!

Drink deep this reality: there is no more sacrifice needed. We do not need to strive to earn God's favor. We do not need to perform to make God love us more than He already *did* through the event of the cross. We do not need to work for salvation to appease God.

Jesus provided the final sacrifice, a sweet smelling offering to God that was pleasing in His sight; the sacrifice was fully paid for the price of our rebellion.

And how do we know this?

One word: resurrection.

Through the physical resurrection of Jesus we know that the sacrifice did something. It worked. It was pleasing to God and absolutely positively defeated evil and sin and rebellion and death. As Paul declares in 1 Corinthians: "Death has been swallowed up in victory. Where, O Death, is your victory? Where, O Death is your sting?"[106]

I love that line: death itself has been swallowed up in the victory of Jesus Christ over the grave. There is now no more sting of death for those who are in Christ Jesus. Because Jesus Christ offered the final sacrifice for all humans, we also have the opportunity to participate in the first re-creative act of God, which is the resurrection of Jesus Christ from the dead. Because of the brutal event of the cross, we have the same hope that we ourselves will be ultimately re-created through the rescue provided by Jesus Christ through an ultimate resurrection.

This is a good, hopeful, (un)offensive gospel, indeed!

Chapter 9
our re-creation

Then I saw a new heaven and a new earth, for the first heaven and the first earth had passed away, and there was no longer any sea. I saw the Holy City, the new Jerusalem, coming down out of heaven from God, prepared as a bride beautifully dressed for her husband. And I heard a loud voice from the throne saying, "Now the dwelling of God is with men, and he will live with them. They will be his people, and God himself will be with them and be their God. He will wipe every tear from their eyes. There will be no more death or mourning or crying or pain, for the old order of things has passed away."

He who was seated on the throne said, "I am making everything new!" Then he said, "Write this down, for these words are trustworthy and true." [107]

"I am making everything new!" What hopeful words from the Book of Revelation. As the statement reveals, God is in the recycling business, He is not a demolition man!

God truly is a re-creator.

The resurrection makes this incredibly clear: the Victorious Obedient Substitute Jesus Christ defeated the consequence of rebellion (death) and was re-created to new life through resurrection. The new life that burst forth from the grave that first Easter Sunday has been fueling re-creation ever since, in both the lives of individual humans and in our collective human societies. The Kingdom of Heaven—this movement to re-create the world that hinged on the defeat of evil, rebellion, and death through the cross—began with the Son of God and continues through His followers, the Church. While we are sent on mission by the Father in the same way Jesus was sent to bring rescue and re-creation, God will Himself finally usher in a new and final epoch of *shalom* for all the earth. What the resurrection and this text from the Book of Revelation make undeniably clear is that God is not through with our world. We aren't just a passin' through! While the Reign of God through Christ has been and is invading the earth through Jesus and His followers, it will also come in a final climactic act when heaven comes to earth.

Will all humans participate in this final re-creative act? Will all humans enjoy a seat at the Wedding Banquet Table of the Risen Lamb of God? What about "That Other Place" so many people discuss? What about hell? If God's posture toward all humans is love, which of course I emphasized in Chapter 3, then will not all people eventually be rescued and re-created through Jesus? If God really loves all humans, how can anyone be sent away to an everlasting torment, where there is screaming, darkness, and gnashing of teeth?

These are the final aspects in God's Story of Rescue. This final act, called re-creation, unpacks the moment for which all creation has been longing and groaning: the moment when Creator re-creates creation by restoring everything to the way He intended it to be at the beginning. While there is much to celebrate in this final act, there are also some things to mourn. A discussion about "final things" cannot avoid a discussion about universalism, judgment, and hell. As we end this Story, let's celebrate the moment at which our Creator will finally re-create creation, while also honestly dealing with the ultimate consequence of willful human rebellion.

This act begins with those who are self-proclaimed followers of Jesus: the Church. While Jesus is our Rescuer and started the re-creation for which all of Creation is groaning, the Church is the vessel through which God is now accomplishing His re-creation on earth in the lives of individuals and the world. While creation is all about God the Creator, rebellion is all about humans, rescue is all about the divine-human Jesus, re-creation is partly about humans again (at least those who have committed themselves to Jesus as devoted followers), while ultimately about God as the Lord of Creation.

On to act four!

Harbingers of Shalom

This phrase, *harbingers of shalom*, was a term conjured up by my good friend Andy to describe our roles as agents of God's Kingdom Reign. Brilliant phrase from a brilliant man. A harbinger is a sign of things to come. Usually in history or literature it signals really bad things to come. I love this term. It just drips with irony! Rather than being a signpost of bad, nasty, horrible things to come, the Body of Christ is a sign of the wholeness and peace and resurrection and re-creation that will ultimately arrive. We Christians are the continuing presence of Jesus Christ in the world and are marked by the wholeness and future re-creation made possible through Jesus.

Since the Body of Christ is the continuing presence of Jesus in the world, we need to recapture the identity and mission of the Church as a show-er and teller of Jesus and His hopeful message. We are Harbingers of Shalom. We need to understand that the mission of the Church is to be a community in which people are discipled in the Way of Jesus. A community that embodies and bears witness to the Reign of God. Because the Church is the presence of Jesus in the world, I hope this understanding of mission will help us faithfully live as the organism through which God is accomplishing His Rescue mission for the world and its progressive re-creation.

The Church is not a mere collection of individuals, a cultural construct, a human institution or a political interest group. The Messianic Community of Jesus does not have its origin in human, social institutions, but rather claims Her origin, and thus Her mission, from God. The first mention of the *ekklesia* (Church) is in Matthew 16, where Jesus said, "*I* will build *my* gathering of called-out ones (Church), and the Gates of Hades will not over come it." [108] Throughout His ministry Jesus set out to raise up and shape a group of people to send them on mission when He ascended to the right hand of the Father, thus extending His presence and work in the world. From the very beginning of Jesus' ministry, creating a Messianic Community was Jesus' goal. Building the Church was not an afterthought or even simply a result of His movement. Gathering a called-out group of people was intentional because we would perpetuate His mission.

As the Father sent Jesus, so Jesus has sent us, the Church. [109] Jesus' mission becomes our mission, because God uses humans to accomplish His re-creative work. While we will often fail and disappoint Him, our role is crucial to the achievement of God's mission, for it is through this flawed and vulnerable group of people that God's Kingdom will be established. He entrusts the proclamation of His Kingdom-movement to a particular group of people whom He has chosen for the sake of rescuing and re-creating the whole world. What is this community to proclaim? They are to proclaim the Reign of God; that God whom Jesus knows as Father is the sovereign ruler over all people and things. This reality is no longer something remote, but now confronts all men and women with a decision. We truly live in a re-creative reality even now.

Just as God set apart a group of people (Israel) to be a blessing to the world around them by testifying to the one true God, so also He chose the Church to testify to the salvation and re-creation found in the Reign of God through Christ. By way of choosing, calling and sending a particular people to be the bearer of blessing for all, God is uniting the whole cosmos through His plan of *shalom* re-creation. How do we explain the moral and ethical truths of this Reign? First, the Church must embed Herself within particular cultures by incarnationally living, eating, and working closely with Her surrounding communities to build strong links between Christians and not-yet-Christians. Second, the mission of the Church in preaching the good news of Jesus must never be separated from demonstrations of God's justice. Doing justice and mercy in concrete situations has always been at the heart of God's deliberate movement and mission in history, and the Church must make them as equal a priority. Third, the Church represents the values, authority, and Way of the Reign of God; She is a preview of what is to come, and points people toward this better way of being human. Ultimately, the Church stands as witness to the powerful, restorative work displayed on the cross through the once-for-all sacrifice of Jesus and final defeat of death for all. This is the worlds true hope. This is the (un)offensive gospel and beautiful Story of Rescue the Church is to tell the world.

I have a confession to make, though: I hate evangelism. Well, not evangelism, per se, but rather the word. I don't like how it is used to define the mission of the church. The word evangelism stems from the Greek *euangelion* for "good news." It is used in the New Testament as a noun, not a verb. The problem is an entire theology of mission has been built on this single word, a word never used for the commission of the Church. When the word was originally used by Jesus to announce the Kingdom of God, He described that invasion of God's Kingdom-movement in the world as good news. He called people to turn from their own Rhythm of Life and believe in this Rhythm by following Him into it. After His resurrection He commissioned His disciples as harbingers of this new Kingdom-movement to share the good news of the Kingdom. Where you would expect Jesus to use the word "preach/proclaim" or "bear witness" in His commission in Matthew 28:19-20, a slower, lower profile verb is used. It's an almost scholastic, schoolish word: "disciple." This verb literally means, "to cause one to be a pupil or apprentice," which is the primary, controlling word for the Church's mission. [110]

Key to the mission of the Church is not "evangelism" but discipleship. We are not to evangelize and colonize the world, but to influence our neighbors, coworkers, and relatives in such a way that they pattern their life and lifestyle after Another. Our goal as the presence of Jesus in the world is to influence people to follow Him as Messiah, Redeemer, and Restorer. Of course, in this process we will proclaim, explain, and bear witness to the amazing, (un)offensive news that is found in Jesus and His teachings. The mission of the *ekklesia*, though, is to step into people's lives and show them a better way of living and being human through Jesus. We are not simply to talk at them about their sin, Jesus' death and resurrection, and possible heavenly bliss (or other place) after they die.

The differences between these two notions of mission are incredibly stark: While evangelism is monological, discipleship is dialogical; evangelism seeks to win people, discipleship seeks to shape people; when we evangelize, we posture ourselves as a sage on the stage, in discipleship our posture is a guide on the side; evangelism is an ephemeral (once-for-all) event, discipleship is an ongoing, progressive effort. I liken evangelism to *Colonialism* and discipleship to *Sustainable Development*. Let me explain.

"Colonialism is the extension of a nation's sovereignty over territory beyond its borders by the establishment of either settler colonies or administrative dependencies in which indigenous populations are directly ruled or displaced. Colonizing nations generally dominate the resources, labor, and markets of the colonial territory, and may also impose socio-cultural, religious and linguistic structures on the conquered population." [111] Have not Christian storytelling, evangelistic tactics often been similar to nineteenth and twentieth century colonial efforts, crossing borders into enemy territory to settle and claim people for our Kingdom? When we Christians enter into a conversation with another, don't we usually dominate all emotional, intellectual, and verbal capital to make that individual our own? Just as colonialism was often based on the ethnocentric belief that the morals and values of the colonizer were superior to those of the colonized, don't we insist that we Jesus followers hold the trump card to all things spiritual? Don't we Christians insist that our morals and spirituality are more superior to our friend or coworker, all the while believing they have nothing to add to the conversation, about their own spirituality?

Rather than colonizing, the Church is called into *Sustainable Development*: We are called to step into the cultures, languages, and customs and lives of real people to show and tell them a better way of being human by showing them Jesus and telling them of God's Kingdom Reign. In other words, we are called to *disciple*. Those in sustainable economic development indefinitely enter the lives of people groups to show them a better, more sound way of growing food, filtering water, or organizing an economy. Similarly, we are called to step into the lives of people indefinitely to show them a better way of being human in Jesus and explain the significance of His death, burial, resurrection, and ascension. Just as sustainable development is about the individuals being helped (rather than the group thats doing the developing), so too are efforts at discipling non-followers about them and their lives. Discipleship is not about us and our church or group. In the same way sustainable development equips people to better grow food or better manage a local economy, discipling non-followers must be about equipping them to follow Jesus and obey His teachings, not simply about a promise to get them to heaven.

As Darrell Guder explains in his book, *The Missional Church*, "The absence of the gospel Jesus preached in the gospel the church has preached has woefully impoverished the church's sense of mission and identity." [112] In other words, how the Church defines and tells the gospel is often very different from how Jesus defined and told the gospel. This results in a misunderstanding of mission and identity. Whether it is the *Four Spiritual Laws*, *Romans Road*, or *Evangelism Explosion*, evangelistic tools used to communicate Jesus' hopeful, (un)offensive message typically invite people to accept Jesus to receive forgiveness of sins to go to heaven. While experiencing both forgiveness (and might I add liberation) from sin and everlasting existence with God are dimensions of the good news found in Jesus, reducing the gospel to those terms alone is woefully inadequate and foreign to Jesus' own definition. For Jesus, the immanent Reign of God was the good news that needed to be proclaimed in Jerusalem, Judea and Samaria, and to the uttermost parts of the world. A Reign that most certainly takes root as the Church lives out God's mission to restore all creation through the death and resurrection of Jesus. While the Church must not be equated with the Reign of God, She is in service to it. The Body of Christ is the result of the breaking forth of an alternative Rhythm of Life and is in humble service to that Reign. She serves the Kingdom by bearing witness to it as Jesus' Harbingers of Shalom embedded within the world in anticipation of God's ultimate re-creative act of earthly renewal as heaven descends to earth.

Heaven Is a Place on Earth

Sing it baby!

At times I think Christianity needs a good dose of Belinda Carlisle. Heaven really is a place on earth. The point of re-creation is not escapism from earth to a distant land in outer space. God did not invade the earth by becoming a human in the person of Jesus Christ to get humans saved to go to heaven when they die. No, no, no. God never intended heaven to be separate from earth nor did He intend to sweep us earthlings out of His *good* creation. From the beginning, the Creator intended to permanently dwell with creation and He has been in the process of making that happen since the dawn of creation. American pastor, Maltbie Babcock, reminds us of God's heaven-earth co-mingling desires in his wonderful hymn, *This Is My Fathers World:*

> This is my Father's world. O let me ne'er forget
> That though the wrong seems oft so strong, God is the ruler yet.
> This is my Father's world: the battle is not done:
> Jesus Who died shall be satisfied,
> And Earth and Heav'n be one.

We really need to remember that this world is still *good* and is still God's, He will eventually re-create what is now not supposed to be, permanently dwelling with His Eikons on the New Earth. Like Babcock, we all long for the moment when earth and heaven will be one. All of creation groans in eager expectation for the day when things are re-created and restored to the way God intended them to be. I think the band *Sleeping at Last* describes this expectation well. Read the words of "Heaven Breaks," from their album *Keep No* Score for a glimpse of the beauty of this expectant moment:

> It always starts like this,
> A harmless and simple thing to fix.
> Contagious and spreading quick...
> Like cracks in ice,
> Wholly claiming our lives
> While we sleep.
>
> We'll pray for Heaven's floor to break,
> Pour the brightest white on blackest space,
> Come bleeding gloriously through
> The clouds and the blue.
> Forcing one place from two,
> Killing formulaic views,
> Only love proves to be the truth.
>
> When heaven meets the earth,
> We will have no use for numbers
> To measure who we are and what we're worth.
>
> When Heaven meets the earth,
> We will have no need for mirrors
> To tell us who to be
> And where we fit into this awkward point of view.
>
> When angels meet the earth, may our bodies be light.
> When angels meet the earth, may our heavy hearts untie.
> When angels meet the earth, may our bodies be light.
> May our bodies be light for you. [113]

We are praying for this very thing, that heaven's floor will finally break and dwell among us. When we recite the Lord's Prayer and pray "Your Kingdom come, your will be done on earth as it is already being done in heaven" we anticipate it. In this prayer of Jesus, we join with legions of Heavenly Hosts, humans from ages past and present, and the Lamb of God Himself by praying that the fabric of our dark earth will tear apart to let loose the Light of Heaven into our space. We pray and anticipate the bursting forth of God's final re-creative effort to unite one place from the two, that earth and heav'n be one.

What I especially love about *Sleeping at Last's* description of that final re-creative event is that when heaven finally does meet the earth and God finally does make His dwelling among us humans, "*We will have no use for numbers to measure who we are and what we're worth; We will have no need for mirrors to tell us who to be and where we fit into this awkward point of view.*" What a vision of a re-created society indeed, a vision of the values and Way of God's beautiful, good and perfect Kingdom Reign replacing those of the Kingdoms of the earth.

When we are resurrected and re-created anew in Jesus Christ, our worth will no longer be defined by the silly, stifling numerical categories of this world. Instead, our worth will be as Sons or Daughters of the living God. Our identity will no longer be shaped by mirrors that scream back to us an identity rooted in rebellion as cracked Eikons. Instead, we will reflect the Lamb of God who came to take away our sins.

What a glorious moment that will be when heaven bleeds forth onto our earth from one reality above to replace our broken, cracked space below!

What a glorious moment that will be when our individual and collective judgment is atoned for by our coming Rescuer; when our robes are washed in the blood of the Lamb of God and we are declared righteous before God's throne!

What a glorious moment that will be when the Victorious Obedient Substitute comes to make all things new, including us His precious Children!

What a glorious moment that will be when God descends to make his permanent dwelling among us, when He finally "tabernacles" among His Image-Bearers to be with them forever and ever! Amen and Amen!

I don't know about you, but I long for the day when all of this is re-created anew, when I am re-created as the human I was intended to be from the beginning.

A lingering question remains, however: is this re-creation intended for all humans? Will there be a universal re-creation, will God re-create all humans anew, or is this final Act in God's Story of Rescue meant for only a few? A conversation on God's act of re-creation cannot escape these pressing questions, and neither will I avoid them.

Universal Re-Creation?

If God's posture toward humans is as hyper-relational Lover, and if Jesus is coming "to make all things new," does that mean that all humans will eventually be part of God's re-creative act and heavenly Kingdom on earth? Can we followers of Jesus acknowledge a universalism to God's movement in the world?

The idea of a Christian Universalism is different from Straight-up Universalism. Straight-up Universalism says that all roads lead to God. It especially jibes well with our postmodern, multicultural sensibilities, because it allows people to believe whatever they wish without any required commitment to one religion or story over another. As you probably detected, I believe that Jesus is the fullest expression of God and *the* Rescuer of the world. Not Muhammad. Not Buddha. Not Madonna's Kabbalah. Jesus Christ. If you're offended by this exclusive claim, just remember that every other religion and story is just as exclusive!

Christian Universalism is the belief that every human will ultimately be saved and rescued through Jesus Christ. Jesus Christ and His once-and-for-all sacrifice is at the center of this idea and still acknowledges one true God. As one author puts it, "[Christian] universalists believe in one God, the creator of heaven and earth, in the goodness of the created order, the severity of sin and its terrible consequences, the necessity of divine action to effect redemption. They believe that salvation is found only through Christ's work in becoming flesh, suffering the consequences of our sins on the cross, being raised to new life in the power of the Spirit, and ascending to reign in heaven." [114] As you can see, Jesus Christ is still at the center of God's plan to rescue and re-create the world. Evil and sin and rebellion are real objective realities that had to be dealt with, and were atoned for through the event of the cross. In fact, Christian Universalists even believe in the necessity of an explicit faith in Jesus Christ, a final judgment, and hell.

What exactly do Christian Universalists believe, then, that is different from regular Christianity? They insist that: 1) it is possible to be saved from hell, and do not think that, when it comes to salvation, there is such a thing as a point of no return and it is never too late to be the recipient of grace and mercy; 2) in the end, everyone in hell will turn and receive divine mercy through Christ. [115] They emphasize the exclusivity of Christ right along side the hyper-sufficiency of Jesus' victory, obedience, and substitution. They also acknowledge the severity of human rebellion and need for rescue, while insisting on the exhaustive grace of God.

To be honest, at times I have resonated with this interpretation of the God we see in Jesus and His Story of Rescue that is offered by Christian Universalists. Karl Barth, for instance, said that the reason we Christians should evangelize the masses isn't simply to tell them about the salvation found in Jesus, but to announce far and wide the reality of the actual freedom all people have through His rescue. We do not simply share the reality of Christ to tell people they are sinners and bound for hell unless they repent and change their ways through Jesus Christ. Instead, we are to proclaim to all people the reality that death and the power of sin have already been defeated through Jesus, so start leaning into that reality right now with full force. It's like telling someone who is in jail that they have been freed from their sentence, yet until they get up, walk out of their cell and begin living out that freedom, they still live in their phony identity as a prisoner instead of their real identity as a freed person. In some ways I like this idea of evangelism, because we are proclaiming to all people that they can begin living as a rescued person now, instead of continuing in their phony identity as a rebel.

I also like the idea that God's heart and posture toward humans is that of a hyper-Lover who will go to any length and exhaust every grain of patience until the very last stray sheep has been found and returned to His pasture. It seems like the Story we find in the Scriptures is written large with this patient, gracious Lover. Just look at the story of the Children of Israel for peet's sake! Their story is one of contestant betrayal, exile, repentance, and restoration. Throughout the whole of the Hebrew narrative we see a very gracious, patient Lover who is in constant pursuit of His people. In the Book of Jonah we see a God who goes to great lengths to give even a pagan nation that is clearly outside the borders of His chosen people the equal opportunity to repent and turn to the one true God, a God who is willing to relent from sending calamity and judgment. Clearly, the Holy Scriptures reveal a hyper-relational, hyper-personal, hyper-patient, and hyper-gracious Lover who is in pursuit of humans for the sake of rescue and re-creation. Even this God of the Bible pursues those not considered part of the inside group.

I like this idea that all humans will eventually accept Jesus' act of rescue and find ultimate re-creation. I really hope that this is the case. You might call me a Hopeful Christian Universalist: I really hope (and I am hopeful) that all will eventually turn to Christ and be rescued and re-created in Him.

But the problem I have is this: what if I'm wrong?

I was voicing this concern to my sharp friend, Andy, with whom I've had several conversations about Christian Universalism. He called my concern a "reverse Pascal's Wager." *Pascals Wager* is a suggestion posed by the French philosopher, Blaise Pascal, that even though the existence of God cannot be determined through Reason, a person should "wager" as though God exists because a person living as if He does exist has potentially everything to gain and certainly nothing to lose. Similarly, since there is ample evidence in the Holy Scriptures to suggest that people who deliberately entrust themselves to Jesus Christ and walk in His Way will be separated from those who do not, the Church should act as if Christian Universalism is not true. Since we really do not know if everyone will eventually be re-created in the cosmic scope of Jesus' rescue, we should not act as though Christian Universalism is possible, because we have *everything* to lose.

While I definitely sympathize with Christian Universalists and love Karl Barth's assessment of our Christian witness, I think there is enough thrust in the teachings of Jesus and Scriptural narrative to suggest not all are included in God's final act of re-creation. Since there is the very real possibility of millions of people experiencing everlasting separation from the Creator, the Church must urgently declare the rescue made possible through Jesus. We must intentionally both *bring* and *be* the remedy for the world. We need to be honest, yet gentle, about the aspects of the teaching of Jesus and the whole of the Holy Scriptures that speak of judgment and the separation between followers and non-followers. If we do not take seriously Jesus' call to embody, demonstrate, and proclaim the rescue and re-creation possible through His Kingdom, the consequences will be catastrophic. Because both the entire Holy Scriptures and teachings of Jesus clearly exhibit a reality of future judgment, I'd say the prospect that some humans will ultimately exclude themselves from the Kingdom is very likely.

That Other Place

By "That Other Place," I mean hell.

Yes, the dreaded 'H' word. You can't talk about these things, however, unless you also talk about the reality and consequences of unbelief; about rejecting God and His Way and choosing to stay in rebellion.

While I think the prospect of a universal re-creation is possible, I find it hard to reconcile that idea with all the different teachings of Jesus which show a separation of people who choose belief from those who choose unbelief. Jesus Himself seems to insist that there is a separation between those who choose to entrust their stories and lives to Jesus in total commitment and those who hold onto the Way of Self while actively vandalizing shalom and rebelling against God and His Rhythm of Life.

I asked my friend Andy about his own struggle with judgment and hell. Like many of us, myself included, he has struggled with the idea that people will be judged and punished forever because of sin. The idea the some will receive eternal heavenly bliss, while others sit in hell has been a struggle for Andy. Recently, though, he's begun to understand why judgment seems to make sense. "For the longest time both judgment and hell made me shudder, leading to a rejection of their existence. But in doing that I rejected the reality of our world. The reality is that there are consequences to our rebellion, which I think is hell. Now it makes sense that there is a hell and judgment because of the that reality."

Unfortunately, sin and rebellion exist. Things are not the way they are supposed to be. We are not the way we were supposed to be and we all continue to actively rebel against God and His Rhythm of Life. While I do think that the (un)offensive gospel of Jesus insists there will be a small population of judged unbelievers, I cannot escape the fact that some will be judged and separated from those who have repented of their rebellion and committed themselves to Jesus Christ as Lord.

That last paragraph may be hard to handle for some. Consider the words of Jesus, however, in a parable of a banquet that He used to illustrate the judgment and separation that would befall those who seek to enter the Kingdom outside of God's terms:

Jesus spoke to them again in parables, saying: "The kingdom of heaven is like a king who prepared a wedding banquet for his son. He sent his servants to those who had been invited to the banquet to tell them to come, but they refused to come.

"Then he sent some more servants and said, 'Tell those who have been invited that I have prepared my dinner: My oxen and fattened cattle have been butchered, and everything is ready. Come to the wedding banquet.'

"But they paid no attention and went off—one to his field, another to his business. The rest seized his servants, mistreated them and killed them. The king was enraged. He sent his army and destroyed those murderers and burned their city.

"Then he said to his servants, 'The wedding banquet is ready, but those I invited did not deserve to come. Go to the street corners and invite to the banquet anyone you find.' So the servants went out into the streets and gathered all the people they could find, both good and bad, and the wedding hall was filled with guests.

"But when the king came in to see the guests, he noticed a man there who was not wearing wedding clothes. 'Friend,' he asked, 'how did you get in here without wedding clothes?' The man was speechless.

"Then the king told the attendants, 'Tie him hand and foot, and throw him outside, into the darkness, where there will be weeping and gnashing of teeth.'

"For many are invited, but few are chosen." [116]

Here we face a story of a king who sends out his servants with an appeal to those already invited to his royal wedding banquet. In the Jewish and ancient Near Eastern cultures, social gatherings and parties had a double-invite: The first one told of the event and sought initial acceptance; the second was a reminder and told the guests that all was ready and they should come. In the story the slaves are not sending out an invitation; they are calling on those who have already been invited and accepted to remind them to come.

These people have already accepted the first invitation, but now they make excuses to reject the second invite. This was a huge act of betrayal because huge social significance was attached to rejecting the second invitation. Apparently, they had better things to do and they put their selfish concerns over their obligations to the king. They cared more about their "farms" and "business" than their social obligation to attend the royal banquet of the king. They even go so far as to subject the king's messengers to violence and death!

In this parable, Jesus is speaking to two religious groups: the Chief Priests and Pharisees. Jesus reminds these leaders of the nation of Israel of their original invitation and subsequent rejection, directly tying into the next part of the story.

Because these originally invited people failed to respond to the second invitation, the king opens the door to everyone in the city. People from all corners of the city are invited to come to the royal banquet and enjoy a feast and festival. All people, both good and bad are invited, irrespective of person. The invitation did not depend on who the person was, but on whom the king chose to invite; he chose to invite everyone in his Kingdom and it didn't matter who they were.

At this point we have two groups contrasted: those who think they have the right to their position as invitees, the right to a place at the banquet table and who think they are "in." Then there are those who are unexpectedly promoted and surprisingly invited to the feast.

Originally, the Jewish people were invited to covenant with God to be His people. They received the first invitation. But throughout their history they did not live up to their obligations to that invitation. In Jesus' story, they are replaced by an unexpected collection of street people. The first invited group who rejected the second invitation are replaced with a second group. As Jesus says, "The first will be last, the last will be first." To be a member of the new group and new nation is no more guarantee of salvation than to be born into old Israel; it still depends on a persons reaction to the invitation, here symbolized by the wedding clothes.

This is where I want to turn our attention as we think about "That Other Place" and the possibility of judgment of humans.

In Jesus' story, we come to a man who is wandering around the king's royal wedding banquet in completely inappropriate attire. He is the guy in Rustler jeans and a Hanes t-shirt at your wedding reception. A sight to behold for sure! The king notices him, calls him friend and asks how in the heck he got into the party without the proper wedding clothes.

Contrary to popular thinking, a special wedding garment was not distributed to guests in the Jewish culture; special garments were not provided or expected to be worn at weddings or special banquet occasions. People were simply expected to wear decent, clean cloths that were *appropriate* for a wedding. In the case of a modern wedding, then, a pair of black khakis and white button down shirt would certainly do, rather than a special outfit like a tuxedo and bow-tie.

The event to which this man was invited required him to make a change, to change his clothes into something that was appropriate to the event for which he was invited. The parable assumes the man had time to change and come in appropriate attire anyone might have. While the cultural context of the parable didn't require a specific type of clothing, any invited person was to come clothed in a way fitting this specific event, nonetheless. Instead, the man made no preparations to wear clothes fitting to the feast he himself chose to attend!

Four years ago when I was working on Capitol Hill, I was invited to attend the official Bush/Cheney Presidential Campaign party in Washington, D.C. The event was quite the affair and was filled with members of the press, cabinet members, lobbyists, thousands of supporters and Administration staff, and then little ol' me. Not only was I invited to take part in the festivities, but I had some responsibilities of my own. I was required to come to the invited event appropriately dressed and to behave accordingly. If I had come dressed in jeans and a flannel shirt I would have been soundly given the boot. If I had come in my old sweatpants and the sweatshirt sporting my fraternity Greeks, I probably would have been arrested! Instead, I came dressed in my black tie garb, the only clothes fitting for a Presidential party.

So here's the question: How are we coming to the banquet at judgment? What clothes are we wearing? How are we coming to this grand banquet at the Day of the Lord?

The first invitation goes out indiscriminately to every person. The second invite begs a response. This second invitation is the other side of the paradox between divine grace and human responsibility. The first invitation was the announcement proclaimed by the Heavenly Hosts in chapter 8: "Glory to God in the highest, and on earth shalom to all humans, on whom His favor rests!" This announcement heralded the coming Lamb of God, the coming Rescuer, an invitation to take part in this new act of rescue by the Creator. The second invitation was by Jesus himself, which we will consider in the next chapter. In this invitation, Jesus announces to the entire world that the good news for which all humans have been waiting (the Kingdom of Heaven) has arrived. We are invited to respond in repentance, belief, and following.

I get the feeling from this parable, though, that there are a whole lot of people who have accepted God's invitation to salvation and *shalom*. Of course everyone wants everlasting life and re-creation at some level. Many people, though, will respond by coming dressed to the banquet as a lumberjack or in their frat house sweatshirt.

This lavish banquet with Jesus as host is for us, and the question is: how are we coming? Are we following the social customs of this Kingdom, or going inappropriately dressed to meet our Creator? Are we clothing ourselves with the righteousness that God requires or are we simply coming, not as we are, but as we insist on being?

These are the questions we need to ask as we think about "That Other Place" and who will or will not go there in judgment. Often, people make hell and judgment out to be God problems, as if the idea of eternal judgment somehow makes Him out to be less than the hyper-relational Lover that He is. Hell and judgment are not God problems, they are human problems. Just as rebellion and the consequences of rebellion are human problems, how we are judged for our willful vandalism of shalom and willful rebellion against the Creator and His Rhythm of Life are also our problems.

Just as the man who decided to show up to the banquet as *he* insisted was thrown out into the darkness in judgment, so too will those who decide to float through life on their terms and approach Jesus' banquet and God's judgment sporting their own outfits.

This brings us to the end of verse 14: "For many are called, but few are chosen." One commentator distinguishes between called/invited and chosen: "*Called* means taking up the initial invitation, chosen means preserving to the end. The word for chosen has exactly the opposite meaning in Matthew that it has in Paul: in Paul it is used mainly to *assure* of salvation's *possession*, whereas in Matthew it is used mainly to warn of its loss. In Matthew's context *chosen* is a goal word, not a *source* word; it is a word of admonition more than of comfort; it is ethical not predestinarian." [117]

Whereas the apostle Paul instructs Christians to live in a way that is worthy of those who are chosen, Matthew urges them to live in a way that would ensure at the end that they are *among* the chosen at all. Jesus is demanding that we do not come to His banquet and final judgment on our own terms and hand him a life lived according to our own Way; Jesus demands that we come to the banquet as a denier of self, a cross-carrier, and a follower of Him and *His* Way of Life. In short, Matthew cautions against the false security which thinks God's salvation is a done deal, "in the bag."

How about you? How are you coming to the king's banquet? How are you approaching our collective final judgment? The ending proverb, "For many are called, but few are chosen" could be put this way, "None are excluded but those who exclude themselves." As I said before, since "That Other Place" and final judgment for continuing in rebellion isn't a God problem, but a personal human problem, are you coming to the Wedding Banquet on God's terms or yours?

While Jesus does indicate a judgment and separation of people who decide to come to the end on their own terms, the Church does need to be careful about declaring who is "in" and who is "out" all by themselves. Far to often I hear the question, "Who goes to heaven and hell?" Usually, the answer is rooted in whether a person subscribes to the particular lists of "do's" and "don't's" of the person asking the question. In chapter three I wrote quoting Jesus:

> Not everyone who says to me, 'Lord, Lord,' will enter the Kingdom of Heaven, but only he who does the will of my Father who is in heaven. Many will say to me on that day, 'Lord, Lord, did we not prophesy in your name, and in your name drive out demons and perform many miracles?' Then I will tell them plainly, 'I never knew you. Away from me, you evildoers!' [118]

Some who thought they were on the "inside" at judgment time will actually be on the outside of the Kingdom; some who claimed the name of Jesus Christ were nevertheless unknown to Jesus. They will be cast out of His presence. While Jesus does talk about judgment and separation of believers from unbelievers, of deliberate followers from deliberate non-followers, the Church needs to be far more careful with Her talk on who is "in" and who is "out." The beauty of the good, hopeful, (un)offensive message of Jesus is that rescue and **re-creation** are continually available for all humans.

God intends to rescue and re-create all of humanity. In coming to earth, Jesus intended to redeem all of humanity through His life, death, resurrection, and ascension. His act of rescue is sufficient for all humans and effective for everyone who will honestly embrace Jesus as Lord.

Despite all of this talk on judgment and hell, the hyper-relational Lover God sent His Son Jesus Christ into the world as our Victorious Obedient Substitute so that any human who entrusts and totally commits their life to Jesus Christ will not taste ultimate death. Instead, they will be resurrected to experience an eternal existence with their Creator, in perfect *shalom* and unity.

That is our ultimate hope: resurrection from the dead into *shalom* and into an eternal relationship with our Creator permeated with love.

Our Ultimate Hope

Ultimately, our hope for re-creation is not in heaven or in escape from hell. Rather, our hope is in the resurrected Christ. As Anglican Bishop N.T. Wright explains, "'Resurrection' doesn't mean 'going to heaven when you die.' It isn't about 'life after death.' It's about 'life *after* 'life after death.' What is promised *after* that interim period [after you die] is a new bodily life within God's New World (life *after* 'life after death')" [119]

Our ultimate hope is not "heaven" or "life after death."

Our ultimate hope is the resurrection!

We look for *resurrection* in eager expectation. We should place our hope entirely in the resurrection from the Dead.

This is the very thing for which Paul waited: "We know that the whole creation has been groaning as in the pains of childbirth right up to the present time. Not only so, but we ourselves, who have the firstfruits of the Spirit, groan inwardly as we wait eagerly for our adoption as sons, *the redemption of our bodies*. For in *this hope* we were saved. But hope that is seen is no hope at all. Who hopes for what he already has? But if we hope for what we do not yet have, we wait for it patiently." [120] What is our hope? Some kind of spiritually disconnected existence in outer space? No. Paul explains that because followers of Jesus possess the Spirit—who is the first gift, a pledge of the fuller gift that is to come—we wait in eager expectation for the climactic revelation of two things: we wait for our full declaration as Sons and Daughters of God; and we wait for the resurrection of our physical bodies to share in that adoption and final liberation from the frustration and slavery to decay wrought through rebellion.

This is our hope: the final defeat of the way things are not supposed to be and a return to the way things were intended at creation. We hope for the final defeat of evil and rebellion and death and establishment of pure, complete *shalom* through resurrection.

This is the final act of the (un)offensive gospel of Jesus.

Hear the applause: "Praise be to God for ever and ever, in the name of the Father, and the Son, and the Holy Spirit! Amen!"

Chapter 10
what to do with Jesus and His Story

I'm sitting at a coffee shop in a small town in Nowheresville, MI, writing this final chapter even before I write the ones preceding it. You see, I stole away for four days from my duties at church and school to get some much needed R & R and work on this book. I'm staying at a Bed and Breakfast and just spent the afternoon wandering around a town that was devastated by a mill closing. After wandering a bit I spent an evening at the local pub downing a thoroughly non-non-fat burger, while scratching out some notes in my handy notebook for the outline of this book. As I sat mulling over the ideas about this (un)offensive gospel of Jesus, I stopped and looked around the restaurant, wondering if this Jesus and Story I'm writing about really matters to the people I saw.

I eaves dropped on a conversation about a so-called "dick-head NASCAR driver" who refused to give his autograph to one of the patrons. I thought about my waitress DeeAnn and the type of life she leads and how in the world she lives off of the paltry wages and tips from a small town pub. To these people who spend most of their time wondering where their next paycheck is coming from, if they'll make next month's rent, and if anyone cares about their life, I wondered if this whole Jesus thing and Story thing really works.

I wondered: Does the gospel work? Does Jesus matter anymore? Is His Story still compelling and effective?

Does it work for these people, for my friends, for me? Is the Story that I and countless others have devoted our lives to worth its salt, or is it like any other ancient religious myth and modern bit of psycho-babble?

Maybe I'm being too pragmatic. I mean, the Christianity with which I am familiar has always been more concerned if the gospel is *true* than if it *works*. While I also care if it is true (and I believe it is), I think the question with which many are grappling is if the gospel really *does* something. People around the world, especially in our postmodern, post-Christian culture, wonder if the good news about the person, reality, and Story of Jesus still connects to our time and space. They wonder how exactly we are to connect both Jesus and His Story of Rescue to modern-day America.

As I sat in that pub eating and drinking, my heart began to well up with hope for the people around me, for the world. While the Church may be showing and telling a poor Jesus and Story, She is still the hope for the world. The Bride of Jesus is still His and still being built by Him. There still is a compelling, hopeful Jesus and Story that, if properly shown and told, still rescues and re-creates.

There's still a true, (un)offensive gospel of Jesus that works.

After I returned from my dinner, I met the patrons of my B&B, Roseanne and her daughter, Miranda, in the kitchen for a little over-the-counter chitchat. Roseanne was baking yummy banana bread and Miranda was telling me about her watercolor paintings. Her mom inquired whether I was a student, and I gave my usual evasive spiel I give almost everyone who asks what I am studying. I talked a bit about my studies and my hope to be a pastor, which I think intrigued them.

Then Miranda broke through the conversation by asking me a simple, four word question: "So, are you saved?"

Internally, I almost lost it because that question and its phrasing was like a question back from the future: it was a question I was thoroughly interested in eons ago, but have somehow lost interest in asking.

"Are you *saved*?" Are you kidding me?

The question is so...pedestrian. It's so politically incorrect. Are you saved? That's almost as bad as asking someone if they're pregnant. For the eleven year old across the stool from me, though, it didn't matter what I thought of her question. She only really cared if I was saved, meaning if I was saved from sin, from death, from evil; if I was saved unto everlasting life and rescue and relationship with God and resurrection.

In the innocent question of this child, I was brought back to the basics, to what matters most about the gospel: finding rescue, forgiveness, salvation, re-creation, and resurrection in the person and Story of Jesus Christ of Nazareth.

After Miranda's question, I learned her mother "got saved" seven years earlier after spending half a lifetime worshipping Buddha. As she told me about how her conversion from Buddhism to the Way of Jesus occurred I sat there thinking, "How does that happen? What did she see in Jesus and His Story that caused her to leave what she was sure about for so long, to something less known?"

I never did get a chance to ask her these questions, but as I finish up this book I think I know how she would have answered: she met the very good Jesus and encountered His hopeful, (un)offensive Story. Somewhere, somehow she met the loving, gentle, caring Jesus of the Scriptures and believed in His hopeful, (un)offensive message. In the words of her daughter: she "got saved." It worked.

It still works.

What do you think about Jesus? What do you think about His Story? Actually, the only thing that matters in the end is not necessarily what you *think* about Jesus and His Story, but what you *do* with them. Like Roseanne and Miranda, everyone faces a choice after encountering Jesus and His Story. In fact, Jesus in announcing the good news of the Kingdom of Heaven drew a line in the sand and invited all people to respond by doing something with His hopeful gospel message of rescue and re-creation.

"The time has come," Jesus said. "The Kingdom of God is near. Repent and believe the good news!"

After announcing the in-breaking presence of the Reign of God into our time-space reality, Jesus made a pretty gutsy, exclusive demand:

Repent. Believe.

The same is true today.

Everyone who encounters the loving, gentle, caring Jesus and His good, hopeful, (un)offensive Story is called to repent and believe. Every human, young and old, male and female, Westerner and non-Westerner, is called to respond to Jesus by turning from their own Rhythm of Life and making a total commitment to the teachings, person, and Way of Jesus Christ of Nazareth. We are beckoned to follow Him with our entire being.

"Repent..." of Your Rhythm of Life

This is probably the least liked word in all of Christian vocabulary: Repent.

Yuck!

Who wants to admit they are wrong and wear the title *sinner*?

Jesus calls *all* people into repentance, however. After he declared the good news for which the whole earth had been waiting in eager anticipation to hear, that the Kingdom of Heaven and Reign of God was finally breaking forth into our time-space reality, He said, "Repent and believe this good news."

Jesus' first words as Messiah called all humans to repent of their rebellion and turn from the Way of Self. In fact, later on Jesus had some deliberate words for everyone who would follow Him. In Matthew 16:24-28, He said: "If anyone would come after me, he must deny himself and take up his cross and follow me. For whoever wants to save his life will lose it, but whoever loses his life for me will find it."

If anyone seeks to experience the Life that Jesus offers by entrusting himself to and following Jesus, he must deny himself and his *own* Rhythm of Life and die to the world by picking up the rugged planks of execution, his cross.

Deny.

Die to self.

Follow me.

All three imperatives describe a deliberate denial of self and a confession of our rebellious attitudes, motives, and actions against God. In fact, confession is at the center of what it means to repent. King David in the Hebrew Scriptures best models these acts of confession and repentance. King David abused his power and committed two grave acts of un-love: adultery and murder.

2 Samuel 11 describes the events in vivid detail. One evening David went out into the cool of the night to get some air. Then he saw her—beautiful bathing Bathsheba. And he wanted her. He wanted her as his own. The only problem was that she was the spouse of Uriah the Hittite. That didn't stop mighty King David, however. He sent messengers for her and she slept with him and became pregnant. Act one complete.

The second act was the result of the first. Uriah was still in the way of David completely having Bathsheba to himself. So he did what we all do when we sin: he tried to cover his tracks by having Uriah killed! Though he didn't do the act himself, he did send this dutiful soldier to the front lines of a brutal military campaign against the Ammonites because David's army was besieging the city of Rabbah. David sent word with Uriah to his commander, Joab, with these instructions: "Put Uriah in the front line where the fighting is fiercest. Then withdraw from him so he will be struck down and die." [121] And die he did.

When Bathsheba heard the news, she was overcome with grief. After the time of mourning Uriah's death was over, David brought her to his house and made her his wife. Then, she gave birth to the son that was conceived in sin and rebellion from the Way of the Lord. The Holy Scriptures say, "The thing David had done displeased the Lord."

God was so displeased that He sent Nathan the prophet to bring a message to King David. Nathan framed the message in a cryptic story that told of two men: a rich man with many sheep and cattle and a poor man with one small baby lamb. The poor man cared deeply for the one little lamb. When a traveler visited the rich man, however, the rich man took the one little lamb that belonged to the poor man to prepare a meal for his guest.

When David heard this story of injustice, he burned with anger against the rich man. David said to Nathan the prophet, "As surely as the Lord lives, the man who did this deserves to die! He must pay for that lamb four times over, because he did such a thing and had no pity." [122]

Nathan replied, "You are the man! This is what the Lord, the God of Israel, says: 'I anointed you king over Israel, and I delivered you from the hand of Saul. I gave your master's house to you, and your master's wives into your arms. I gave you the house of Israel and Judah. And if all this had been too little, I would have given you even more. Why did you despise the word of the Lord by doing what is evil in his eyes? You struck down Uriah the Hittite with the sword and took his wife to be your own. You killed him with the sword of the Ammonites.'"[123]

Needless to say David got the point! He and his rebellious acts were completely laid bare before both God and man. In response he could only utter, "I have sinned! Against Yahweh I have rebelled!" David composed a poem about these sinful, rebellious acts and about his later confession and repentance before the Lord. Psalm 32 reads:

> Blessed is he
>> whose transgressions are forgiven,
>> whose sins are covered.
>
> Blessed is the man
>> whose sin the LORD does not count against him
>> and in whose spirit is no deceit.
>
> When I kept silent,
>> my bones wasted away
>> through my groaning all day long.
>
> For day and night
>> your hand was heavy upon me;
>> my strength was sapped
>> as in the heat of summer. *Selah*

Then I acknowledged my sin to you
    and did not cover up my iniquity.
    I said, "I will confess my transgressions to the LORD
    "—and you forgave the guilt of my sin. *Selah*

Therefore let everyone who is godly pray to you
    while you may be found;
    surely when the mighty waters rise,
    they will not reach him.

You are my hiding place;
    you will protect me from trouble
    and surround me with songs of deliverance. *Selah*

I will instruct you and teach you in the way you should go;
    I will counsel you and watch over you.

Do not be like the horse or the mule,
    which have no understanding
    but must be controlled by bit and bridle
    or they will not come to you.

Many are the woes of the wicked,
    but the LORD's unfailing love
    surrounds the man who trusts in him.

Rejoice in the LORD and be glad, you righteous;
    sing, all you who are upright in heart!

Embedded within the cadence and flow of this poem is both the blunt confession of David's acts of rebellion and his earnest desire to shed his self, turning from his rebellious way. He also writes a plea to others to join in with his confession and repentance and to fully devote themselves to the Lord and His Ways. Right along side the repentance is a total recommitment to the Lord. Along with confession and repentance is a belief in the Lord and commitment to Him. Jesus calls us into the very same twofold act of repentance *and* belief.

"Believe..." in Jesus With Your Life

Belief is one of the most foundational ideas to Christian spirituality. People are beckoned by God to believe certain things are real about Him and His reality. In fact, Christian doctrine was often formulated directly in response to aberrant beliefs. The Church, then, has always been concerned with what people believe and that people believe rightly. The word *orthodoxy* means right thinking/ belief. In the Gospel of John, belief is the central idea of John's witness to Jesus. The word occurs ninety-eight times, denoting a major idea of importance to this beloved disciple. No other verse in the Gospel of John and in the whole New Testament is more well known than John 3:16. This one verse is memorized by most and makes more TV appearances thanks to ambitious sports fans with their John 3:16 emblazoned poster boards. The apostle John declares, "For God so loved the world that he gave his one and only Son, that whoever believes in him will not perish but have eternal life."

The word here—*believes*—however, does not mean mere intellectual acknowledgement of certain facts and truth claims. Instead, John's use of "believes in" means to trust oneself to an entity in complete confidence and implies a total commitment to the one in whom a person is entrusting himself. As we'll see shortly, for John belief is always connected to actions. Actions are signposts of this "total commitment."

John 1:12 emphasizes this exact notion of belief when John uses the word *received* to convey the need to actively embrace, rather than simply passively accept, Jesus. For John, believing and receiving are equivalent terms. Believing on Jesus' name is the key to receiving the revelation of the Word that has come into the world. Both terms declare the ability and opportunity to receive this revelation and belief in Him for eternal life. While John 3:16 assures us that the Father gave His Son in incarnation and death so that the believer might have eternal life, verse 17 expands the scope to salvation for the entire world. This passage also reveals that the very presence of Jesus in the world is judgment in the sense that it provokes men to judge themselves by deciding either for Jesus or against Him, either to believe or reject. All people are faced with the real choice between belief in and receipt of Jesus, or rejection and unbelief. All people are called to actively place their entire trust and commitment in Jesus.

Throughout his Gospel, John emphasizes that belief is an action rather than simply a state or quality. Belief, according to the Gospel of John, is the deliberate, consciously chosen commitment to a person or principle. That commitment cannot end with simply thinking correctly about doctrine. Rather, believing must translate into following Jesus. Believing must translate into a nailing of one's colors to the mast, to *show* one's beliefs by living them each day through deliberate actions.

Earlier this year, I wrote a blog post entitled, "Which is Better: Following or Believing?" I wrote it in reaction to a conversation I had with someone over the wording of a sentence taken from a new monastic community website, *The Simple Way*. On this website, this individual had a problem with the wording of the community's commitment to Jesus. The problem sentence reads, "We affirm the importance of calling all persons to personal faith and faithful discipleship in following Jesus Christ."

For my friend, this statement created questions about the community's actual commitment to faith in Jesus. His problem was the use of "following" in relationship to Jesus Christ and especially faith in Christ. He wondered why a person or a community would affirm the importance of calling people to "personal faith...in following Jesus Christ," rather than simply faith *in* Jesus Christ. Why would they call someone to faith in following, rather than simply belief in Jesus? While he didn't want to get nit-picky and had not read the complete "statement of faith" on the website, the wording did create red flags for him.

Those red flags relate to a broader concern with emerging conversations in the church that emphasize doing or following over merely believing. While he affirms our need as Christians to live out our faith and do what Jesus did, he fears that following and doing is largely at the expense of belief. Often these postmodern innovators do not come out and say they are in support of certain historically Christian Orthodox beliefs (like the Trinity or resurrection). They even revise other ones, like hell. These maneuvers reinforces my friends concerns. He wants to scream, "Don't stop believing!"

I did think he was being a bit nit-picky, however. I said that using the "following" terminology is better and stronger than simply using "belief." Following and doing *incarnate* the belief.

In his book, *The Hermeneutics of Doctrine*, Anthony Thiselton says this about belief: Belief is a nailing of ones colors to the masts because one's beliefs must be daily lived through deliberate actions. [124] Throughout the first 60 pages of his authoritative tome on the communal process of doctrine, he writes at length of this notion that belief is really not belief until and unless it is incarnated, that is until one "nails their colors" to the mast of life by existentially living out their beliefs. He coins the term *dispositional belief* as the kind of belief to which Christians are called.

Dispositional beliefs are action-oriented, situation-related, and embedded in the particularities and situations of everyday living. Viewing belief in this manner helps us realize that belief is a disposition to respond to situations both by expressing and by standing behind beliefs in situations that challenge belief or that demand actions appropriate to belief. Belief, then, must be explicit, active, and public. Belief in Jesus can only truly be demonstrated. The living out of faith, thought, and discipleship takes the form of visible, tangible, practical, bodily modes of existence; a disposition, habit and action. [125]

This is why I think "following" is better and stronger than "belief." By stopping at belief, we allow space for people to simply sit in their intellectual embracement of an idea rather than forcing them to act and incarnate that idea. With "following," all the bases are covered: You cannot follow something or someone without holding to a belief in the reality and validity of that something or someone. In order to follow Jesus, there are a number of things that must be believed: Jesus is the promised Messiah; Jesus' Way is what it means to be truly human; Jesus bodily rose from the dead by defeating death and providing the forgiveness of sins; Jesus is the fullest expression of who God is and truly is God; Jesus offers a way out of the mess of this world and into a relationship with God. Following Jesus doesn't mean we check our brains at the door and stop believing. While all forms of 'following' begin with belief, I say a true following doesn't end there. In order for our belief in Jesus to be real, rather than fake, we must deliberately and actively nail that belief to the mast of life. By truly believing in Jesus we must follow Him into His Way and explicitly, actively, publicly, tangibly, practically, bodily, and existentially live out our belief in Jesus by obeying His teachings and living in His Way.

Recently, a large number of Christians are beginning to emphasize the need for orthopraxy instead of simply orthodoxy. Theologians rightly concern themselves with ortho*doxy*, a commitment to right beliefs and ideas. We all should be grateful that they are committed to helping provide a framework for good biblical teaching and insisting on believing rightly. The Church, however, must also be committed to ortho*praxy*, a commitment to right practices and actions. Because She is the presence of Christ in the world, the Church must show what She believes by her everyday actions, conversations, and mission.

The apostle John insists as much in his First Letter: "We know that we have come to know Him if we obey his commands." [126] Here, John links a person's claim of knowledge and belief in God to visible characteristics of that belief, mainly demonstrable, tangible actions. This is exactly what Jesus himself said in John 14:12: "Anyone who believes in me will do what I have been doing." The context of this verse relates to the works and deeds Jesus did to show He was in the Father and the Father was in Him. While some of those deeds were certainly miraculous, most paralleled Jesus' own self-proclaimed mission in Luke 4, where He declared that he was sent to preach good news to the marginalized, to heal the blind, to bring release to those who were captive, and bring in the Lord's favor. The life of Christ was marked by doing acts of love and restoration (physical, economic, spiritual, and social restoration), and the life of His followers are to imitate this mission.

John continues by saying that if a person does not do what Jesus commanded, that person is a liar and an unbeliever. [127] Whoever claims to live and believe in Him must live and walk as Jesus did. A person who claims to believe in the Son of God must do what Jesus did and walk as he walked. [128] In the end, John's insistence of belief in his first letter parallels the one who "does the truth," as he wrote in his Gospel. He that commits his life to the Light of the World must keep the faith by doing acts of Truth, by living as Jesus lived. [129]

This most surely is why early Christians weren't called "believers" but rather "followers of the Way." Instead of merely believing some truths, they were living a Way of Life. To live Jesus' Way and truly follow Him they of course needed to believe. Likewise, may we not merely believe, but live and follow in the Way of Jesus. May we not stop believing, but may we not simply stop at believing. Instead, may we cultivate a robust believing that incarnates a full-bodied following that authentically lives out the Way of Christ, demonstrating that we are passionately believing it.

"Follow…" Jesus and His Rhythm of Life

As Jesus was walking beside the Sea of Galilee, He saw two brothers, Simon called Peter and his brother Andrew. They were casting a net into the lake, for they were fishermen. "Come, follow me," Jesus said, "and I will make you fishers of men." At once they left their nets and followed Him.

Going on from there, He saw two other brothers, James son of Zebedee and his brother John. They were in a boat with their father Zebedee, preparing their nets. Jesus called them, and immediately they left the boat and their father and followed Him. [130]

Look at these first words of Jesus as he embarked on ministry. They were not "obey me!" or even "believe me!" No, no, no. Jesus' first words to specific individuals as He set out on His mission were:

"Come follow me!"

Come *follow*.

Jesus literally says, "Come hither! Fall in behind me!" He called them out from where they were and who they were into an apprenticeship with Him and His mission. No longer were they to be who they were before that calling. Instead, they would be a different people, called to a different mission.

The same is true for us: Jesus calls us out from a previous community and identity. He rescues and transforms us out of our former identities as rebellious, cracked Eikons and calls us to entrust our entire life and Way of Living to Him by nailing our colors to the mast of *His* Life and Way. Like these early disciples, we are called to leave our former identities and both follow after Jesus and engage in His mission.

From what communities and identities did Jesus call these guys? What did they leave behind?

Obviously they left behind their jobs as fishers; they abandoned their nets and boats. These were young men (probably 16-20 years old) who were part of a culture that did not provide upward mobility like America. No American Dream for them. They were born into a fishing family and would be fishers for the rest of their lives. Contrary to popular belief, fishing was a fairly lucrative job. Since fish were a staple of the Judean diet, they probably lived a fairly comfortable life. Their identity as men were marked by nets and boats, an identity that would have provided a fair living.

But they abandon that identity to follow Jesus. The dramatic language used indicates an immediate abandonment of their previous identity as fishers. "At once they left their nests and followed Him." While they didn't exactly know what they were signing up for or even who this Jesus person really was, they knew enough to devote themselves to this man. This person and this mission were better than their lives as fishers. They wanted in.

What's interesting is they not only abandoned their very livelihoods and identities, but also their families. James and John leave their father Zebedee to follow Jesus into His mission. They "immediately they left the boat and their father and followed him."

James and John were still under the household, protection and authority of their father, fishing away with their papa and along came Jesus. He beckoned them to "come hither" and follow Him into His mission and they wanted in. Whatever it meant to be "in," they wanted it. They jumped out, left the boat, and abandoned their father. Poor Zebedee! He probably thought, "What are my boys up to now?!"

As I write this I am also reminded of the story of the prophet Isaiah. Isaiah chapter 6 recounts this young Temple clerk's early dramatic encounter with Yahweh:

One day, in the year that King Uzziah died, young Isaiah was working in the temple, minding His own business, and the curtain separating his reality from the Divine fell. Suddenly smoke began to fill the Temple and he could see the Lord high and exalted, seated on a throne. The train of Yahweh's majestic and massive robe filled the entire Temple. What an experience!

Beings that could only be described by someone like C.S. Lewis or J.R.R. Tolken began flooding the Temple and flying around the Throne of God. These Beings were chanting in unison:

Holy, holy, holy is the Lord Almighty;
The whole Earth is full of His glory.

Every door post shuddered and threshold shook at the sound of their majestic, powerful voices.

In the face of the glory of God, the majestic scene of seraphs praising the Creator and the overwhelming presence of Yahweh Himself, Isaiah could only cry: "Woe to me! I am ruined! I am a man of unclean lips, and I live among a people of unclean lips, and mine eyes have seen the King, the Lord almighty!" [131]

Isaiah was completely laid to waste by the power and presence of God. How did he respond to His encounter with His Creator? "I am a rebel. And I am surrounded by other rebels. Surely I am ruined and in deep trouble, for I have seen the pure, holy Lord!"

Yahweh's response is quite different, however. He sends a seraph with a live coal to purify and cleanse Isaiah. A seraph flew down to him, and with a live coal in hand the angel touched Isaiah's lips and declared, "See, this has touched your lips; your guilt is taken away and your sin atoned for." [132] The very objects that were sinful and rebellious (apparently, Isaiah's mouth and lips) were cleansed. After he recognized the glory and holiness of God and his own sin (repentance), Isaiah was forgiven, cleansed, and set right before the very throne of God.

We all feel like Isaiah, that we are too dirty to follow Jesus and be in the presence of God because of our sin, because we think we are unclean. Perhaps you think you are too:

impatient

unmerciful

selfish

materialistic

unloving

greedy...to follow Jesus.

Friend, if you have repented and believe in Jesus, you are cleansed, you are released and freed up to follow Jesus and serve His mission.

This is exactly what Yahweh does: He calls Isaiah to follow Him, and especially follow Him into His mission. God asks, "Whom shall I send? And who will go for us?" [133]

You can almost see Isaiah sitting like a little kid in preschool at the feet of God going: "Oh, oh, pick me! Pick me!!"

That was exactly Isaiah's response: "Here I am. Send me!"

He doesn't even know to what or to whom or to where God is intending to send Him. All that matters is that God is asking, and he will obey and go.

The same call is made to all of us: God is calling to us, "Whom shall I send; who will go for us?"

Who will follow in my Way? Who will join me on mission as I go to the Section 8 housing in Grand Rapids to breath new life into the darkness? Who will go to the divorcing neighbors down the street to show them a better way of being married? Who will follow me in befriending and loving the alcoholic coworker who finds no other comfort than in bottles of J. D.? How about the depressed college student who really needs a friend, who will follow Jesus into his or her life? Who will be Jesus to the racially segregated pockets of our country to declare that there is a better way of living in community as fellow human beings? Who will go and tell the empty suburban soccer mom that a life outside of mindlessly spending money and suffocating schedules is possible?

Who will follow Jesus by stepping into the lives of the marginalized to bring, healing, restoration, release, and rescue? Who will leave behind their rebellious attitudes and selfish Ways to pursue relationship with God through Jesus and the Way of Christ? Who will follow and bring the good news of the Kingdom of Heaven to the world?

I think about myself when I ask these questions. I think about the Church, this ragamuffin group of broken, normal, ordinary, crazy people who have been called out from who they were and set apart for global, massive mission. I wonder:

- What do we need to leave behind as individuals to more passionately and deliberately follow Jesus and His mission?
- What do we as the American Church need to leave behind to fully embrace our identity as a called out and sent people who fully participate in Jesus' mission, who show Jesus and tell His hopeful Story well?

When we "become a Christian" or choose to enter into relationship with God through Christ, we are not simply signing-up to something like a bowling league. No, no. We are in large ways leaving and stepping away from an identity and our own Way of Life. We are giving up everything to follow Jesus and are stepping into His Way and His mission. I love this episode in Luke 5 where Jesus calls the first disciples because it portrays a sudden and complete change of lifestyle, involving leaving both work and family behind to follow behind Jesus into His mission of "catching people."

That's what we are called to do, too: Leave behind our identities as rebels, our rebellious attitudes, and Way of Self. We are called to entrust our entire lives by totally committing ourselves to Jesus and following Him in His Way by deliberately living out the teachings and Way of the Rescuer Troublemaker Jesus.

Only one question remains, then: Will you repent of your rebellion, believe that Jesus is who He said He was as the Son of God who came to rescue all of humanity, and follow Him in total commitment by deliberately living out His teachings and Way?

Are you willing to drink and breath in the delicious (un)offensive gospel of Jesus down to the very last drop? Are you ready to wholeheartedly dive into the reality of Christ by repenting of the Way of Self and giving your life in total commitment to Jesus?

"Lord After You, To Whom Shall We Go?"

In the end, I realize that much of what you've read still may be hard to grapple. Maybe you grew up on "Jesus Juice" and you're left with nothing but bitterness. Or maybe you're a non-theist or an other-theist and somehow stumbled across this book and you still find the Jesus Person and Jesus Story uncompelling, though if that's the case, then *I* have failed, not Jesus.

I leave you, the reader, with one last thought. It's a thought from the Book of John. In chapter 6, the author tells of an episode Jesus had with some Teachers of the Law in Israel. He always had "episodes" with them folk! On my blog, novuslumen.net, I recounted this story, adding my own little twist. I leave you with the same words Jesus had for some people who were interested in following Him and the Life He offered:

"How can this man give us his flesh and blood? This is absurd!" A sharp argument broke out among the Jews, centering on this graphic teaching of the Man from Nazareth.

"I tell you the truth, my friends, unless you eat the flesh of the Son of Man and drink his blood, you have no life in you," Jesus responded.

"Absurd," called out one of the more orthodox Jews.

"Whoever eats my flesh and drinks my blood has eternal life, and I will raise him up at the last day."

"Ghastly! This flesh and blood teaching is simply ghastly," quipped another pious, clean Israelite.

"Whoever eats my flesh and drinks my blood remains in me, and I in Him."

"Uh, Rabbi," cautioned one of his disciples, "maybe you should stop with this flesh and blood business. Not really good for publicity if you know what I mean!"

Jesus continued, "Just as the living Father sent me and I live because of the Father, so the one who feeds on me will live because of me. This is the bread that came down from heaven. Your ancestors ate manna and died, but he who feeds on this bread will live forever."

The synagogue where Jesus was teaching was stunned into silence. They remembered the story of their ancestors and God's provisions of life in the wilderness through the life-giving manna. That they got. But this teaching of feeding on the flesh and blood of the One the Father sent was a mystery wrapped in an enigma.

After Jesus finished, a heated discussion began among His many followers: "What in the world! Feeding on His flesh and blood?" "This is really confusing, hard teaching!" "How can anyone embrace this sort of idea, much less stomach it?"

Aware of the grumbling among His own circle of friends, Jesus approached them saying, "Does this really offend you? What if the Son of Man ascends right now to heaven to where He was before, before your very eyes? The Spirit gives life; the flesh counts for nothing. The words I have spoken to you are spirit and they are life. Yet there are some of you who do not believe..."

From that point on many of his followers turned back and no longer followed Him. One by one they left Jesus to pursue other ventures, other less insane ideas, leaving Jesus and His crazy "flesh and blood" teachings behind.

"You're still here?" Jesus said to the remaining Twelve. "Don't you want to pursue other, more digestible, more logical notions on Life? You do not want to leave, too, do you?"

Simon Peter, one of Jesus' more skeptical disciples, replied, "Well, after that rousing homily I guess it would make sense to leave," eliciting a few chuckles from the other eleven. "But Lord," Peter continued, "to whom or to what shall we turn?

"Shall we go to Oprah or Dr. Phil? In the face of your difficult teachings, does the Church of Oprah offer the life giving sustenance we need for healthy, integrated living?

"Or maybe we should turn to Nietzsche, Camus, or Foucault, those great modern thinkers who have bleached the world of the Spiritual and Divine, stripping it of it's need for You, our Messiah, or Yahweh for that matter. They seem to do a good job of pointing out the absurdity of belief in Yahweh and, to be honest, they seem to offer a rational alternative. After we leave you, are they and their philosophies all that's left?

"Would those other religions be better? Though it is hopeless to try to create shalom through our own efforts, no matter how spiritual those efforts are, if we leave you, isn't that what's left? A grace-less life of hopeless striving for Divine approval, a grasping at the wind? Would they be better than you, Jesus?

"How about we give up on religion altogether and pursue hard reason and verifiable science, the opiate for the modern Enlightenment world? Would rationalism satisfy the soul of man and repair our broken world? Can we humans put to rights the world and give each other the life for which we all long? Can Man triumph over Man and consummate a Brave New World devoid of social evil?

"Or maybe MTV has the answers? Maybe we could get ourselves a celebrity-made Crib, pale around with Jay-Z and Snoop or Britney and Paris, bling out our sandals and pimp our camels? Isn't it written in one of the Wisdom Books to eat, drink and be merry for tomorrow we die? Maybe we should leave you for the Real World and pursue every materialistic pleasure and sexual fetish known to man to find true Nirvana?

"Jesus, after you what else is there? If we leave you, what else is left to believe? Who else is there to follow?"

Peter continued, *"You and you alone have the words of Eternal Life. Oprah, Dr. P, Camus, the modern Enlightenment project, and MTV offer no Life; they do not satisfy, they are Life-less. If we left you, we would be wandering nomads in a dry and thirsty land where there is no water.*

"Jesus, you ask if we, too, will leave?

"Well, I ask you: After you to whom or to what shall we go?"

231

Afterword

I am both a full-time student as well as a blogger, so I've written before. During my first year of seminary, I wrote over 60,000 words, enough for a nice sized book. As a blogger, I've written over 350 blog posts with an average word count of 1200 words. That's over 420,000 words, enough for five very large books. I can say, though, without a doubt, this project has been the most challenging, exhausting, and rewarding adventure I've ever experienced. There's something about whittling away at a ream of paper and forming it into a book that marks a man for life. Consider me marked!

I've been marked primarily spiritually because of the impact the content of this book has had on my own soul. In some ways I feel like the Unseen Hand from the heavens burning the Hebrew letters onto the two stone tablets and declaring them the Ten Laws. While I totally understand the difference, in some ways writing this book has been just as declarative! Writing this book has declared to the world an alternative to the status quo, while helping further articulate my own beliefs and understandings of Jesus and His Story.

I've also been marked personally by this adventure. Author Scot McKnight once wrote that writing is a community affair. He's right. I could never have birthed this thing without several midwives: Andy, John, Jason, Taylor, Ben, Cameron, and Rachel were theological dialogue partners in the best definition of the word, helping me come to some understandings about many of the ideas here. My professor and academic mentor, Dr. Michael Wittmer, provided the intellectual sharpening for this undertaking. My friend and colleague in ministry, Dr. John W. Frye, was my cheerleader as much as he was my editor. I needed both roles to accomplish this thing called a book. Finally, my parents modeled for me throughout my life the good Jesus and hopeful story I speak of in these pages. This book was indeed a communal affair, a community to which I am greatly indebted.

As I was finishing up this book I was asked several times, "Who is your audience?" That's a tricky question because I see three people: Christians who are trying to show and tell, but are missing some key pieces in the showing and telling; de-Churched people, those who've grown up "Christian" and embraced Jesus and His Story at one point in their life, but have since walked away; and finally non-Christians, people who have really never interacted with the good Jesus and hopeful Story of the Holy Scriptures nor have made any kind of commitment to Jesus. I hope that after reading this book, these three groups have been affected by the (un)offensive gospel of Jesus as much as I have been by writing it. If you're a follower of Christ, I hope you've been affected. I hope you've learned a thing or two about how to better show and tell Jesus and His Story. If you're not a follower of Christ, I hope you're able to glimpse a good Jesus and hopeful Story, a gospel that is inviting you to dive in even now.

As I mentioned before, everyone who comes across Jesus and His Story is left with two choices: follow or walk away. When you come across the Jesus of the New Testament and God's Story of Rescue, you need to *do* something with both. Perhaps I should have mentioned that in the preface, as a disclaimer. Sorry, now you're stuck! You, Christian or not, now have to do something with both Jesus and His Story. You can either follow Jesus or walk away.

I hope you choose the former.

As a de-Churched person, maybe you're just sick and tired of the crap that's found in American Churchianity. I know I've been there and nearly walked away myself. I really hope, though, that you will take a second look at Jesus and a second read of His hopeful Story. I really hope that something in this book sparked something in you to reengage the life, teachings, and person of Jesus. I hope that you will sit at His feet and just drink Him in. I guess I would hope after reading this that you will pick up the Gospels and plant yourself in them for a year. That's what I did when I was fed-up with the Church. Give it a year. Sit with Jesus and His Story a year. I'll bet you that it will mark you forever. If it doesn't, write me a note and I'll refund the money you spent on this book!

If you're not a follower of Jesus Christ, I hope that you have been equally impressed by Jesus and His Story. I don't necessarily claim to write anything new in this book. Most of what I've written has been penned elsewhere, so the Jesus and Story found herein is consistent with how much of the Church throughout history and the world has understood Him. I think in recent years, though, that understanding has been clouded and stifled by well-meaning but misguided Christians. My guess is that some of these folk have shown you a pretty crappy Jesus and told a pretty lame or offensive Story which has left you jaded, offended, and dry, yet still spiritually hungry for relationship with God. Please reconsider. After finishing this book I urge you with the same challenge of the de-Churched person: for an entire sit with Jesus and His Story found in the books of Matthew, Mark, Luke, and John at the beginning of the New Testament. That's only one book every three months. You can handle that. If at the end of the year you're unconvinced that Jesus is who He said He was and you're not interested in following His Way, write me and I'll refund you the price of this book. It's the least I can do considering how passionate and convinced I am of Jesus and His Story.

Finally, for the committed Christian I ask two things: think about the Jesus you're showing and the Jesus the world around you sees; examine the Story you're telling and the Story your world is hearing. While I think the Church does do both well at times, Lord knows an entire generation is disinterested and disengaging from Jesus' community precisely because of our shabby show and tell efforts. In this book I hope you've received a glimpse of how it might look to show Jesus well in our twenty-first century postmodern, post-Christian world. Also, I hope you see a greater depth and majesty in the good, hopeful message of Jesus than ever before. I hope you see how important it is to begin well and tell a holistic, (un)offensive gospel of Jesus that connects to the individual stories of those floating around you. Finally, I hope you are more passionate about the good Jesus and hopeful Story of God's rescue than you were before you began reading this book. Sorry, no refund deal for you!

As I close this my first book, I can think of no better way to end than by paraphrasing the lines from Peter in John Chapter 6 that you read at the end of the last chapter:

> Friend, if you abandon Jesus and His hopeful message, to whom or to what will you turn? After the (un)offensive gospel of Jesus, what else is there?

Appendix
God's story of rescue

Putting it all together, then, what is the (un)offensive gospel of Jesus? If you are a Christian and wonder how to retell God's Story of Rescue, here is a simple version of the Story I hope will prove useful as you tell Jesus' hopeful message. Or maybe you're still trying to figure out Jesus and His hopeful Story and just need the basic rundown of what that Story is about. Either way, here is a condensed version of God's Story of Rescue:

When everything began, there existed one eternal God who created all that exists. Most importantly, people were the culmination of God's purposeful Act of Creation. We were created on purpose, with purpose in the Image of God to reflect, enjoy, worship, and love Him forever.

This is the key to God originally creating us: we were originally created to exist in an eternal relationship with Him, defined by mutual love. Humans were intended and invited to be in an eternal, loving relationship with their Creator, an invitation that allowed room for both acceptance and rejection.

Unfortunately, humans rebelled against God and rejected His Way. There was a real time-space event when humans sinned and rebelled by loving Self rather than God. This act of relational rejection first occurred through Adam and Eve, which resulted in the Fall of all of creation, including humans.

Now, God did not intend for sin and evil to be part of creation. Because sin is the result of rejecting the Way of the Creator, it was a potential possibility, but not an intended component of God's reality. The result of sin is brokenness and death, both physical and spiritual. Because of our willful choice to rebel against God, all of creation is broken and in need of rescue and re-creation, including us. Without rescue through the provisions of God we earn eternal brokenness, death, and ultimately separation.

God, though, wants nothing more than to restore the God-Human relationship and all creation to the way He originally intended them to be. Even in the beginning, God promised an Anointed One, someone who would eliminate this brokenness and alienation, and rescue humans and creation.

He was described as a King who would someday reign, a Servant who would suffer and die, and a Judge who would someday return. In fact, He was declared to be God Himself in human form.

The high-point of God's Story of Rescue is the arrival of the promised Anointed One. The means by which God desired to rescue us was through sending His Son Jesus Christ. God enfleshed Himself in the person of Jesus Christ to demonstrate the fullest extent of His love for humans. The full vision of rescue and expression of that love was displayed and communicated through the cross.

Jesus is the Victorious Obedient Substitute, and His redemptive act rescues and restores creation in this way: Through His Life, Jesus obeyed God perfectly after the First Adam did not, while demonstrating how we are to live as humans; through His death, Jesus paid the final penalty to God for rebellion on behalf of all humans through a final sacrifice, thus restoring humans to relationship with God; through His resurrection, Jesus defeated the dark powers to liberate all humanity from Satan's control and free us from the bondage of evil and sin, and validated the sacrifice and completion of that payment. He was the One to whom the Bible had been pointing and the One for whom our restless hearts have been thirsting. Through Him we all find forgiveness for and salvation from our sin and rebellion, restoration to relationship with God, and holistic re-creation.

But it doesn't end there, because the Bible ends with bringing to completion what God began at the beginning: the re-creation of humans and all creation. At the end of the Story, we have a beautiful picture of Eternity when all the restored, re-created humans relate to their God with perfect intimacy. Fulfilling the very way they were originally created, they worship God the way He deserves and without hinderance of sin, sickness, sadness or death. If we respond to this Story as God desires us to, we will experience an abundant everlasting life with our Creator-Rescuer God.

God says we respond to this Story by confessing with our mouth and believing in our heart that Jesus is Lord; confessing our sin and rebellion, while seeking forgiveness and rescue; and finally we are called to respond to God's Story by denying our own story, by laying down our lives and own selfish agendas and surrendering ourselves to Him.

What I love about the Holy Scriptures is that it's Story connects with our own story at our point of deepest need.

What do you think about this Story? What do you think about God's desire to restore you to the way you were originally created to be? I hope you can see that Jesus and His hopeful Story is what all people have been waiting for their whole lives. The beauty is that you can receive God's rescue, right now.

As I mentioned in Chapter 10, after Jesus announced that the new Reign of God had invaded the world, He called all people to both *repent* and *believe*.

Repenting means to turn from your own story and your own Rhythm of Life that mirrors the patterns of this world, while acknowledging that you are a rebel and that you sin.

We are also called to trust ourselves to Jesus Christ for rescue and re-creation. Often we think that we need to earn God's favor and forgiveness through our own effort. We try to please God by doing or saying good things. The Holy

Scriptures tell us, though, that God's rescue and love does not come through ourselves and our own works, but instead through the sacrifice and rescue of God's one and only Son Jesus Christ. We are called to believe in Him and in nothing else for our rescue and re-creation.

What exactly does *believe* mean? How does belief in Jesus Christ look? First, it doesn't mean simply thinking rightly about God or Jesus or His rescue. Instead, it means entrusting our entire self, totally committing our life and story to the teachings, person, and Way of Jesus Christ. It means following Jesus and His Way and them alone. In the Holy Scriptures, God seeks out relationship with other people and desires them to bind themselves to Himself by following Him and His Way. The same is true for us today.

This is probably why early Christians weren't called "believers" but rather "followers of the Way." Instead of simply believing, they were living. But to live Jesus' Way and truly follow Him, they needed to believe some things. Similarly, we are called not merely to believe, but rather to live and follow in the Way of Jesus. Ultimately, this is what the whole Jesus Story is about: following Him totally by denying our own Rhythm of Life, dying to self, and following Jesus' teachings and Way into relationship with God and as a restored human being.

May you fall in love with the hyper-relational Lover we find in Jesus Christ and be captivated by His good, hopeful (un)offensive Story. May you fall in love with God's Story that begins with creation and ends with re-creation. May you recognize your own willful vandalism of *shalom* and constant rebellion against God and His Rhythm of Life. May you embrace the forgiveness, restoration, and rescue found in Jesus Christ of Nazareth. In the end, may you entrust your life and totally commit your own story to Jesus, while following Him and His Way passionately until that glorious and hopeful day when our Lord Jesus Christ returns to resurrect and re-create all things.

Do you want a discussion?

I figured you would! That's why I created a site where you can wrestle with the content of this book in virtual community. On this forum, you will have the opportunity to interact with the content of this book chapter by chapter. You may ask me questions, give comments, or push back against my ideas. I also hope that this space will be a catalyst for creating dialogue with others, Jesus-follower or not, regarding Jesus and His hopeful, (un)offensive gospel message.

Log onto **http://discuss.unoffensivegospel.com** to begin painting an alternative following of Jesus and discussing how to share Him and His hopeful Story well.

discuss.unoffensivegospel.com

Notes

[1] A comment on an editorial by Mike S. Adams entitled, "Forward This Column of Get Stuck on Stupid." Accessed 8/9/08 at http://www.onenewsnow.com/Perspectives/Default.aspx?id=75211.

[2] David Kinnaman and Gabe Lyons, *unChristian* (Grand Rapids: BakerBooks, 2007) 71.

[3] Luke 18:18.

[4] John 6:35.

[5] John 6:54-56.

[6] See John 4:1-42.

[7] See Matthew 9:9-12.

[8] See Luke 7:36-50.

[9] Matthew 9:36.

[10] Anthony C. Thiselton, *The First Epistle to the Corinthians* (Grand Rapids, Eerdmans Publishing, 2000) 171.

[11] Ben Witherington III, *Conflict and Community in Corinth: A Socio-Rhetorical Commentary on 1 and 2 Corinthians* (Grand Rapids: Eerdmans Publishing, 1995) 108-113.

[12] Gordon Fee, *The First Epistle to the Corinthians* (Grand Rapids: Eerdmans Publishing, 1987) 75.

[13] Withingington III, *Conflict and Community*, 113.

[14] Yann Martel, *Life of Pi*, (New York: Harvest Book, 2001) 54.

[15] Martel, *Life of Pi*, 54.

[16] Martel, *Life of Pi*, 54.

[17] Luke 7:22.

[18] Klyne Snodgrass, *Stories with Intent* (Grand Rapids: Eerdmans Publishing, 2007) 171.

[19] 1 Thessalonians 2:6-12/

[20] Kinnaman and Lyons, *unChristian*, 28. This page also shows a larger table with the top 10 impressions of Christianity.

[21] Kinnaman and Lyons, *unChristian*, 24.

[22] Kinnaman and Lyons, *unChristian*, 24.

23 See the very insightful report by the Pew Forum on Religious Life at religions.pewforum.org for more trends in the spiritual dynamic of America.

24 Pew Forum on Religious Life at religions.pewforum.org.

25 Luke 7:37.

26 Joel B. Green, *The Gospel of Luke* (Grand Rapids: Eerdmans Publishing, 1997) 309.

27 Green, *Luke*, 310.

28 Kinnaman and Lyons, *unChristian*, 32.

29 Kinnaman and Lyons, *unChristian*, 32.

30 Dan Kimball, *They Like Jesus But Not The Church* (Grand Rapids: Zondervan, 2007) 236.

31 Dan Kimball, *They Like Jesus*, 236.

32 Kyle Meinke, "Outspoken Preacher Sparks Controversy," *Grand Valley Lanthorn*, 20 September 2008. Accessed October 11, 2008 at: http://www.lanthorn.com/11-preacher.

33 Meinke, "Outspoken Preacher Sparks Controversy," http://www.lanthorn.com/11-preacher.

34 You can watch the full YouTube video through this link: http://www.youtube.com/watch?v=bOTrDtCvj3E.

35 Kinnaman and Lyons, *unChristian*, 16.

36 Donald Miller, in his book *Blue Like Jazz*, wrote about how he and some of his friends did this very thing on the campus of Reed College. Needless to say it turned some heads and opened doors to share Jesus and His Story.

37 I credit New Testament scholar Scot McKnight with reframing humanity as Image-Bearers from the classical *Imago Dei* to this better, more nuanced *Eikon* term. You can read more about the *Eikon* in his book, *Embracing Grace* (Brewster, MA: Paraclete Press, 2005).

38 Paulo Freire and Donaldo Macedo, "A Dialogue: Culture, Language, and Race." *Harvard Educational Review*, 65 (1995): 379.

39 Kinnaman and Lyons, *unChristian*, 74.

40 Kinnaman and Lyons, *unChristian*, 74.

41 Kinnaman and Lyons, *unChristian*, 28.

42 John Piper, *Putting My Daughter to Bed Two Hours After the Bridge Collapse*. Accessed August 8, 2006 at http://www.desiringgod.org/Blog745_putting_my_daughter_to_bed_two_hours_after_the_bridge_collapsed.

43 John 11:33.

[44] John Piper, *Putting My Daughter to Bed Two Hours After the Bridge Collapse.*

[45] John Piper, *Putting My Daughter to Bed Two Hours After the Bridge Collapse.*

[46] Clark Pinnock, *Most Moved Mover*, (Grand Rapids: Baker Academic, 2001), 1.

[47] Roger Olson, *The Story of Christian Theology* (Downers Grove, IL: IVP Academic, 1999), 57.

[48] Olson, *Christian Theology*, 57.

[49] Pinnock, *Mover*, 4.

[50] Pinnock, *Mover*, 132.

[51] Pinnock, *Mover*, 172.

[52] Luke 4:18-20.

[53] Luke 8:40-56.

[54] Fredrick Dale Bruner, *Matthew: A Commentary* (Grand Rapids: Eerdmans Publishing, 2004), 651.

[55] Mark 14:32-42.

[56] Hebrews 5:8-9.

[57] This describes a church of which I was a part outside Washington, D.C. for over a year.

[58] Luke 19:1-9

[59] Luke 10:25-37

[60] John 5:19-20.

[61] John 15:1-5.

[62] Merrill C. Tenney, *John: The Gospel of Belief* (Grand Rapids: Eerdmans Publishing, 1976) 228.

[63] John 15:7.

[64] Acts 1:8.

[65] John 14:15-16; 16:-5-7.

[66] Philippians 2:13.

[67] Matthew 28:20.

[68] James K. A. Smith *Who's Afraid of Postmodernism* (Grand Rapids: BakerAcademic, 2006) 39.

[69] Jaques Derrida, *Writing and Difference* (Chicago: The University of Chicago Press, 1978) 10.

[70] Smith, *Who's Afraid*, 64.

[71] Smith, *Who's Afraid*, 65.

[72] Smith, *Who's Afraid*, 69.

[73] Smith, *Who's Afraid*, 84.

[74] Deuteronomy 29:29.

[75] Scot McKnight, *Embracing Grace* (Brewster, MA: Paraclete Press, 2005).

[76] From Robert Alter's masterful book *The Five Books of Moses* (New York: W.W. Norton & Company, 2004), 18-19.

[77] Psalm 8:3-8.

[78] Psalm 8:9.

[79] J. Richard Middleton, *The Liberating Image* (Grand Rapids: BrazosPress, 2005), 28.

[80] Middleton, *Liberating Image*, 88.

[81] Middleton, *Liberating Image*, 104.

[82] Middleton, *Liberating Image*, 121.

[83] James D. Dunn, *The New Perspective* (Grand Rapids, Eerdmans Publishing, 2008) 6.

[84] Jacques Ellul, *The Humiliation of the Word* (Grand Rapids: Eerdmans Publishing, 1985) chapter 7.

[85] Cornelius Plantinga, *Not the Way It's Supposed to Be* (Grand Rapids: Eerdmans Publishing, 1995) 14.

[86] Romans 8:22.

[87] McKnight, *Embracing Grace,* 29.

[88] John 1:14.

[89] Exodus 25:8.

[90] Olson, *The Story*, 76.

[91] Romans 5:12:18-19.

[92] Olson, *The Story*, 77.

[93] Brian McLaren, *The Story We Find Ourselves In* (San Francisco: Jossy-Bass, 2003) 102.

[94] Thomas R. Schreiner, "Penal Substitution View," in *The Nature of Atonement* (ed. James Beilby and Paul R. Eddy; Downers Grove, Ill: IVP Academic, 2006), 72.

[95] See Leviticus 1-7.

96 Schreiner, "Penal," 89.

97 Romans 5:7-11.

98 Shane Claiborne and Chris Haw, *Jesus for President* (Grand Rapids: Zondervan, 2008), 131.

99 Doug Pagitt, *A Christianity Worth Believing* (San Francisco: Jossey-Bass, 2008), 181.

100 Pagitt, *Christianity*, 181.

101 Pagitt, *Christianity*, 194-195.

102 See Romans 6:1-23.

103 See Romans 7:14-25.

104 Ephesians 6:12.

105 Hebrews 10:7.

106 1 Corinthians 15:55.

107 Revelation 21:1-5.

108 Matthew 16:17.

109 John 20:21.

110 Bruner, *Matthew*, 815-816.

111 "Colonialism," in Wikipedia: The Free Encyclopedia; (Wikimedia Foundation Inc., updated 22 July 2004, 10:55 UTC) [encyclopedia on-line]; available from http://en.wikipedia.org/wiki/Colonialism; Internet; retrieved 26 May 2008.

112 Darrell Guder, *Missional Church* (Eerdmans Publishing: Grand Rapids, 1998) 88.

113 From the Album *Keep No Score*. Copyright 2006, Sleeping At Last.

114 A post written by Gregory McDonald in explanation of his book *The Evangelical Universalist*. Accessed at http://www.jasonclark.ws/2008/02/25/evangelical-universalism-oxymoron.

115 McDonald at http://www.jasonclark.ws/2008/02/25/evangelical-universalism-oxymoron.

116 Matthew 22:1-14.

117 Bruner, *Matthew*, 392.

118 Matthew 7:21-23.

119 Wright, *Simply Christian*, 219.

120 Romans 8:22-25.

[121] 2 Samuel 11:15.

[122] 2 Samuel 12:5-6.

[123] 2 Samuel 12:7-9.

[124] Anthony Thiselton, *The Hermeneutics of Doctrine* (Grand Rapids: Eerdmans Publishing, 2007), 21.

[125] Thiselton, *Hermeneutics*, 21.

[126] 1 John 2:3.

[127] 1 John 2:4.

[128] 1 John 2:6.

[129] Brown, *The Gospel According to John*, 135.

[130] Luke 4:18-22.

[131] Isaiah 6:5.

[132] Isaiah 6:7.

[133] Isaiah 6:8.

Printed in the United States
128251LV00004B/1-117/P